anglistik & englischunterricht

Teachable Poems. From Sting to Shelley

Manfred Beyer · Hans-Jürgen Diller · Joachim Kornelius · Erwin Otto
Gerd Stratmann (Hrsg.)

anglistik & englischunterricht

Band 53

Teachable Poems. From Sting to Shelley

HEIDELBERG 1994
UNIVERSITÄTSVERLAG C. WINTER

Teachable Poems
From Sting to Shelley

Verantwortlicher Herausgeber für den thematischen Teil dieses Bandes:

Manfred Pfister

HEIDELBERG 1994

UNIVERSITÄTSVERLAG C. WINTER

Die Deutsche Bibliothek - CIP Einheitsaufnahme

Anglistik & Englischunterricht: A & E. - Heidelberg: Winter.

Früher Schriftenreihe
ISSN 0014-2328

NE: A & E; Anglistik und Englischunterricht

Bd. 53. Teachable poems. - 1994

Teachable poems: from Sting to Shelley / verantw. Hrsg. für den thematischen Teil dieses Bd.: Manfred Pfister. - Heidelberg: Winter, 1994

(Anglistik & Englischunterricht; Bd. 53)
ISBN 3-8253-0252-0

NE: Pfister, Manfred [Hrsg.]

ISBN 3-8253-0252-0
ISSN 0344-8266

Anschrift der Redaktion:
Achim Stahl, Ruhr-Universität Bochum, Englisches Seminar
Universitätsstraße 150 · 44801 Bochum
Verlag: Universitätsverlag C. Winter Heidelberg GmbH
Gesamtherstellung: Universitätsverlag C. Winter, Hans-Bunte-Str. 18, 69123 Heidelberg

Printed in Germany · Imprimé en Allemagne

anglistik & englischunterricht erscheint in drei Bänden pro Jahrgang. Der Gesamtumfang beträgt ca. 540 Seiten
Preis des Einzelbandes DM 28,-
Jahresabonnement DM 60,-. Studentenabonnement DM 50,-, zuzüglich Versandspesen.
In diesen Preisen sind 7% Mehrwertsteuer enthalten
Für unverlangte Einsendungen von Manuskripten wird nicht gehaftet
Mitarbeiter erhalten von ihren Beiträgen 30 Sonderdrucke und 2 Freiexemplare. Honorar wird nicht bezahlt
Der Verlag trägt die Kosten für die von der Druckerei nicht verschuldeten Korrekturen nur in beschränktem Maße und behält sich vor, den Verfassern die Mehrkosten für Autorkorrekturen zu belasten

Inhalt

RUBRIK

Manfred Pfister, Berlin

Preface

Teachable Poems: this is not an attempt to discover or proclaim a new genre of poetry. Teachable poems are not 'didactic poems' (or 'Lehrgedichte') and they can be found in all poetic genres of all periods. *Teachable Poems* is, rather, a series of modest – and, occasionally immodest – proposals for bringing the teaching of poetry up-to-date by suggesting new poems and new approaches for the classroom or seminar-room.

The editor and his authors believe that such an *aggiornamento* is possible and not untimely at a time when poetry is in danger of being faded out of the teaching of English in favour of, say, the obligatory Shakespeare play, the odd contemporary short story and piecemeal excerpts of *landeskundliche Texte*, or retained, in mere lip service to High Culture, as the occasional *pièce de résistance* in which teachers and students alike have lost all confidence. The 'Dead Poets Society' formula of whipping up enthusiasm for the all-time masterpieces of English Poetry will be of little avail here, as it entirely falls back upon the charismatic leader-teacher that we have rightly come to distrust. What might be more helpful is to look out for new poems beyond the canon of schoolsoiled anthology pieces that are interesting to the students because they relate to, or challenge, their interests and their assumptions about themselves and the Other, about subjectivity, reality and language. And, moreover, to propose ways of reading these poems that would help to break down the widespread aversion against reading poetry, based on traditional notions of poetry and its appreciation as a rarefied mystique inaccessible to ordinary reason.

What qualifies a poem for teachability? What makes it a teachable poem? Only one of the contributors to this volume, Günther Jarfe, engages with this question in a direct or systematic fashion; for the others, the proof of the poem is in the teaching and most of the poems have, indeed, already been tested in class or seminar. Our project being rather the practical one of making concrete suggestions, and not a theoretical exercise in methods of *Fachdidaktik*, we need not theorize a poem's teachability factor at great length and can leave the criteria of our selection largely implicit in our arguments and strategies of reading. And when the final contribution, by Christoph Bode, calls into question the teachability of poetry altogether, we take this as an exhortation to devise new and more dialogical ways of going about our business.

Teachable poems have been written in all periods and some of them by the canonized masters of English poetry. Our collection, however, focusses on the nineteenth and particularly the twentieth century, emphatically privileging the contemporary and highlighting recent writing as we feel that the new and exciting departures of the last twenty years have not yet really reached the classroom. What characterizes this new state of the art of poetry is, above all, a pluralisation of the poetic voice. This can take many different forms, ranging from a new orality, a new audible presence of the spoken voice that (re-)turns the poem into something to be performed (Langston Hughes, Sista Rootz, Derek Walcott), to an intermedial dialogue with other arts, with painting (U.A. Fanthorpe) or with pop music (Sting). Its most important form is, however, the refracting of the traditionally dominant voices of white, male and educated poets – here represented by W.H. Auden, Philip Larkin and Adrian Mitchell – in the prisms of race, class and gender.

The impact of this can be readily gauged by comparing our collection of essays with a collection of similar scope and intent, *Moderne englische Lyrik: Interpretation und Dokumentation*, edited by Elke Platz-Waury in 1978, only one and a half decades ago. Of the twelve poems presented in the earlier collection, eleven are by male poets (with Sylvia Plath, hardly an English poet anyway, as the only female voice), and all the poets are white and Anglo-Saxon. Our baker's dozen of poets in contrast balances six female voices against seven male ones, and six non-Anglo-Saxon against seven British writers. What this comparative arithmetic reflects is a shift in gravity from the centre to the margins, from male to female and from English Literature to the New English Literatures written by "Writers from Elsewhere", writers with a Caribbean background, for instance (Derek Walcott, Sista Rootz, Grace Nichols) or, in the case of the USA, from a WASP tradition to Black American (Langston Hughes) or Jewish Eastern European ethnic cultures (Irena Klepfisz).

Our interpretations, written by six female and seven male critics (as opposed to the 2:10 ratio in the Platz-Waury collection), respond to this changed set-up with a new kind of critical engagement and with a whole gamut of theoretical frames. They share a basis of structural analysis in paying attention to metre and metaphor, but they go beyond structuralism in diverse ways that all lead to the correlative questions of how the poem is inscribed into history and how history has inscribed itself into the poem. Psychoanalysis (Evelyne Keitel) and sociography (Hans Ulrich Seeber), discourse and intertextuality (Günther Jarfe, Karl J. Häußler, Andreas Mahler), feminism (Ingrid von Rosenberg) and deconstruction (Anna Maria Stuby, Christoph Bode), post-colonialism, ethnicity and multiculturalism (Klaus Ensslen, Gisela Ecker, Elfi Bettinger, Barbara Korte, Peter O. Stummer) – these are the theoretical key concepts with which the teachability of the poems selected is to be unlocked, and, of course, all the interpretations rubricked here under one single heading bring more than one of these concepts into play. Each interpretation does not only present a particular poem but also a particular approach, a particular way of reading poetry that is put to the test in the discussion of the poem.

Each interpretation thus aims at offering a concrete example for what theory can do and, presenting theory in action, it tries to contribute towards closing the gap between critical theory and teaching practice. While Addison was ambitious to have it said of him that he has "brought philosophy out of closets, and libraries, schools, and colleges, to dwell in clubs and assemblies, at tea-tables and in coffee-houses" (*Spectator*, No. 10), we, in our own small ways, aim at bringing post-structuralist theory out of the *Oberseminar* into the classroom and the tutorial.

What remains to be said for the editor of this volume are two words of thanks – to the editors of *A&E* for having responded so enthusiastically to the project of *Teachable Poems* (and even appreciating the self-irony of its mock-pedantic title!), and to the contributors, whose proposals have given the volume a shape substantially different from what the editor had originally envisaged.

Andreas Mahler, München

Singing in the Echo-Chamber – Postmodernist Play and Simple Song: Sting's "Sister Moon"

> But what man under his powere
> Is bore, he shall his place chaunge
> And seche many londes straunge.[1]

Sister Moon

Sister moon will be my guide
In your blue blue shadows I would hide
All good people asleep tonight
I'm all by myself in your silver light
  I would gaze at your face the whole night through
  I'd go out of my mind, but for you
  I'd go out of my mind, but for you

Lying in a mother's arms
The primal root of a woman's charms
I'm a stranger to the sun my eyes are too weak
How cold is a heart when it's warmth that he seeks?
  You watch every night, you don't care what I do
  I'd go out of my mind, but for you
  I'd go out of my mind, but for you

My mistress' eyes are nothing like the sun
My hunger for her explains everything I've done
  To howl at the moon the whole night through
  And they really don't care if I do
  I'd go out of my mind, but for you

Sister Moon

The moon has many signifieds. On the one hand, it is a "Sister fair" that does "bless everywhere, with silver lip/ Kissing dead things to life", it is "the deep glen -/ [...] the mountain top – the sage's pen -/ The Poet's harp – the voice of friends – the sun", a "gentle Orb" and "airy planet"[2], "Queen both for beauty and for majesty"[3]; on the other hand, however, it may also be that, despite all this culturally produced surplus of meaning, the moon which seems "so far away/ Is but a child's balloon, forgotten after play."[4] Empty signifier and semantic heavyweight, inane object and life-giving essence – the moon has always been a target of solitary and wistful projection, with its semantic potential waxing and waning, signifying all and nothing. Common cultural practice has identified it with "changeableness", "fickleness", "lunacy", "coldness", and "chastity"[5], opposing it to the normality, reliability, fruitfulness, constancy, and warmth of the sun. Above all, the moon is "nothing like the sun".[6]

"Sister Moon" is the title song of Sting's 1987 album ... *Nothing Like the Sun.*[7] The transcription of the lyrics, the "words on the page"[8], can be divided into twenty lines, two stanzas of equal length and a shorter third stanza with a concluding invocation. Its *dispositio* follows a pattern of progression and repetition, each stanza ending in a reiterated refrain (ll. 6-7; 13-14; [18]-19) prepared by verbal echoes (ll. 5/12; 5/17; 12/18) and finally leading back to the first two words (1/20), thus closing the cycle. The structure of the stanzas can be schematized as a-b/a-b/a-b/a-b/c/d/d with the last stanza reducing the 'a-b'-sequences by two and textually altering the first 'd'-line.

The lyrics build up a "world within the poem"[9], in which a speaker/singer addresses the moon, gazing at it in the middle of the night. This world-constructing process is brought about by the use of deictic expressions. In ordinary language use, deictics such as first and second person pronouns as well as adverbials of place and time are – in the words of Jonathan Culler – "'orientational' features of language which relate to the situation of utterance". In poetry, however, as in fictional texts in general, the "importance of such deictics as technical devices [...] can scarcely be overestimated [...]. The deictics do not refer us to an external context but force us to construct a fictional situation of utterance"[10]. In "Sister Moon", there is an overall and consistent evidence of a poetic *persona*, beginning with the possessive pronoun "my" (l. 1) followed by diverse uses of other first person pronouns such as "I" (ll. 2, 4, 5, 6ff.) and "myself" (l. 4) and running through the whole text up to line 19. The predominant use of the present tense suggests the simultaneity of the situation of utterance and the situation described; at the moment of utterance, the solitary speaker/singer finds himself in the sole company of the moon ("I'm all by myself in your silver light" – l. 4) longing for its "blue shadows" (l. 2) to give him shelter. The adverbials of time first situate the contents of the utterance at a given point in the present ("tonight" – l. 3), conveying to it a sense of duration ("the whole night through" – ll. 5,17) and finally implying the iterative act of endless repetition ("every night" – l. 12). The interplay of progression and repetition is thus not only a structural feature, but also part of the contents of the song.

In the analysis of the situation of utterance, the position of the addressee has so far been left out. It is interesting to see that each stanza begins with third person references to the moon (ll. 1, 8-11, 15-18), thus establishing it as the principal object of discourse, but then switches to second person pronouns ("your" – ll. 2, 4, 5; "you" – ll. 6, 7, 12-14, 19) addressing it directly (ll. 2-7, 12-14, 19-20). This shift from third to second person is indicative of the overall movement of the song opening with a statement about the moon ("Sister moon will be my guide" – l. 1) and closing with an appeal to it ("but for you/ Sister Moon" – ll. 19, 20). That way, the moon is part of the enunciation as well as of the enounced[11], creating an amount of pragmatic instability which is not only typical of post-romantic *avantgarde* poetical practice[12], but which can also be read as an iconic recoding of the inconstancy of the moon itself, of its vicinity and distance. As principal object of discourse and addressee of the utterance, the moon is thus focalized from two different angles at the same time: the song is not only a song *about* the moon, it is also a song *to* the moon.

Semantically, the moon is constructed as belonging to the realm of the feminine, thus following a long-standing tradition in English poetry in which it is "often personified, always as a female"[13]. The lyrics qualify the moon as a being with a "face" (l. 5), as "[s]ister" (ll. 1, 20), "mother" (l. 8), "woman" (l. 9), "mistress" (l. 15), and "her" (l. 16), endowing it with an isotopy of the feminine[14] which opposes it to the masculinity of the speaker whose gender specification is alluded to in his male heart ("he" – l. 11) and extratextually corroborated by Sting's male voice. Again, there is a movement from mere denomination to direct appeal which results in the singer finally addressing the moon as "you/ Sister" (ll. 19, 20). This face-to-face situation between the 'I' of the utterance and the moon is, however, characterized as being highly asymmetrical; it suggests a relationship of unrequited love with the speaker resorting to all kinds of activity in order to attract attention ("gaze at your face" – l. 5; "howl at the moon" – l. 17) and the moon remaining as passive as ever: "You watch every night, you don't care what I do" (l. 12). This indifference is reflected in the moon's "eyes" (l. 15), which do not betray any sign of interest in the lover's singing his song: "And they really don't care if I do" (l. 18).

The lyrics thus oppose a male lover and a female beloved in a relationship of frustrated adoration. And yet, the moon does not prove to be altogether unhelpful. The speaker characterizes himself as someone who prefers the night to broad daylight ("I'm a stranger to the sun" – l. 10), who considers himself to be different from normal society ("[a]ll good people asleep tonight" – l. 3), who is consequently on his own ("I'm all by myself" – l. 4) and who sees himself potentially jeopardized ("out of my mind" – ll. 6, 7, 13, 14, 19). Interestingly enough, the song constructs the moon as an exact semantic counterpart to the speaker. The moon as phenomenon of the "night" (ll. 5, 12, 17) soothes the speaker's loneliness in appearing to him as "[s]ister" (ll. 1, 20), "mother" (l. 8), "mistress" (l. 15) and manages to give him orientation and security in serving as "guide" (l. 1) and shelter to "hide"

(l. 2) in, thus diminishing his fear of going mad: "I'd go out of my mind, *but for you*" (ll. 6, 7, 13, 14, 19). Consequently, the relationship between speaker and moon also presents itself as one of potential fulfilment: the 'I' of utterance who "seeks" (l. 11) and desires ("[m]y hunger for her" – l. 16), hopes ("*will be* my guide" – l. 1) and wishes ("I *would* hide" – l. 2; "I *would* gaze" – l. 5), finds orientation and protection, the "primal root" (l. 9) and the desired "warmth" (l. 11), in the moon's mere presence. Seen that way, the moon and the speaker belong to the same realm, corresponding to each other as brother and sister, man and mistress, knight-errant and guiding star. The text thus establishes a structural homology in which the speaker belongs to the moon just as much as all *good* people belong to the daylight sun: 'I'::moon':good people': sun'.[15]

The findings so far can be schematized as follows:

I	MOON
male	female
man of the night	phenomenon of the night
solitary	company
in search	guide
"out of my mind"	"but for you"

Speaker and moon appear as semantic complements, both set apart from the 'normality' of ordinary society. For the speaker to be 'under the moon', therefore, constitutes a normality of his own. That way, the womanly lunar "charms" (l. 9) enticing his "weak" (l. 10) eyes precisely enable him to support his intentional keeping aloof from an ordinary-world lunacy, from the suggested madness of every-day life. Instead of being the cause of mental derangement, the moon manages to guarantee the speaker's health. The song thus produces a semantic subversion attributing to the moon the function of guardian angel and celebrating it as saviour.

Once again, however, the relationship between speaker and moon eludes reciprocity with the 'I' of the utterance "gaz[ing]" (l. 5) at the moon and the moon merely "watch[ing]" (l. 12). Cultural practice has identified the gaze with wishful thinking, with a kind of semantic projection by means of which a male subject manages to eradicate the difference between himself and a female object, thus endowing the object with a semantics of his own. This has been called an "allegorising gaze"[16]. Therefore, what is built up in "Sister Moon" as genuine suffering from unrequited love or as authentic adoration of a higher essence may turn out to be nothing but the imagination of a speaker who constructs an addressee according to his will. The addressee thus appears as a mere effect of the speech acts used by the 'I' of the utterance. The stanzas begin with statements describing the semantic qualities attributed to the moon by the speaker, then go on to articulate complaints about the moon's detachment and end in a laudatory refrain. This movement from description to complaint and then to praise is indicative of the lyric forms alluded to in the lines of the song: what first appears to be a romanticist contemplation turns into a Petrarchan love song and finally takes on the guise of a quasi-religious hymn.

Real or imagined, the moon exerts an enormous influence on the speaker, constituting a source of energy that, in his eyes, accounts for practically all his productivity: "My hunger for her explains everything I've done" (l. 16). The most obvious activity of the 'I' of utterance in a song is, of course, to sing. In "Sister Moon", this is explicitly referred to in the last stanza when the 'I' describes his main preoccupation as "[t]o howl at the moon the whole night through" (l. 17). This does not only take up the 'lonesome wolf' motif introduced in the first stanza; it also brings in an element of self-reflexivity by virtue of which the production of the song itself is thematized.[17] This self-reflexiveness opens up the possibility of a metapoetic reading which attributes to the speaker's "mistress" (l. 15) the role of muse, showing the moon to be the central source of inspiration and creativity. Whatever the relationship between man and moon, the song then seems to exist solely because of it. What remains is a piece of art.

That art is foregrounded in "Sister Moon" becomes most evident when one takes a look at the intertextual play on which the song is based. The most obvious quotation in the song is line 15, which takes up the title of the whole album and which is the first line of Shakespeare's widely anthologized sonnet 130:

> My mistress' eyes are nothing like the sun;
> Coral is far more red than her lips' red;
> If snow be white, why then her breasts are dun;
> If hairs be wires, black wires grow on her head.
> I have seen roses damasked, red and white,
> But no such roses see I in her cheeks,
> And in some perfumes is there more delight
> Than in the breath that from my mistress reeks.
> I love to hear her speak, yet well I know
> That music hath a far more pleasing sound.
> I grant I never saw a goddess go;
> My mistress when she walks treads on the ground.
> And yet, by heaven, I think my love as rare
> As any she belied with false compare.[18]

The sonnet thematizes an overall negation of common expectations, subverting not only the stock comparisons of Petrarchan love poetry but also the need to compare in general. "Sister Moon" refers to the sonnet in reproducing the Petrarchan situation of unrequited love and in projecting it onto an equally alternative object, thus questioning the validity of discourses used to construct expectable 'normalities' such as a fair-haired beauty or a daylight existence. Repeating this gesture of subversion, the song contributes to celebrating the marginal: In the CD booklet, Sting tells a story of a drunk who, demanding threateningly, "How beautiful is the moon?", would only be pacified by a recitation of sonnet 130, and he comments on this by saying that he has found Shakespeare "always useful [...] for calming down violent drunks if only because it gives them the impression that you're crazier than they are."

The intertextual play with Petrarchan motifs is connected with another reference alluded to in the title. In the 1993 album *Ten Summoner's Tales*, which significantly combines the singer's real name with one of Chaucer's *Canterbury Tales*, the song "Saint Augustine in Hell" consists of a number of references that can be brought together with Sting's Catholic upbringing. Among others, the song mentions Francis of Assisi who, in his *Canticle of Brother Sun* of 1225, was the first in European literature to coin the phrase of "Sister Moon"[19]:

> Most High, omnipotent, good Lord
> To you alone belong praise and glory,
> Honor and blessing.
> No man is worthy to breathe thy name.
>
> Be praised, my Lord, for all your creatures.
> In the first place for the blessed Brother Sun,
> Who gives us the day and enlightens us through you.
> He is beautiful and radiant with great splendor,
> Giving witness of thee, Most Omnipotent One.
>
> Be praised, my Lord, for Sister Moon and the stars
> Formed by you so bright, precious and beautiful. [...]

The *Canticle of Brother Sun* is a hymn, a laudatory poem in praise of God. In giving to the sun the "first place", Saint Francis simply reiterates one of the basic elements of the common medieval Christian world picture with the sun as "the eye and mind of the whole universe"[20]. Sting's song to "Sister Moon" can be read in the tradition of complementary answers to such orthodox celebrations of the sun. The intertextual play thus combines the Petrarchan motif of the sun-mistress with an ongoing religious scepticism. "You could say I lost my belief in the Holy Church", is a line Sting sings in the Prologue song to the Summoner's Tales, "If I Ever Lose My Faith In You". The celebration of the sun's cultural opposite is an adequate illustration of this loss of faith; it makes "Sister Moon" appear as a counter-hymn.

The most powerful site of the celebration of the marginal in European cultural history, however, is Romanticism with its valorisation of nocturnal situations and melancholic moods. Here the relationship is less one of immediately identifiable intertextuality than that of an overall systemic reference.[21] The "blue blue shadows" (l. 2), the speaker's solitude and the moon's "silver light" (l. 4) refer most clearly to the characteristics of a Romantic discourse, integrating the Petrarchan concept of *acedia* into the notion of Romantic melancholy. "Sister Moon" thus seems to appertain above all to the Romantic genre of the night song.

This impression is enhanced by the music which follows the structure of the lullaby.[22] The lullaby is a soft, slow song sung to a child "[l]ying in a mother's arms" (l. 8), causing the child to fall asleep. Right from the start, the syncopated rhythm of the bass produces a softening effect with two notes moving upwards and three quicker ones going back down again, each movement being followed by an orchestral chord, thus imitating a cradle gently rocking to and fro. This question-and-answer-like structure underpins all the 'a'- as well as the 'b'-sequences with the text being sung on the downward sections exclusively. Above this regular movement, the sad, wistful sound of an improvising saxophone adds to the atmosphere of a nocturnal situation. In addition to that, it also expresses the feeling of unfulfilled desire, thus blending – on the musical level as well – the motif of unrequited love with the Romanticity of the night song. Besides, "Sister Moon" also attains the quality of a hymn. According to the pattern of progression and repetition, the 'd'-sections of the refrain vary in that the last "you" changes from a fall in lines 6, 7 and 13 to a significant rise in line 14 with Sting's falsetto voice prefiguring the howl thematized in the third stanza. This change of tone does not only support the speech act change from the descriptive to the appellative noted above; it also leads to an interposed saxophone solo with an ensuing transposition of the tonality, as a consequence of which the shorter third stanza begins in a higher key, thus focussing more intensely on the most prominent intertextual quotation. The last "you" (l. 19) of the song is sung in the highest pitch so far, only to be surpassed by the final invocation of "Sister Moon" (l. 20) which then gives way to a jubilant celebratory improvisation of the saxophone. Romantic night song, melancholic love call, and religious hymn thus find themselves also musically amalgamated.

This juxtaposition of the heterogeneous, "giv[ing] equal value to the self-reflexive and the historically grounded"[23], makes "Sister Moon" appear as an instance of postmodernist art where intertextuality/intermediality "is not just used as one device amongst others, but is foregrounded, displayed, thematized and theorized as a central constructional principle".[24] The song thus follows the same *avantgarde* poetics as, say, Derek Jarman's filmic essay on the Shakespearean sonnets in *The Angelic Conversation* (1985) or Peter Greenaway's multi-medial play in *Prospero's Books* (1991).

Popular music, however, as all art, is "not essentially either subversive or conformist. [...] Every ideological effect can be deconstructed, no subcultural alignment is permanent, all forms can be appropriated."[25] Self-consciously deploying an intricate play of cultural references, "Sister Moon" can therefore at any time be also just 'consumed' as a simple, pleasant song.

Notes

1 J. Gower: *Confessio Amantis.* Ed. H. Morley. London, 1889, p. 349, VII, ll. 745-747; this is one of the few instances in English literature in which the moon is still linguistically conceived of, as in Old English times, as masculine.
2 J. Keats: *Endymion: A Poetic Romance* (1818). – In idem: *The Complete Poems.* Ed. J. Barnard. Harmondsworth, [3]1988, pp. 106-216, III, ll. 42; 56-57; 162-165; 175; 185.
3 W. Wordsworth: "'With How Sad Steps, O Moon'" (1807). – In idem: *Poems.* Sel. W.E. Williams. Harmondsworth, repr. 1986, pp. 50, l. 14; the title of this poem refers, of course, to sonnet 31 of Sidney's *Astrophel and Stella.*
4 T.E. Hulme: "Above the Dock" (1912). – In A.R. Jones: *The Life and Opinions of T.E. Hulme.* London, 1960, pp. 158, ll. 3-4.
5 *OED*, [2]1989.
6 "[S]o long as it remains an opposition, the contrast between the sun and the moon can signify almost anything" (Cl. Lévi-Strauss). For a discussion of this opposition as "powerful mythological operator with great semantic potential" see J. Culler: *Structuralist Poetics. Structuralism, Linguistics and the Study of Literature.* London, repr. 1989, pp. 52-53, both quotes on p. 52.
7 Sting *alias* Gordon Matthew Sumner was born October 2, 1951 in Newcastle-upon-Tyne as the eldest of four. He is a Catholic of working-class background and has worked as bricklayer, teacher, model, actor, and singer (with *The Police* and as a soloist).
8 "Nothing better demonstrates the inadequacy of words-on-the-page criticism than attempts to analyse the lyrics of popular songs." For a discussion of the problematics of such an approach and a few valuable "caveats" see A. Ross: "Poetry and Motion. Madonna and Public Enemy". – In A. Easthope, J.O. Thompson (Eds.): *Contemporary Poetry Meets Modern Theory.* London, 1991, pp. 96-107, pp. 96 ff., for the quotation p. 96. The transcription of "Sister Moon" does not follow the text printed in the CD booklet accompanying ... *Nothing Like the Sun* (A&M Records, Los Angeles, 1987). I have added one additional line (7), which is sung but not printed, and have transcribed lines 10 and 11 as two long lines rather than four short ones, in general trying to retain the symmetries of the song in the layout.
9 "The first few lines of a poem are naturally the most important for establishing an inferred situation." For the world-constructing qualities of poetry and the notion

of 'inferred situations' see G.N. Leech: *A Linguistic Guide to English Poetry*. London, [6]1977, pp. 189 ff., for the quotation p. 191.

10 J. Culler: *Structuralist Poetics*, pp. 165-166.

11 For the use of the terms 'enunciation' for the inferred situation of utterance and 'enounced' for its contents and a detailed discussion of their applicability to the analysis of poetry see A. Easthope: *Poetry as Discourse*. London, New York, 1983, pp. 40 ff.

12 "Modernist poetry can be seen as denying a position for the transcendental ego." (Ibid., pp. 134 f.) The dissolution of pragmatic coherence in poetry begins in France with Baudelaire and can be traced as a common feature throughout his successors in modernist/postmodern poetry. For a highly suggestive discussion of the poetics of post-romantic poetry see V. Forrest-Thomson: *Poetic Artifice. A Theory of Twentieth-Century Poetry*. Manchester, 1978.

13 *OED*, [2]1989. See also G. Genette: "Le jour, la nuit". – In idem: *Figures II*. Paris, 1969, 101–122, who, tracing the opposition of night and day in French poetry, finds that "la nuit n'est que *l'autre* du jour" (p. 106) and concludes: "le rapport entre *jour* et *nuit* est homologue [...] au rapport entre *homme* et *femme*" (p. 104).

14 The notion of isotopy as developed by the French semiotician A.J. Greimas designates groups of words with a common semantic denominator whose recurrences guarantee the lexical coherence (cohesion) of a text. For a critical discussion see J. Culler: *Structualist Poetics*, pp. 79-83 and 87-95.

15 For a discussion of the concept of homology and its notational conventions see M. Titzmann: *Strukturale Textanalyse. Theorie und Praxis der Interpretation*. München, 1977, pp. 152ff., for an application see pp. 404ff.

16 E. Bronfen: *Over Her Dead Body. Death, Femininity and the Aesthetic*. Manchester, 1992, p. 227.

17 For the idea of literary self-consciousness, mainly in narrrative, see P. Waugh: *Metafiction. The Theory and Practice of Self-Conscious Fiction*. London, New York, 1984, pp. 21ff.

18 W. Shakespeare: *The Sonnets and A Lover's Complaint*. Ed. J. Kerrigan. London, 1986, p. 141.

19 For a discussion of the *Canticle of Brother Sun* see L.S. Cunningham: *Saint Francis of Assisi*. Boston/Mass., 1976, pp. 51-59; the Italian text and its English translation are reprinted on pp. 57-59, I quote the first three stanzas of Cunningham's English rendering.

20 C.S. Lewis: *The Discarded Image. An Introduction to Medieval and Renaissance Literature*. Cambridge, repr. 1988, p. 106; for the moon as agency of restlessness see p. 109. See also E.M.W. Tillyard: *The Elizabethan World Picture*. Harmondsworth, repr. 1978, pp. 17-25 and 95-101.

21 For a discussion of intertextuality as one-to-one reference of a text to its 'pretext' see M. Pfister: "How Postmodern is Intertextuality?" – In H.F. Plett (Ed.): *Intertextuality*. Berlin, New York, 1991, pp. 207-224, 210; for the notion of "Systemreferenz" see K.W. Hempfer: "Überlegungen zu einem Gültigkeitskriterium für Interpretationen und ein komplexer Fall: Die italienische Ritterepik der Renaissance". – In K.W. Hempfer, G. Regn (Eds.): *Interpretationen. Das Paradigma der europäischen Renaissance-Literatur*. Wiesbaden, 1983, pp. 1-31, 15.

22 For a highly stimulating exploration of the analogies between music and language see L. Bernstein: *The Unanswered Question. Six Talks at Harvard*. Cambridge/Mass., 1976.

23 L. Hutcheon: *The Politics of Postmodernism.* London, New York, 1989, p. 2; Hutcheon derives this basic description of postmodernism from its traditional paradigm of architecture.

24 M. Pfister: "How Postmodern", p. 214.

25 A. Sinfield: *Literature, Politics and Culture in Postwar Britain.* Oxford, 1989, p. 178; for further discussions of aesthetizing uses or consumer-oriented reappropriations of mass/élite culture see D. Hebdige: *Hiding in the Light. On Images and Things.* London, New York, 1988.

Anna Maria Stuby, Hannover

Watching Man Watching Woman: Christina Rossetti's "'Reflection'"

'Reflection'

Gazing thro' her chamber window
    Sits my soul's dear soul;
Looking northward, looking southward,
    Looking to the goal,
    Looking back without control. –

I have strewn thy path, beloved,
    With plumed meadowsweet,
Iris and pale perfumed lilies,
    Roses most complete:
    Wherefore pause on listless feet? –

But she sits and never answers;
    Gazing gazing still
On swift fountain, shadowed valley,
    Cedared sunlit hill:
    Who can guess or read her will?

Who can guess or read the spirit
    Shrined within her eyes,
Part a longing, part a languor,
    Part a mere surprize,
    While slow mists do rise and rise? –

Is it love she looks and longs for;
    Is it rest or peace;
Is it slumber self-forgetful
    In its utter ease;
    Is it one or all of these?

So she sits and doth not answer
    With her dreaming eyes,
With her languid look delicious
    Almost Paradise,
    Less than happy, over wise.

Answer me, O self-forgetful –
    Or of what beside? –
Is it day dream of a maiden,
    Vision of a bride
    Is it knowledge, love, or pride?

Cold she sits thro' all my kindling,
    Deaf to all I pray:
I have wasted might and wisdom,
    Wasted night and day:
    Deaf she dreams to all I say.

Now if I could guess her secret
    Were it worth the guess? –
Time is lessening, hope is lessening,
    Love grows less and less:
    What care I for *no* or *yes*? –

I will give her stately burial,
    Tho', when she lies dead:
For dear memory of the past time,
    Of her royal head,
    Of the much I strove and said.

I will give her stately burial,
    Willow branches bent;
Have her carved in alabaster,
    As she dreamed and leant
    While I wondered what she meant.

After a first or second reading "'Reflection'"[1] looks (and sounds) like one of those 'good old' reliable poems whose interplay of skilfully chosen poetic elements (an ear-catching metre and an ingratiating rhyme scheme, a wealth of recognizable and thus pleasurable figures of speech, a melodious and richly modulated sound pattern etc.) seems to warrant poetic power of expression and hence meaning. A closer look at "'Reflection'", however, reveals that such a conventional approach moves on treacherous ground. The reader begins to recognize a striking contradiction between the poem's clear-cut prosodic structure or its elaborate patterns of repetition such as anaphora ("looking northward, looking southward, / looking [...], / looking [...]" – ll. 3-5; "Is it love [...], Is it rest [...], Is it slumber [...]" – ll. 21-23), anadiplosis ("Who can guess or read her will? // Who can guess or read the spirit" – ll. 15-16), polyptoton ("Time is lessening, hope is lessening / Love grows less and less" – ll. 43-44), alliteration, assonance etc. and the confusing content of its mytho-ideological, iconographical and allegorical allusions.

What the reader first tends to classify as a traditional treatment of a traditional theme in Romantic and Victorian painting and literature: the motif of "the woman at the window" with its well-known implications of female immobility, spiritual enclosure and liminality is subtly questioned, parodied and inverted as the poem progresses. One of its basic statements seems to be: "Nothing is authentic, nothing is what it pretends to be."

This does not only apply to the remote and silent woman with the (pretended?) secret, who is alternately watched, addressed, read and described by a male counterpart, who stages himself in a recognizably post-Petrarcan, post-troubadour fashion of the romantic lover, but also to the poem itself, which, in a self-conscious mode, points to its own 'unreliability' by posing as a riddle that subverts its own meaning by highlighting it. The very title of the poem is the first prominently placed signifier to its ambiguity and doubleness: Semantically, 'reflection' oscillates between 'meditation' and 'mirror-image', and, in addition to this, the inverted commas around the title de-naturalize a conventional reading based on public consensus and point to Rossetti's self-contradictoriness as an aesthetic strategy.[2]

While the poem's title draws the readers' attention to the doubleness or ambiguity of the poem's own mode of representation, the first stanza swiftly ensnares them in a dramatic tableau, whose power of visualization is extraordinary.

Readers and listeners of the poem are thus forced to take the roles of spectators in a drama whose main action – that of watching and being watched – is divided between a male and a female protagonist, and where the gender-specific attributation of the roles of subject and object of the gaze is staged as invariable.

The scene laid out in the first lines of stanza 1 seems familiar enough, although its allusions may have been more accessible and self-evident to Rossetti's contemporary public. A woman gazing through a window was an obsessively re-produced image in her time. The enclosed woman was generally conceived of as an icon of female passiveness and seclusion, a woman either desperately waiting for the return of her lover to rescue her from her death-in-life position, or a woman who has become weary with waiting for her tarrying lover and is ready to embrace death instead.[3] That Christina Rossetti was well acquainted with this topic, is proven by such poems as "The Prince's Progress" (*CP*, I, p. 95), "Repining" (*CP*, III, p. 17), "From the Antique" (*CP*, III, p. 231) and many others that can be read as variations on this theme, in which the poet tries out the viability of different female positions within the given framework. The female protagonist in "Repining" e.g. (written at the age of 16), whose opening lines run like this: "She sat alway thro' the long day / Spinning the weary thread away; / And ever said in undertone: 'Come, that I be no more alone.'" is summoned forth by an angelic visitant for a panoramic view of the horrors of the world until she begs to return to her quiet and protected isolation, whereas the weary woman in "From the Antique" (there are many echoes of Tennyson's famous poem "Mariana") wishes to be dead: "It's a weary life, it is; she said: – Doubly blank in a woman's lot".

The fact that Rossetti frames her lyrical picture of the solitary woman with a chamber window points to her awareness of another implication of the iconographical tradition which she invokes. Her picture recalls those portraits of "royal [female] heads" (l. 49) in which the painters of the Pre-Raphaelite Brotherhood immortalized their models and muses.[4] Rossetti was one of those models, while at the same time she strove to become an artist (poet) in her own right.[5] "From her earliest years she sat for some forty-five portraits and photographs, ranging from watercolor when she was seven to Dante Gabriel's [her brother's] last chalk portrait of her, done when she was forty-six".[6] How much she was aware of the problematic power-relation between the artist and his model is documented in her sonnet "In an Artist's Studio" (*CP*, III, p. 264, also unpublished during her lifetime), which pays tribute to Elizabeth Siddal, her brother's model and presumably mistress before he eventually married her.

> One face looks out from all his canvasses,
> One selfsame figure sits or walks or leans.
> We found her hidden just behind those screens,
> That mirror gave back all her loveliness.
> [...]
> He feeds upon her face by day and night,
> And she with true kind eyes looks back on him
> Fair as the moon and joyful as the light:
> Not wan with waiting, not with sorrow dim;
> Not as she is, but was when hope shone bright;
> Not as she is but as she fills his dream.

Unlike the speaker in "'Reflection'", who apostrophizes the woman he watches[7] as his "soul's dear soul" (l. 2) – another indication that here already he is staged in the role of the artist[8] – the watcher and speaker in the sonnet

> witnesses the discrepancy between the artist's frail illusion and the woman's unpicturable reality [...]. The woman vampirized by art, in life more dead than alive, in art endowed with ghostly life, suggests the kind of depersonalization that woman-as-model experiences. The watcher commemorates her symbolic death.[9]

The watcher in "'Reflection'" is irritated by the fact that the gazing woman does not look 'out from the canvas' into his face, that his soul is not mirrored in hers, that her gaze is unsteady, uncontrollable. It moves in all directions (stanza 1) and yet it remains unaware of the speaker's presence. This could either indicate that the speaker's position is an oblique one (he watches her from somewhere beneath her window, posing in a troubadour-like fashion and using the woman as a muse to stimulate his lyrical effusions of love, "feeding upon her face by day and night"), or that he watches her from within her chamber (a frequent perspective in 19th century paintings), but that the woman deliberately ignores him. Both interpretations seem to corroborate each other: compared with a 'true' bard of love[10] the speaker in "'Reflection'" turns out to be emotionally limited and extremely conventional in his concept of the relation between the sexes. What he is saying in the second stanza is nothing else but that for him love is a calculable equation of 'give and take', in which his part consists in giving away flowers and hers in giving away herself (... of being deflowered). Rossetti's flower imagery[11] in stanza 2 also points to a fundamental cultural and aesthetic constellation in Western discourse: the interrelation between femininity and death. Whereas the phallic "meadowsweet" ("growing with erect, rigid stems to the height of about two feet" – *OED*) alludes to the speaker's sexual desire, the rose, lily and iris traditionally function as a suitor's love-tokens for his wife-to-be and, simultaneously, as symbols of mourning for a dead bride. Thus stanza 1 and 2 (the redoubled aesthetization of the window-framed woman killed into art as a dead bride) can be read as the speaker's subconscious/repressed anticipation of the final two stanzas, where he eventually decides to save himself from the threat of the uncontrollable, enigmatic, 'over wise' and sphynx-like woman by *having* her carved in alabaster (my italics).[12] Here, Rossetti ironically points to the speaker's duplicity, who only *poses* as a lover and an artist in a Pygmalion-like manner but proves to be neither the one nor the other.

His impatience and impotence as a lover become manifest in the 3rd stanza already: he gives up wooing his beloved i.e. addressing her personally, and instead turns to the reader inviting him to become a complice in his view of the mirrored, 'speculated' woman, whose secrets he so desperately wishes to disclose.

The 'framed' woman is thus doubly isolated as the 'Other'. As a dead bride endowed with statuary qualities, as an art object, she can be read like a text that poses a hermeneutic task for the lover-artist-analyst: "Who can guess or *read* her will?" (my italics). The catalogue of possible answers in stanzas 4 to 7 is long – partly repetitive – but, significantly, it is not exhaustive. The speaker can only imagine that his mute epipsyche's "languid look" (l. 28) expresses "[...] a longing, [...] a languor, [...] a mere surprize" (ll. 18-19), that her 'dreaming eyes' speak of love, rest, peace, self-forgetful slumber or of a combination of all these things. What he dares not overtly consider is the threatening possibility that the object of his desire has made itself unattainable, that the sphynx-like, over wise woman has her revenge on those who would read her as a conventional sign: that rather than mean what the lover wants, she will mean nothing at all. In this respect "'Reflection'" can also be read as an early critique of influential myths of femininity such as the Mona Lisa cult, which gained importance as the century progressed, and which inspired such well-known works of art as Walter Pater's "La Gioconda", Oscar Wilde's "Sphynx Without A Secret", or Franz von Stuck's "The Sphynx's Kiss".[13]

In another poem written only two months after "'Reflection'", entitled "Winter: My Secret", Rossetti suggests that the lyrical I wears her "mask" for "warmth" having her say: "my secret's mine, and I won't tell. / Or, after all, perhaps there's none." (*CP*, I, p. 47, ll. 6-7)

> Like the sphynx of 'Day-Dreams' [R. Crump's third volume of the *Complete Poems* of Christina Rossetti with the text of "'Reflection'" was not available yet when Rosenblum wrote her book, A.M.S.], this enigma may be empty as enigma, but more important, the speaker, the owner of the 'mask' asserts her right to think her own thoughts. [...] The self-display that falsifies the self becomes a means to compose a self that sees while being seen, and the model turns out to be none other than the artist.[14]

For the sake of his own survival the artist-lover in "'Reflection'" must suppress the possible knowledge that his model may lead an independent existence beyond his creative powers, that the female figure whose self is presented as 'spectacle', may convert her reification into an inward pose of female self-creation.

The increasing tension, suspense and irritability of the speaker culminates in his anacoluthic imploration in stanza 7:

Answer me, O self-forgetful –
Or of what beside?-

where the dashes indicate his growing incapability of mastering the situation linguistically and point to the effort which is necessary to suppress the knowledge that his beloved's absent-mindedness surpasses his explanatory powers.

The chance of an insight into the true nature of his relationship with the impenetrable woman is short-lived, however; it does not survive the first two lines of the 7th stanza. The woman's threatening silence is quickly filled with yet another series of potential answers (day-dream, bridal vision, knowledge, love, pride) that add nothing new but only echo the old ones without attaining their intensity.[15]

How can the speaker escape from this vicious circle? In stanza 8 his suspense eventually turns to petulance. Confronted with the fact that the woman remains "Deaf to all I pray" – an imperceptible shift in "pray" from 'beg, implore' to 'preach' can be discerned here – he takes refuge in his original (but not openly acknowledged) concept of love as a form of calculable cash-nexus. He realizes that he has been deceived into investing too much, wasting "might and wisdom", "night and day", his man-power and his invaluable time. The accountancy of emotions in the next stanza is revealingly at variance with the pose of the romantic lover.

> Now if I could guess her secret,
> Were it worth the guess? –
> Time is lessening, hope is lessening,
> Love grows less and less:
> What care I for *no* or *yes*?

The colon in line 44 suggests that the last line of stanza 9 ("What care I for *no* or *yes*?") amounts to the total sum of his calculations.

The seeming facility with which the speaker shrugs off his irritation about the unsolvable problem of femininity by reducing his relationship with the woman to a mere matter of economic balance is belied by his fear to be eternally thrown back on a question that may turn out to be less rhetorical than it seems: "What care I for *no* or *yes*?" To end his reflections on a note of possible *da capo* seems inadmissable. Two stanzas are added to reassert his shaken identity. If the lover cannot survive, the artist, at least, must. The elaborately balanced structure of these two final stanzas (especially the anaphora of their first lines) points to the speaker's will to aesthetic mastery. So does his projected *mise-en-scène* of a stately burial for his dead beloved (or rather, for his badly invested love): "For dear memory of the past time / Of her royal head, / Of the much I strove and said." (ll. 48-50)

A *Mariana*-figure, who rejects the traditional concept of suicidal female love (the "Willow branches bent" [l. 52] evoke the poetic fates of many an Ophelia, Lady of Shalott and Elaine) but constructs a sign of self-possession out of her petrifaction[16] poses such a threat that she must be killed once more. The persona of the suitor-artist ultimately "kills off this idol / model, who is already 'dead' anyway, in order to make an art object that commemorates her fixity and his obsession [...]."[17]

The prominently placed "I" as the first word of each of the last stanzas draws the reader's 'eye' away from the woman, who vanishes behind her carved image on the alabaster-gravestone. The latter is not only evocative of the Pygmalion-myth (which is obliquely and critically inscribed into Rossetti's poem), its whiteness reduplicates the image of the dead bride. But in spite of all these gestures of re-assertion the reader remains unconvinced of the artist-lover's ultimate victory. "Even if we are given an image of death engendering a stabilizing self-representation, we are asked to acknowledge that the ensuing self-construction is neither original, unique nor authentic."[18]

And what about the woman at the window?

> [...], and she, by the inevitable logic of his desires, will be as much alive in stone as she seemed dead to him in life. The punitive and acquisitive motives behind this inflicted death-wish are clearly audible. Meanwhile, however, [...] this woman dreams on, 'deaf' (37) to all her lover's morbid romancing. The sense of her 'secret' in the poem makes all his speculation irrelevant. 'What' she means is an object outside his frame of reference, intact and inviolable. Such a secret is both the object of the poem and also its negation; its sense and also its nonsense. 'While I wondered what she meant' rings, at the end, with an irresistible double reference both to the woman at the window and also to the woman poet who has played this toying game of meaning with the very house of courtly love.[19]

Much of Christina Rossetti's poetry which was so long forgotten, misread or devalued in the twentieth century[20] is surprisingly postmodern in the sense that it challenges and subverts traditional modes of perception.

> If the mastering gaze which separates the subject from the object of the gaze, projecting desire onto that object, is inherently masculine, as many feminists argue, could there ever be such a thing as women's *visual* art? I think this may potentially be a very real impasse, but nevertheless one which postmodernist parody has offered at least one possible exit strategy – a compromised one, but one with some possible political efficacy. By using postmodern parodic modes of installing and then subverting conventions, such as the maleness of the gaze, representation of woman can be 'de-doxified' [de-doxify (R. Barthes) = de-naturalize, A.M.S.].[21]

The pleasure of reading and teaching a poem of the mid-nineteenth century like "'Reflection'" lies, to a great extent, in the discovery of the poem's modernity, in its adaptability to our own aesthetic and political needs.

Notes

1 "'Reflection'" was composed on Sept. 8th, 1857, when Christina Rossetti was 26 years old. It belongs to the many poems that she decided not to publish during her lifetime. Two years after her death in 1894 her brother William Michael Rossetti included it under the title of "DAY-DREAMS" in an edition which he called *New Poems by Christina Rossetti.* His printed version of the poem follows the manuscript in Christina's notebook, which is now in the British Library. R.W. Crump's version in her variorum edition of *The Complete Poems of Christina Rossetti*, 3 vols., Baton Rouge, London, 1979-1990, cited as *CP* in my article, is based on a fair copy of this first manuscript, which is in the Princeton University Library, and which was revised and signed by Christina Rossetti. This version forms the textual

basis of my analysis. The most remarkable difference between the first and second manuscript is the poem's title. Rossetti changed it from "Day Dreams" to "'Reflection'". Her resoluteness in doing so is all the more surprising as "Christina always struggled with titles" (K. Jones: *Learning Not To Be First: The Life of Christina Rossetti.* Moreton-in-Marsh, 1991, p. 33). Some of her most famous lyrics (e.g. "When I am dead, my dearest") are simply called "SONG" or "Song".

2 The correspondences between L. Hutcheon's theoretization of postmodernism and its political functions and Rossetti's aesthetic practice of distancing, posing and masquerading are striking. "In general terms", writes Hutcheon, "[postmodernism] takes the form of self-conscious, self-contradictory, self-undermining statement. It is rather like saying something whilst at the same time putting inverted commas around what is being said. The effect is to highlight, or 'highlight', and to subvert, or 'subvert', and the mode is therefore a 'knowing' and an ironic – or even 'ironic' – one. Postmodernism's distinctive character lies in this kind of wholesale 'nudging' commitment to doubleness, or duplicity." (L. Hutcheon: *The Politics of Postmodernism.* London, New York, 1989, p. 1)

3 See E. Shefer's article on "The Woman at the Window in Victorian Art and Christina Rossetti as the Subject of Millais's *Mariana*" (*Journal of Pre-Raphaelite Studies* 4, 1983, 14-25) and my discussion of the *Mariana* and the *Lady of Shalott*-motif in *Liebe, Tod und Wasserfrau. Mythen des Weiblichen in der Literatur.* Opladen, 1992, chps. IV and V. Ironically, the 21-year-old Christina Rossetti herself posed as the model for Millais's famous picture *Mariana* to which he was inspired by Tennyson's eponymous poem, in which the solitary female protagonist wishes to be dead: "She only said, 'My life is dreary, / He cometh not', she said; / She said, 'I am aweary, / I would that I were dead!"

4 See G. Daly: *Pre-Raphaelites in Love.* London, 1989; see also the three monographs by J. Marsh: *Pre-Raphaelite Sisterhood.* London, 1985; *Pre-Raphaelite Women. Images of Femininity in Pre-Raphaelite Art.* London, 1987; *The Legend of Elizabeth Siddal.* London, 1989; and the recent essay by N. Grundmann et al.: "Original oder Kopie? – Die Frauen der Präraffaeliten". *Gulliver* 34, 1993, 70-101.

5 The strategies she employs to find "her place" as a female poet without being trapped in the pitfalls of melancholy romantic love lyricisms like her predecessor Laetitia Elizabeth Landon (1802-1838), to whom she dedicated her poem "L.E.L." (1859), and without having to emulate the overtly political poetry of Elizabeth Barrett Browning are discussed in A. Leighton: *Victorian Women Poets. Writing Against the Heart.* Charlottesville, London, 1992, pp. 118-163; in D. Rosenblum: *Christina Rossetti. The Poetry of Endurance.* Carbondale, Edwardsville, 1986, ch. 3; and in my article: "'I tell my Secret? No, indeed, not I'. Zur poetischen VerStellungskunst Christina Rossettis". *Gulliver* 34, 1993, 109-128.

6 D. Rosenblum: *The Poetry of Endurance*, p. 114.

7 In her article on "Christina Rossetti's Religious Poetry: Watching, Looking, Keeping Vigil" (*Victorian Poetry* 20, 1982, 33-49), Rosenblum assesses the secular tradition of watching as follows: '[...] the metaphor of sight, particularly as it involves gazing upon a face, belongs also to the secular tradition, where it has acquired specific and fixed gender assignments: from Sidney through Keats and Shelley to Dante Gabriel Rossetti, the poet writes as a male "seer" who gazes upon a beloved – or calm and cold, even terrifying – female face. This face answers his look, or does not; mirrors his soul, or does not; in any case, it is always an *object* of vision. As a woman poet, then, Rossetti must deal with the fragmentation of her

poetic consciousness into an observer and an observed. Characteristically, she takes on both roles, becoming the observer seeing herself observed, the witness of the reification of self, very often precisely as a visual object." (p. 37)

8 As Rossetti was well acquainted with the poetry of the Romantic Age, it is highly probable that "my soul's dear soul" refers to Shelley's poem "Epipsychidion" (1821). The word "epipsychidion" is an invention of Shelley's, and in the poem he translates it as "this soul out of my soul". The male genius's feminized soul also plays a central role in Dante Gabriel Rossetti's narrative *Hand and Soul*, where a "fair woman, that was his soul" visits the painter Chiaro and begs him: "Chiaro, servant of God, take now thine Art unto thee, and paint me thus, as I am, to know me [...]. Do this; so shall thy soul stand before thee always and perplex thee no more". (D.G. Rossetti: *Poems and Translations 1850-1870.* London, ^{8}1986, p. 168). See also D.G. Rossetti's poem "The Portrait", whose first stanza runs like this: "This is her picture as she was: / It seems a thing to wonder on, / As though mine image in the glass / Should tarry when myself am gone. / I gaze until she seems to stir,- / Until mine eyes almost aver / That now, even now, the sweet lips part / To breathe the words of the sweet heart:- / And yet the earth is over her." (Ibid., pp. 73-76)

9 D. Rosenblum: "Christina Rossetti's Religous Poetry", p. 39. In a lucid analysis of Erica Pedretti's postmodern novel *Valerie oder Das unerzogene Auge* (1986) G. Ecker discusses the possibilities and limits of the female protagonist's complicitous critique of her roles as lover, muse, model, and as creator of texts. There are striking parallels with the diverse strategies Rossetti employs in her poems to secure female self-possession. (G. Ecker: "Der andere Blick? Erica Pedrettis Roman 'Valerie oder das unerzogene Auge'". – In S. Weigel [Ed.]: *Leib- und Bildraum.* Köln, Weimar, Wien, 1992, pp. 77-99)

10 In A.C. Swinburne's poem "A Leave-Taking" the speaker's/singer's sadness about the deafness of his beloved rings much more true because the singer without hope will eventually be silenced: "Let us go hence, my songs; she will not hear. / Let us go hence together without fear; / Keep silence now, for singing-time is over, / And over all old things and all things dear. / She loves not you nor me as all we love her. / Yea, though we sang as angels in her ear, / She would not hear." (A.C. Swinburne: *A Selection.* Comp. with an Introd. by E. Sitwell. London, 1960, pp. 82-83, 1st stanza)

11 The American critic J.J. McGann ("Christina Rossetti's Poems: A New Edition and A Revaluation". *Victorian Studies,* Winter 1980, 237-254), who was among the first to point out that Christina Rossetti's "work does often cultivate the manner (and hence the poetic illusion) of a clear simple surface", suggested that readers of her poetry "be supplied with a floral dictionary, for example, if they are to deal with one of her most elementary, and pervasive, symbolic structures" (240).

12 In a chapter entitled "The speculated woman" E. Bronfen (*Over Her Dead Body. Death, Femininity and the Aesthetic.* Manchester, 1992) discusses the interrelation between death and femininity in Western discourse with reference to Freud's theories of femininity, where "Woman as patient is transformed into the bearer of a secret which the analyst brings out into the open. The implication is that Woman readily serves as metonymy for any other question not solved, such as death. The riddle of death can be solved by solving the riddle of Woman and vice versa with the speculating man in the position of the analyst trying to discover the concealed secret. In Freud's construction of femininity, the enigma that Woman is thought

to pose readily transforms into dissimulation. Because Woman is silent about herself, she creates an excess of mystery and obscurity, turns herself into an undecipherable riddle, and her inability to disclose herself turns into a lack of sincerity. In his search for truth, the masculine speculator takes on the position of one who watches the other, tries to decipher the riddle she incorporates, tries to solve what she is silent about. The crux is whether Woman has a secret of which she is ignorant and which she is hiding from herself or whether she knows her secret and is wilfully hiding it." (p. 264)

13 For further examples in literature and the visual arts see B. Dijkstra: *Idols of Perversity. Fantasies of Feminine Evil in Fin-de-Siècle Culture*. New York, Oxford, 1986.

14 D. Rosenblum: *The Poetry of Endurance*, p. 123.

15 S. Rimmon-Kenan ("The Paradoxical Status of Repetition". *Poetics Today* 1, 1980, 151-159) suggests that an undifferentiated oversameness without variation comes close to complete death, beyond life and narrative. This destructive repetition in "'Reflection'" threatens to eventually silence the speaker.

16 See Rosenblum's discussion of Christina Rossetti's sibylline power and her self-image as a "stony woman" in the poem "From House to Home" (*CP*, I, pp. 82-88, ll. 205–6): "Therefore in patience I possess my soul. / Yea, therefore as a flint I set my face." (*The Poetry of Endurance*, p. 118)

17 Ibid, p. 122.

18 E. Bronfen: *Over Her Dead Body*, p. 8.

19 A. Leighton: *Victorian Women Poets*, p. 157.

20 As late as 1971 the following critique could still reckon with public consensus: "With few exceptions her gifts were for lyrics of great felicity, but somehow removed from a world in which real tragedies happen and in which man is confronted with real conflicts, real doubts, real decisions, and indeed real truths – [...]. Her aims were small and her gifts were small". (St. Curran: "The Lyric Voice of Christina Rossetti". *Victorian Poetry* 9, 1971, 299, 287-299)

21 L. Hutcheon: *The Politics of Postmodernism*, p. 151.

Günther Jarfe, Passau

W. H. Auden's "Roman Wall Blues" and What to Consider When Teaching a Simple Poem

A Few Opening Remarks About Teachability

Although the teachability of this particular piece need not and cannot be shown here I should like to point out very briefly what to me are the most important aspects of teachability:

(1) whether something is teachable and what constitutes 'teachability' is a very urgent question for the secondary school teacher (teachability at the university level is an altogether different matter);

(2) since the majority of pupils cannot be expected to be more than superficially interested in whatever is taught in an English lesson the choice of subject matter and the method of teaching are of supreme importance;

(3) the pupils ought to be readily able to relate to a given subject or topic;

(4) since their attention is limited the text shouldn't be too long;

(5) the language should be easy enough not to cause too many obstacles;

(6) the students' own ideas, expectations etc. must be activated by means of advance organizers[1] and other methodological measures;

(7) meaning ought to be seen as a result of a negotiating process between the text and the reader's proposals;[2]

(8) this negotiating process must be realized in the form of a 'classroom discourse'[3], not by the teacher imposing his ideas on the group.

How the Poem Came to be Written

In the case of this particular poem it is possible to reconstruct the larger frame of reference which qualified the original meaning of the text. "Roman Wall Blues" wasn't written separately. Initially it was part of a larger piece called *Hadrian's Wall* which was commissioned by John Pudney, a former schoolmate of Auden's who had in the meantime become a producer with the BBC. Auden wrote it in the autumn of 1937, and it was broadcast on Nov. 25th, 1937 but not published until 1989.[4] One of several possible reasons may have been its explicit and rather unambiguous political message which the later Auden may have disapproved of. At any rate, at the time Auden left no doubt about it that the programme about the Roman wall was meant to criticize "a certain imperialistic conception of life".[5] The narrator concludes:

> The Roman Empire has disappeared, but other empires have taken its place, and the virtues and the vices of Imperialism, its ideals and its scandals, are as great a problem now as then.[6]

"Roman Wall Blues" was the only part that was salvaged from the programme. It was first given its title and published in 1940.[7] Auden must have liked it because not a word of it was ever changed; neither was it dropped from the canon altogether as so many other poems from the 30ies. It was in fact republished again and again in almost all of his collected and selected editions.[8] In spite of its popularity with the author this little poem seems not to have gained his critics' attention: In all of the huge Auden industry "Roman Wall Blues" has never been allowed more than an occasional couple of lines. Here is the poem:

Roman Wall Blues

Over the heather the wet wind blows,
I've lice in my tunic and a cold in my nose.

The rain comes pattering out of the sky,
I'm a Wall soldier, I don't know why.

The mist creeps over the hard grey stone,
My girl's in Tungria; I sleep alone.

Aulus goes hanging around her place,
I don't like his manners, I don't like his face.

Piso's a Christian, he worships a fish;
There'd be no kissing if he had his wish.

She gave me a ring but I diced it away;
I want my girl and I want my pay.

When I'm a veteran with only one eye
I shall do nothing but look at the sky.[9]

After reading this poem once or twice pupils may very well come to the conclusion that it is a very simple poem indeed. There are hardly any unknown or difficult words. It consists of 14 lines only. And contrary to a sonnet which is a very complicated structure with quatrains and tercets and varying rhyme schemes etc. this is just a sequence of seven couplets. And as regards the content, there is nothing much to be uncertain about, is there? The speaker, a poor Roman "Wall soldier" (l. 4), is fed up with his job and his living conditions and puts all his pent-up frustration into this complaint. What else is there to think and talk about? But the matter isn't as simple as all that. Writing in the 30ies, why should Auden choose a Roman soldier as his speaker? And what about his denseness?

For choosing a simple soldier with an impoverished range of feelings as the speaker of a poem confronts the poet with a difficult task. On the one hand, he must express and show his simplicity and lack of imagination, not just in so many words, but by making (at least some of) his formal principles reflect the same idea, too. On the other hand, his poem, *qua* poem, has to transcend this spiritual poverty. So the shape of the poem must both imitate and transcend the impoverished reality which is its subject. Thus there may be more to the poem than meets the eye at first inspection. To find out I propose to take a closer look at the speaker, the poem and the title.

The Speaker

From what the speaker says it becomes perfectly clear that he is a plain, unassuming, and simple-minded man and a poor fellow at that. He not only confesses to having no idea why he is doing his job, but there is nothing he can think and speak of except his own physical needs, his lack of physical and material gratification. He is frustrated by the permanently bad weather, his girlfriend's absence and the lack of payment. About seven lines (6-12), i.e. half the poem, refer to his girlfriend. It is because of her that he cannot recognize and accept Aulus and Piso as comrades but only as impediments to his own well-being. What he says about Piso:

> Piso's a Christian, he worships a fish;
> There'd be no kissing if he had his wish. (ll. 9-10)

shows a total failure to understand. He mistakes a pictorial symbol the early Christians used to communicate with each other for God, and Piso's belief in something spiritual is quite beyond him.

The speaker's range of vocabulary and choice of sentence patterns also point to a limited capacity. There are hardly any complex sentences and their 'complexity' is negligible. Except for the last couplet, each line is made up of one or two simple sentences as for example line 6: "My girl's in Tungria; I sleep alone."

Syntactically speaking, then, the whole poem is astoundingly simple. This simplicity on the one hand corresponds to the speaker's narrow-minded egotism, his parochial fixation on frustrated personal needs. On the other hand, simple as they are, the things, conditions, and feelings described evoke a striking atmosphere of immediacy and provide a means for the author to succinctly and tersely convey the pathos and misery of the speaker's situation. As a soldier to have to do one's duty far away from home, on the most northern edge of the Roman empire, cut off from civilization, exposed to the barbaric British weather, with nobody there to explain to him what all this suffering is good for – this is more than a normal human being can bear. And maybe he isn't even a genuine Roman soldier but a native from Tungria (today in Belgium) who was conscripted and sent to Britain against his will. Nowhere does the pathos become more poignant than in the last stanza which puts forward the speaker's idea of a satisfying and happy life in the future:

> When I'm a veteran with only one eye
> I shall do nothing but look at the sky. (ll. 13-14)

If all the soldier wants is to "do nothing but look at the sky" (even if it should be an Italian sky he is dreaming of) – this quintessence of happiness for the speaker is a measure of how restricted, degrading and desperate life as a wall soldier is felt to be. Choosing such a speaker gives the poem a decidedly anti-heroic quality.

The Poem

Although the speaker's choice of words and syntactical structures is very limited, his message is conveyed and confirmed by subtle rhythmical means and sound structures. Within the narrow confines of a 14-line poem consisting of seven couplets Auden manages (so to speak) to outwit his obtuse speaker. Behind his simple tune a more subtle melody becomes audible. Here is a brief analysis of how his thought is structured and how it is metrically conveyed.

The first three stanzas each begin by describing an aspect of the nasty weather and continue by stating the psycho-physical situation of the speaker, e.g.

> Over the heather the wet wind blows,
> I've lice in my tunic and a cold in my nose.

The next three stanzas refer to three people the soldier knows (two men and his girlfriend first mentioned in line 6) and determine his attitude towards them. The longing for his girlfriend colours all his human relationships. Because of her he is jealous of Aulus, feels resentment against Piso's spirituality, and has a bad conscience since he staked and lost the girl's ring. That stanzas 1-3 and 4-6 are to be seen as distinctive groups can also be shown by the way the rhyme words of the first and third stanzas, and the fourth and sixth stanzas, respectively, are linked by means of assonances: "blows" and "alone" [əʊ] go together just as "place" and "pay" [eɪ] do. Six stanzas as against one. The last couplet with its vague dream of infinite leisure in the future cannot quite counterbalance the two heavy blocks of three stanzas each evoking an oppressive experience of privation. It is true, the speaker's attempt to project his thoughts into the future and imagine a life free from the present restrictions is partly confirmed by the syntactic structure of this couplet (it's the only one composed of a whole sentence). On the other hand, the speaker imagines himself as a handicapped person ("with only one eye"), and the rhyme-word "sky" refers back to the second couplet emphasizing the speaker's ignorance ("I don't know why"). Thus the end isn't too hopeful, after all. The speaker's life has been too impoverished to leave him much chance of leading a full life later.

As for metre, the basic metrical pattern is dactylic as is clearly visible and audible in line 9:

> Piso's a Christian, he worships a fish;
> x̲́xx/x̲́xx/x̲́xx/x́

But each line realizes the pattern in a (slightly) different way. Some lines begin with an upbeat such as line 11:

> She gave me a ring but I diced it away;
> x/x̲́xx/x̲́xx/x̲́xx/x̲́

Others may introduce a secondary stress or shift the stress within a foot as does line 10:

> There'd be no kissing if he had his wish.
> x̲x́x̀/x̲́xx/x̲́xx/x̲́

Some may even redefine the basic metre as seems to be the case in line 12:

> I want my girl and I want my pay.
> x/x̲́x(x)/x̲́xx/x̲́x(x)/x̲́

Here the metre is almost iambic, the deviation stressing the urgency of the speaker's needs. A comparable redefinition of the metre occurs in the fifth line which seems to topple the dactyls completely:

> The mist creeps over the hard grey stone,
> x/x̲́x̀(x)/x̲́xx/x̲́x̀(x)/x̲́

This most spectacular deviation is not due to the speaker's incompetence but goes to show the unsettling effect the slow, oppressive mist has on the soldier. The rhythm, it seems, is subtly controlled by the implied author.

The Title

The title is significant in that it combines two very different things, the "Roman Wall" from the second century AD and the "Blues". The primary association is between the *Roman Wall* and the melancholic form of song popular in the 20s and 30s. But extrinsic knowledge enables us to make the secondary association with the plight of the black slaves in USA who invented and practised the blues. Thus the poem manages indirectly to link being a Roman soldier in ancient Britain with being a black slave in the North America in the 17th, 18th, and 19th centuries. The soldier's fate foreshadows the sadness, the lack of freedom, the restrictedness of life of the American slaves; the slave's blues harks back to the longings, the anxieties, and the lack of orientation of the Roman soldier who does his duty in a foreign country. Both the soldier and the slave have to spend their lives in countries they haven't chosen to live in and under conditions extremely difficult to bear. The title of the poem juxtaposing ancient remains in Britain and a modern type of slow, melancholy song explicitly points to the fact that the text is dealing with an experience which is neither restricted to the past nor the present, an experience which, in fact, is seen to be universal.

Thus the seemingly unassuming little poem spoken by an anonymous Roman soldier also makes its comment on the contemporary situation. By choosing, in 1937 (while the Spanish Civil War was still raging), a plain ordinary Roman soldier as the speaker of a poem that expresses his complete dissatisfaction, disillusion, and despair at being cut off from a happy, civil life, Auden makes his listeners aware of what Western civilization - progress in certain fields notwithstanding - has failed to achieve. Though the crumbling remains of the wall will testify to the limitations of everything human and, in particular, to the futility of war and the building of empires imperialism is still there as are the struggle for power and war. And it is still the plain soldiers who suffer acutely from this state of things. By first publishing the poem in 1940 and only then giving the text its title "Roman Wall Blues" Auden uses the pathetic perspective of the simple Roman soldier to expose and attack the senselessness and cruelty of Hitler's imperialistic war.

That it is indeed also contemporary soldiers' attitudes and experiences (such as he himself may have seen when he went to Spain early in 1937)[10] that Auden makes his speaker articulate can be easily demonstrated. *On the Frontier*, a topical play condemning fascism and war by several means and on different levels and written at roughly the same time as "Roman Wall Blues"[11], contains a "Soldiers' Song" expressing very similar sentiments and in some places even using the same words and ideas as "Over the heather...". Here are three stanzas from the contemporary play's song:

> The biscuits are hard and the beef is high,
> The weather is wet and the drinks are dry,
> We sit in the mud and wonder why.
> [...]

I'd rather eat turkey than humble pie,
I'd rather see mother than lose an eye,
I'd rather kiss a girl than die.

We're sick of the rain and the lice and the smell,
We're sick of the noise of shot and shell,
And the whole bloody war can go to hell![12]

If we compare the two songs it is easier to appreciate the greater complexity and depth of "Roman Wall Blues".

There is one aspect, in particular, that the word 'blues' from the title can draw the reader's attention to which otherwise might remain unnoticed. In the songs of the black slaves often an especially intense piety made itself felt which helped them to cope with the humiliating conditions of their lives. Of course the Roman soldier is anything but pious. But the Piso stanza, insignificant as it may seem, does contain hints of the Christian belief as an alternative hidden possibility. This stanza is unique in the great number of short and long [i(:)] sounds it presents and also because it's the only stanza in which the speaker does not refer to himself. In itself this may not mean very much. But since the Latin word for "fish", i.e. 'piscis', can be detected in the initial sounds of the words *"Piso"* and "*kis*sing", it seems only fair to conclude that the frequent occurrence of [i(:)] sounds is not accidental but meant to remind the reader of the Greek "ἰχϑυς" (= ichthys) and the Latin 'piscis' and of the significance the pictorial symbol of the fish had for the early Christians. The Greek word "ἰχϑυς" the early Christians understood as an acronym (i.e. a word made up of the initial letters of a group of words), in this case meaning

Jesus Christ God's Son the Saviour.
I CH TH Y S

To emphasize this religious undercurrent in an otherwise profane poem may appear far-fetched. And yet, to Auden's own surprise, it was the very experience in Spain of Republican soldiers pointlessly destroying the churches and killing the priests that initiated his slow return to the Christian belief.[13] And this in turn may have suggested to him the idea of introducing a Christian element into the "Roman Wall Blues".

Notes

1 A term coined by David P. Ausubel. An "advance organizer" helps to bridge the gap "between what the reader already knows and the propositions in the text that it is hoped he will understand and learn." Cf. P.L. Carrell, J. Devine, D.E. Eskey (Eds.): *Interactive Approaches to Second Language Reading.* Cambridge, 1988, p. 41.

2 The reader interested in modern reading research is referred to the book mentioned in the previous note and to P.D. Pearson (Ed.): *Handbook of Reading Research.* New York, London, 1984.

3 Cf. H. Weber (Ed.): *Aufforderungen zum literatur-didaktischen Dialog.* Paderborn, 1979, pp. 122-124.

4 The text of *Hadrian's Wall* and some important information about its genesis are now easily accessible in W.H. Auden, C. Isherwood: *Plays and Other Dramatic Writings 1928-1938.* Ed. E. Mendelson. London, 1989, pp. 441-455, 674-676.

5 Ibid., p. 675.

6 Ibid., p. 455.

7 The title of Auden's volume of poems was *Another Time.*

8 The first edition not to reprint the poem was *Selected Poems.* Ed. E. Mendelson, London, 1979.

9 Reprinted by kind permission of Faber & Faber Ltd. from *The English Auden. Poems, Essays and Dramatic Writings 1927-1939.* Ed. E. Mendelson. London, 1977, pp. 289f.

10 One of the reasons Auden gave for going to Spain was to find out what it was like to be a soldier. In a letter he wrote: "I shall probably be a bloody bad soldier but how can I speak to/for them without becoming one?" Quoted in H. Carpenter: *W.H. Auden. A Biography.* London, 1981, p. 207. For details about the Spain episode cf. the same book, pp. 206-216.

11 According to E. Mendelson the "Soldiers' Song" from *On the Frontier* was written in August 1937, "Roman Wall Blues" in October 1937. Cf. *The English Auden,* pp. 289f.

12 W.H. Auden: *Plays 1928-1938,* pp. 403f.

13 Cf. "To my astonishment, this discovery left me profoundly shocked and disturbed. [...] I could not escape acknowledging that, however I had consciously ignored and rejected the Church for sixteen years, the existence of churches and what went on in them had all the time been very important to me." Quoted in H. Carpenter: *W.H. Auden,* pp. 209f.

Karl J. Häußler, Inzell

Europe's Vicious Circle: Adrian Mitchell's "Autobahnmotorwayautoroute"

Around the gleaming map of Europe
A gigantic wedding ring
Slowly revolves through Londonoslowestberlin
Athensromemadridparis and home again,
Slowly revolving.

That's no ring,
It's the Great European Limousine,
The Famous Goldenwhite Circular Car

Slowly revolving

All the cars in Europe have been welded together
Into a mortal unity,
A roundaboutgrandtourroundabout
Trafficjamroundaboutagain,
All the cars melted together,
Citroenjaguarbugattivolkswagenporschedaf.

Each passenger, lugging his
Colourpiano, frozenmagazines, high-fidog,
Clambers over the seat in front of him
Towards what looks like the front of the car.
They are dragging behind them
Worksofart, lampshades made of human money,
Instant children and exploding clocks.

But the car's a circle
No front no back
No driver no steering wheel no windscreen no brakes no[1]

To my mind, any 'teachable poem' must meet one basic requirement: It must be – or at least turn out to be – interesting to the students, and this interest must arise out of the students' awareness that they themselves can contribute to the insight into the poem's meaning. This progressive deepening of understanding may be brought about by their supplying biographical, historical, philosophical, literary or any other background information, or by their detecting and pointing out basic poetic strategies the author has used. The more this happens, the higher will the didactic value of such an enterprise be. Experience with my students has proved "Autobahnmotorwayautoroute" to meet this requirement.[2]

1. The Circle

The most obvious image in Mitchell's poem is that of the circle. Direct references occur all through: "Around [...] Europe" (l. 1), "(wedding) ring" (ll. 2, 6), "revolving" (ll. 3, 5), "Circular car" (l. 8), "roundabout" (ll.12, 13) "grandtour" (l. 12), "clock" (l. 22), "circle" (l. 23) and "(steering) wheel" (l. 25). "Roundabout" evokes two, maybe even three various meanings: the children's merry-go-round, the traffic circle and, in its adjectival use, 'not in a direct or straightforward way'.

However, these semantic references to different circular objects, movements or concepts form only part of the cyclic connotations of the poem. The ring and the circle have always been symbols for connecting, combining and bringing together. The poem talks a lot about combining: about welding together (l. 10), about melting together (l. 14). From the point of word formation, the welding together of individual words is the most striking stylistic feature. It starts with the title's "Autobahnmotorwayautoroute", goes on with Europe's capitals in "Londonoslowestberlin / Athensromemadridparis" (ll. 3-4), connects individual circular concepts into bigger ones with "roundaboutgrandtourroundabout" (l. 12) and "Trafficjamroundaboutagain" (l. 13). Famous European car trademarks are combined into the rather monstrous single brand of "Citroenjaguarbugattivolkswagenporschedaf" (l. 15). Other examples of words welded together into one occur with "Colourpiano", "frozenmagazines", "high-fidog" (all l. 17) and "Worksofart" (l. 21). Their connotations, however, do not extend towards the circular.

If the unusual word formation conveys the idea of the circle, even more so does, in some cases at least, the concept behind it. If one follows up the tour through Europe as expressed in "Londonoslowestberlin / Athensromemadridparis and home again" (ll. 3-4), one realizes that it describes a clockwise circular tour through all of Western Europe, a tour that – at least in its southern semicircle – has been the "grand tour" of the educated Englishman for several centuries. It is referred to again in line 13, sandwiched in between the word "roundabout". Certainly the initial "roundabout" is to be understood as meaning 'circular', whereas the repetition refers to the traffic circle. All of Europe becomes a huge traffic roundabout, made up, as we see, of only one car: "The Famous Goldenwhite Circular Car" (l. 8) that is depicted more closely right at the end: "the car's a circle / No front no back / No driver no steering wheel no windscreen no brakes no". (ll. 23-25) When the poem breaks off at this point, its overall structure recurs to the circular as well: There is no end, you are either lost in infinity, or you can start all over again.

2. *Where the Circle Fails*

It does not take any reader long to realize that Mitchell's poem is critical and satirical, and that its criticism is epitomized in the European consumer good *par excellence*, the car, and all that follows in its wake: motorways, traffic jams and congestion, car fetishism, road casualties. (Strange to say, pollution does not seem to have been so very topical in the late sixties.) However, what exactly is it that the poem finds fault with in this Brave New European Car World? The criticism falls into various categories.

2.1 *Loss of Proportion*

The new European road system has lost all sense of proportion. European motorways form a ring around its member countries, but the initial positive connotation underlying the concept of a 'ring', here even enhanced by the adjunct 'wedding', is refuted straightaway by various pejorative additions: It is a "gigantic", i.e. disproportioned ring, and it is "slowly revolving" (ll. 2, 5), a statement that develops menacing overtones by being twice repeated. In the end we are told that there is no ring at all: There is only "the Great European Limousine, / The Famous Goldenwhite Circular Car" (ll. 7-8). Biblical associations impress themselves upon the reader: the image of the Golden Calf, round which the Jews danced in blasphemous adoration. The car has become Europe's idol.

This idolized car has lost all its usual earlier connotations of progress, mobility and status symbol. It has been "welded together" into a "mortal unity", and it is even equated to the nominal monstrosity of a "roundaboutgrandtour-roundabout / Trafficjamroundaboutagain" (ll. 10-13). The megalomania in the semantic field is even outdone by the monstrous word formation.

2.2 *Loss of Individuality and Identity*

There are no longer any specifically French, English, Italian, German or Dutch cars left, but only the one "Citroenjaguarbugattivolkswagenporsche-daf" (l. 15) that is stuck in the one huge European traffic jam. The result is not only "a mortal unity", it is more than just that: By losing their separateness, the objects lose their identity. Europe's "gigantic wedding ring" at the beginning, suggesting an initially positive conception of the European unification, is soon revoked as being an illusion, one might even say a deception: "That's no ring. / It's the Great European [...] Circular Car" (ll. 6-8). Of course, a circular car mocks any reasonable concept of a car, and so does the poem. As it goes on, it refutes such a car's existence by pointing out its absurdity and illusiveness: "Each passenger [...] / Clambers over the seat in front of him / Towards what looks like the front of the car." (ll. 16, 18-19) The last three lines deconstruct the car even further. Once again it is only a "ring", and all the components of the common car have ceased to exist with this specific 'Great European Circular Car': "No front no back / No driver no steering wheel no windscreen no brakes no" (l. 25).The European unifying process has led to an idolatrous monstrosity first, and in the end to an annihilation of the basic concept of any object. Not without reason is the poem's last word "no".

Further instances of welding words together occur, and this process has led to other hybrids. "Colourpiano", "frozenmagazines" and "high-fidog" (l. 17) make the reader stumble at first, but he will immediately realize that a rearrangement of the components produces two generally acceptable combinations, namely 'colour magazines' and 'high-fi piano', both indicative of common European consumer culture as well. However, neither 'frozen' nor 'colour' go easily together with 'dog', and thus one is left to let one's imagination roam in search of more associations. They come in rather great numbers, some of them may seem more convincing, others less, and I leave it to the reader to decide on that matter. If one recombines the components of the hybrid words, the following connotations can be suggested: Frozen food, dog food, hot dogs, magazines advertising or offering food for the deep freeze (instant or fast food), the dog of His Master's Voice ("high-fidog"), frozen smiles in colour magazine ads, Elton John's colour pianos. Whether kitchen gadgets, musical appliances or posh publications, they all have one thing in common: They are status symbols of our modern West European culture, and form part of our everyday life just as much as the car. And just like the car, they are seen in a critical and satirical context.

2.3 Loss of Humanity

The disappearance of proportion denotes an inhuman world, as does the dissolution of individuality. This aspect of inhumanity pervades the whole poem. Against the background of the huge European car stuck in a huge traffic jam, man is not only dwarfed, he has also lost every command over the situation. All that is left to him is toiling his way through his mobile environment: "*lugging* his / Colourpiano [...]", "They are *dragging* behind them [...]" (ll. 16-17, 20 – my italics). The absurdity of the situation is obvious: The automobile, invented as a means of conveyance and transport, has stopped fulfilling its original purpose. Now man has to sweat and toil inside his almost stationary car that is only "Slowly revolving", to toil just as much as a miner or any other manual worker in earlier centuries. The difference lies only in the objects he has to drag now: They are no longer the raw materials that made the Industrial Revolution possible, now they are indicators of our West European consumer society. We have already dealt with the "Colourpiano, frozenmagazines, high-fidog"; other items that burden and encumber his life are to follow: "Worksofart, lampshades made of human money, / Instant children and exploding clocks" (ll. 21-22). Here the connotations of inhumanity loom even larger. The orthographically compressed 'works of art' lure the reader into interpreting them – at least for a short moment before he realizes the grammatical inadequacy of such a phrase – as 'work so fart'. I doubt whether Mitchell could have had the rather recent expression of "arty-farty" in mind in this context, but even if he didn't, we as readers can. Be that as it may: modern art and culture find themselves deflated and transformed into a mere flatulence.

But the aspect of inhumanity reaches even deeper. Nobody will escape the associations with medical experiments during the Nazi regime when he reads about "lampshades made of human money". True, 'money' replaces an expected 'skin', but nothing is detracted from the original bestiality except that Nazi ideology may have become replaced by capitalist ideology. The ensuing "Instant children", possibly triggered off by the similar sound of 'infant', takes up inhuman medical experimenting. Test tube babies come to one's mind, but also the worst possible excesses of genetic engineering. Finally the "exploding clocks" evoke the cruelty of terrorist time bombs on the one hand, they may also refer to an ever-increasing flux of time which leaves the human being without any chance of leaning back and enjoying life any more. And Europe on the whole might be regarded as a time-bomb, environmentally, economically, politically, ethnically.

2.4 Loss of the Sense of Reality

A great number of the concepts, images and ideas behind "Autobahnmotorwayautoroute" mock any realistic approach to the world we live in. Our West European world has turned into a gigantic closed circuit through which we drag the paraphernalia of our culture. We have lost all sensible proportions. All the things and objects we have taken for granted are now transformed beyond recognition; the "wedding ring" (l. 2) reveals itself as a huge motorway roundabout, which undergoes a metamorphosis into a huge circular car, which again reveals itself as being nothing but a circle in the end, a vicious circle starting all over again. All we are left with are illusions and a sense of the absurd. The trip through Europe, once the epitome of cultural education, has turned into an absurd, monstrous circular movement through Europe's self-destruction.

3. The Man and the Message

Ride the Nightmare is the title of the anthology in which "Autobahnmotorwayautoroute" was first published. That was in 1971. The title is indicative of the general atmosphere of those poems: They deal with the Vietnam War, the occupation of Czechoslovakia by the troops of the Warsaw Pact States, with China, Cuba, South Africa and Rhodesia, European and British foreign and interior politics, British-Irish relationships and social problems in Britain and all over the world. Among others, President Johnson and Enoch Powell have the honour of figuring in titles ("Ode To Enoch Powell" and "Ode On The Assassination Of President Johnson"). Hardly any nightmare of the sixties is left out. And Mitchell talks about Mitchell in his poems, about what made him that angry, even if no longer so young, man. "My brain socialist / My heart anarchist / My eye pacifist / My blood revolutionary" – thus his later self-characterization in "Loose Leaf Poem".[3]

Born in 1932 in London as the son of a father who was a scientist and a mother who was a teacher, Adrian Mitchell went through school in Wiltshire, did his military service in the Royal Air Force from 1951 to 1952 and went on to Oxford to read English literature. He became president of the Oxford Poetry Society, published the student magazine *The Isis*, and his first poems appeared in print. He reacted with increasing aggression against the elder statesmen of Modernism, who had gathered in the literary group of 'The Movement'. From 1955 onwards he worked for various newspapers, and in 1963 he left for America to take up the first of his visiting lectureships at the State University of Iowa; several more Creative Writing Fellowships were to follow in later years. Journalism and the development of politics in the United States of the late fifties and early sixties turned him into a keen observer and an ardent critic of the political development both that and this side of the Atlantic. His ideological home was the left wing of the Labour Party.

Mitchell, like so many others in his days, believed in the revolutionary power of the poetic word. His creed, prefixed as a motto to his first volume of collected poems from 1969, reads: "Most people ignore most poetry because most poetry ignores most people". Thus poetry has to become 'democratic', it has to move away from the academic tradition of esoteric literature. And poetry has to be brought to the masses by word of mouth, not by way of the sterile printed book. The theory was put into action, and the flame seemed to have spread to the masses on more than one occasion: At the first International Poetry Incarnation in June 1965, an event which gathered critical poets from all over the world in London, Mitchell read his Vietnam poem "To Whom It May Concern" to an enthusiastic audience of 7000 at the Royal Albert Hall, and the same poem was recited by Peter O'Toole in London's Trafalgar Square when the Easter marchers for nuclear disarmament had gathered there. This was 'Poetry in Action', in events like these the poetic word could mobilize the masses.

To reach that aim, not only new forms of public presentation of poetry had to be found; new literary strategies had to be developed as well. The Beat Generation of American and then British poets – Allen Ginsberg above all, and the Liverpool group with Roger McGough, Brian Patten and Adrian Henri – had approached rock, beat and pop music in their lyrics. Repetition, refrain, catchphrases are their hallmarks. Poetry for the masses cannot be poetry for the academics. Several of Mitchell's anthologies – *Ride the Nightmare* is among them – start with the following warning: "None of the work in this or any other of my books or articles is to be used in connection with any examination whatsoever". A poem is not for defining its metre and analysing its rhyme pattern, its function is to carry simple, but vital messages. If you want to talk to the masses in your poem, you have to use a language they understand. Mitchell, through his education an academic literary critic himself, reveals the reasons for most critics' fear of simple poetry:

> The critics are scared [...] because we are doing something very simple – trying to talk directly and honestly to people about the things which matter most to us – and the critics want complexity, they want exclusiveness. And it is easy to be complex and hard to take those parts of your vision which are most important and convey them, even if they are so simple that it's embarrassing to everyone who's even sniffed a university.[4]

In his time, Mitchell was seen as belonging to the group of British 'Underground Poets'. Thus thirteen of his poems were included in Michael Horovitz' Penguin anthology *Children of Albion. Poetry of the 'Underground' in Britain* from 1969. The phrase may seem strange today, as the 'Underground' activities were very much above ground. 'Underground' denoted nothing but the fact that official government and party politics were openly and actively attacked, and that literature was meant to manipulate public opinion towards a revolutionary insight into a reality that was different from what politicians made us believe. The central topics were the great issues of the sixties: Vietnam, human rights and racial equality, post-imperialist exploitation of the Third World, fascism, drugs, and last but not least, Europe.

In Britain, entry into the European Community had been a bone of contention all through the sixties. The Conservatives were mainly against it for fear of jeopardizing British national sovereignty and British identity. The Labour party around Harold Wilson had always been pro-European, partly at least owing to a more internationalist attitude of socialism on the whole. In the end a Labour government negotiated the entry, a Conservative government ratified it on January 22, 1972, on January 1, 1973 Britain's membership came into effect, and in 1975 a referendum about the entry was held in which two thirds of the British voted for it. But before that the rift between anti- and pro-marketeers had gone through all political factions, and the left-wingers in the Labour Party had been outspoken adversaries to joining the Common Market. Of course, the reasons were different from those of the Conservatives. It was the conviction that the European Community was nothing but a huge capitalist enterprise that made them suspicious of it. It is this aspect that Mitchell takes up in his "Autobahnmotorwayautoroute".

We have already dealt with the points of criticism in this poem. The projected Europe appears as something forcefully "welded together", not as something that has grown organically. It seems too gigantic, too impersonal, too much orientated along the lines of a consumer society. It will not lead up to an understanding of its individual members, but to an absurd conglomeration of supranational megafirms that disregard all needs of the individual. In its message the poem is truly Mitchellesque. In its form, however, it is less so, as it depends very much on its visual impact, and as understanding it is anything but simple. Here Mitchell the academic, who relishes images, allusions and a rather esoteric use of language, seems to have triumphed over the propagator of popular poetics.

The poet Mitchell seems to have fallen silent now. In 1982 a selection of poems from his earlier anthologies, entitled *For Beauty Douglas. Adrian Mitchell's Collected Poems 1953-79* was published, and two years later his to date latest collection of poems appeared under the title *On the Beach at Cambridge: New Poems*. He seems to have ended up with what Anthony Thwaite said of all the fellows in battle from days of yore:

> In an odd way these poets, too, are now seen as belonging to an 'establishment', having been taught in schools and enthused about by teachers with supposedly progressive notions.[5]

This may seem bad enough, though not quite as bad as Mitchell's own vision of the poet's reduction to complete and utter uselessness with which his hilarious, but also bitterly sarcastic poem "The Oxford Hysteria of English Poetry" ends:

> Finally I was given the Chair of Comparative Ambiguity
> At Armpit University, Java.
> It didn't keep me busy,
> But it kept me quiet.
> It seemed like poetry had been safely tucked up for the night.[6]

Notes

1 A. Mitchell: *Ride the Nightmare*. London, 1971. Author's Note: "None of Adrian Mitchell's poems are to be used in connection with any examination whatsoever." Mitchell's poem is also reprinted in the Klett reader *Learning English. Top Line*. Stuttgart, 1992, p. 32. The *Teacher's Book* to accompany this reader provides useful annotations.
2 I would like to thank the Leistungskurs Englisch 1992/94 at the Karlsgymnasium Bad Reichenhall for their willingness to join me in the attempt at squaring Mitchell's vicious circle. Quite a number of the associations to be found in the following analysis are theirs.
3 A. Mitchell: *For Beauty Douglas*, pp. 61-69.
4 Cf. M. Horovitz (Ed.): *Children of Albion*, p. 357.
5 A. Thwaite: *Poetry Today*, p. 124. It must be added that Mitchell has also written several novels and plays. I have ignored that part of his work.
6 A. Mitchell: *Ride the Nightmare*, p. 32–34. There is an Adrian Mitchell who, in the 1980s, wrote children's books about the adventures of the Baron of Münchhausen. They constitute a rather unimaginative conglomeration of literary motifs borrowed not only from Bürger, but also from the Bible. Homer, the medieval German "Spielmannsepos" *Herzog Ernst* and possibly other sources. Should this A.M. be identical with the A.M. of our poem, then his development as a writer may be deemed a fate worse than his having got a chair at Armpit University.

Bibliography

1. Collected Poems by Adrian Mitchell

Poems. London, 1969.
Out Loud. London, 1969.
Ride the Nightmare. Verse and Prose. London, 1971.
For Beauty Douglas. Adrian Mitchell's Collected Poems 1953-1979. London, New York, 1982.
On the Beach at Cambridge. New Poems. London, New York, 1984.

2. Critical Literature

Booth, M.: *British Poetry 1964 to 1984. Driving through the Barricades*. London, 1985.
Bülow, F.M. et al.: *Learning English. Top Line, Teacher's Book*. Stuttgart, 1992.
Horovitz, M. (Ed): *Children of Albion. Poetry of the Underground in Britain*. Harmondsworth, 1969.
Oeser, H.-C.: "Adrian Mitchell". – In Thwaite, A.: *Twentieth Century English Poetry*. London, New York, 1978.
Thwaite, A.: *Poetry Today. A Critical Guide to British Poetry 1960 – 1984*. London, New York, 1985.

Hans Ulrich Seeber, Stuttgart

Philip Larkin's 'The Building' and the Art of Sociography

The Building

Higher than the handsomest hotel
The lucent comb shows up for miles, but see,
All round it close-ribbed streets rise and fall
Like a great sigh out of the last century.
The porters are scruffy; what keep drawing up
At the entrance are not taxis; and in the hall
As well as creepers hangs a frightening smell.

There are paperbacks, and tea at so much a cup,
Like an airport lounge, but those who tamely sit
On rows of steel chairs turning the ripped mags
Haven't come far. More like a local bus,
These outdoor clothes and half-filled shopping-bags
And faces restless and resigned, although
Every few minutes comes a kind of nurse

To fetch someone away: the rest refit
Cups back to saucers, cough, or glance below
Seats for dropped gloves or cards. Humans, caught
On ground curiously neutral, homes and names
Suddenly in abeyance; some are young,
Some old, but most at that vague age that claims
The end of choice, the last of hope; and all

Here to confess that something has gone wrong.
It must be error of a serious sort,
For see how many floors it needs, how tall
It's grown by now, and how much money goes
In trying to correct it. See the time,
Half-past eleven on a working day,
And these picked out of it; see, as they climb

To their appointed levels, how their eyes
Go to each other, guessing; on the way
Someone's wheeled past, in washed-to-rags ward clothes:

They see him, too. They're quiet. To realise
This new thing held in common makes them quiet,
For past these doors are rooms, and rooms past those,
And more rooms yet, each one further off

And harder to return from; and who knows
Which he will see, and when? For the moment, wait,
Look down at the yard. Outside seems old enough:
Red brick, lagged pipes, and someone walking by it
Out to the car park, free. Then, past the gate,
Traffic; a locked church; short terraced streets
Where kids chalk games, and girls with hair-dos fetch

Their separates from the cleaners – O world,
Your loves, your chances, are beyond the stretch
Of any hand from here! And so, unreal,
A touching dream to which we all are lulled
But wake from separately. In it, conceits
And self-protecting ignorance congeal
To carry life, collapsing only when

Called to these corridors (for now once more
The nurse beckons-). Each gets up and goes
At last. Some will be out by lunch, or four;
Others, not knowing it, have come to join
The unseen congregations whose white rows
Lie set apart above – women, men;
Old, young, crude facets of the only coin

This place accepts. All know they are going to die.
Not yet, perhaps not here, but in the end,
And somewhere like this. That is what it means,
This clean-sliced cliff; a struggle to transcend
The thought of dying, for unless its powers
Outbuild cathedrals nothing contravenes
The coming dark, though crowds each evening try

With wasteful, weak, propitiatory flowers.[1]

Larkin's Lyrical Sociography

The choice of a poem by Philip Larkin (1922-1985) for teaching purposes is not difficult to justify. Both his topics and his manner of speaking in poems are quite accessible. His preoccupation is contemporary urban English life seen from the vantage point of one who has lost all illusions. The point of his achievement and his widespread popularity[2] lies in the fact that he manages to convey this stance in a way which, despite its accessibility, is poetically subtle, thoroughly contemporary and yet traditional. "The Building", first published 1974 in *High Windows*, both demonstrates these characteristics and Larkin's well-known obsession with death. Before embarking upon a more detailed examination of "The Building" I should like to place the poem (1) systematically, (2) individually and (3) historically.

(1) Lyrical poetry is notoriously difficult to describe as such because, unlike novels and plays, it does not seem to be based on a dominant mode of writing or speaking such as narration or dialogue. If there exists a dominant mode at all, apart from rhythmic speech not necessarily bound by metre and rhyme, it is the more or less enthusiastic, impassioned 'apostrophe'[3] of an object by a speaker – God, the beloved, mountains etc. In German criticism this speaker or voice is usually called "das lyrische Ich". The speaker's privilege is not to be hampered by constraints. His most uncommon perception, experience, thought or intuition may be expressed in a structured, yet unexpected pattern of words, of visual and acoustic signs, called 'poem'. Since it is not certain that apostrophe is the dominant feature of poetry, I suggest that a poem frequently focuses upon one of the following four modes whose various combinations form the communicative structure of a poem.

(a) A poem, often making use of the figure of *prosopopeia* (*Personifikation*), can be a solemn extended *apostrophe* which is normally linked to description. A famous example of this kind of poetry is Coleridge's "Hymn Before Sun-Rise in the Vale of Chamouni" (1802). Like a magician the poet uses language to create and to conjure up reality in the act of naming.

(b) In other cases the emphasis is clearly on autobiographical *narrative*, as is often the case in Wordsworth ("I wandered lonely [...]"), Edward Thomas and Seamus Heaney. It is not surprising, therefore, to learn that the use of the preterite is quite frequent in English poetry. However, short lyrical narratives, as for example E. Thomas's "A Tale", are far more charged with meaning and emotional intensity than prose narratives normally are.

(c) A huge section of European poetry, for example the poetry contributing to the culture of the court ('wit') or to religious meditation, employs *argumentation* and *meditation* as its chief vehicle of communication. For, as the Metaphysical Poets already knew, poetry is not only a child of Platonic enthusiasm, but also a child of wit (Thomas Randolph).[4]

(d) Finally, laudatory, derogatory or meditative *description* of people, towns, houses, nature etc. falls within the province of poetry proper, frequently combined with apostrophe. Clearly Larkin's "The Building" belongs to this category. It integrates description, apostrophe and commentary (reflection, meditation).

(2) It is my claim now, paradoxical as it may seem, that the powerful individuality of Larkin's poetic work has to do with his use of a mode of perception and interpretation which I call lyrical sociography. Since the appearance of *The Less Deceived* (1955) Larkin's imagination became increasingly spatial. His aim is to present people in a recognizably social space or environment such as railways, towns ("Here" = Hull), offices ("Toad"), hospitals ("The Building"), and the like. This is both true for his self-portraits and his portraits of social types ("Mr. Bleaney"). His characteristic mode is sociographic. According to Steinmetz, the founder of the school of "Soziographie", "geübte Wahrnehmer" are expected to discover new social facts and modes of perception ("neue Tatsachenarten und neue Wahrnehmungsmethoden")[5] and to describe the social reality of a specific place at a specific time.

Larkin's lyrical explorations of contemporary England are very much reminiscent of this method. Leaving, unlike T.S. Eliot or C.H. Sisson, literary tradition and traditional poetic subjects aside, he concentrates on rendering his experience of the here and now. This private experience, including the categories which it uses for its self-interpretation, is deeply influenced by social modes of perceiving, thinking and valuing. In his poetry Larkin presents himself as someone who is very much part of the social system he describes. For a speaker who implicitly defines himself as a social self, as someone who views his personal situation in the light of socially sanctioned norms such as work and leisure, success and failure, prosperity and poverty, adaptation and rebellion, sexual gratification and asceticism, order and chaos, it is only consistent to mobilize the suggestive potential of contemporary English places and localities for the purpose of self-representation:

No, give me my in-tray
My loaf-haired secretary,
My shall-I-keep-the-call-in-Sir:
What else can I answer,

When the lights come on at four
At the end of another year?
Give me your arm, old toad;
Help me down Cemetery Road.[6]
("Toads Revisited")

The speaker of these lines is a person in an office, who, as we know, shares Larkin's views. He has obviously internalized the norms of the world of work ("old toad"). All this is incompatible with the traditions of romantic or modernist poetry. Such a speaker as Larkin's would have been the butt of ruthless cultural criticism. Larkin, however, turns the unresolved conflicts of the average modern man between conformism and imagined rebellion, between social life and individualism, into a poetic source of strength. In his poetry the romantic sublime, hinting at a metaphysical realm of stability and meaning, is only present as a nostalgic gesture of negation ("High Windows"):

And immediately

Rather than words comes the thought of high windows:
The sun-comprehending glass –
And beyond it the deep blue air, that shows
Nothing, and is nowhere, and is endless.[7]

Larkin's sad, disillusioned, conservative voice is unmistakable and quite unlike that of post-1945 'nature poets' (Tomlinson, Hughes) precisely because he stays within a social world whose development he deplores.

On the whole, Larkin's statements on his own art are quite consistent with his poetic practice. Experience, not tradition or language or form, is at the centre of his thinking about poetry. This is a romantic approach which, however, results in radically unromantic, realistic poems. Yet romantic yearnings are discernible in his constant preoccupation with the experience of a lost 'home'. Again and again he insinuates that modern reality is sadly incompatible with a term suggesting a secure, fulfilled and meaningful life (cf. "Friday Night in the Royal Station Hotel").

Placing experience at the top of his poetological priorities implies a series of structural consequences for his lyrical sociography. First of all, the act of perceiving the often shabby surfaces of contemporary England is linked to an act of reflexion which transforms the impression of the momentary encounter (experience in the sense of *Erlebnis*) into social knowledge (experience in the sense of *Erfahrung*, *Wissen*). Experience does not simply mean that perception and reflexion merely confirm preconceived notions about reality. It is rather a process which in the typical Larkin poem leads up to a climactic and pointed phrasing of the insight won in that process. Accordingly, a poem by Larkin conveys a sense of movement.

For Larkin, only the poet who is true to his experience can produce an original poem. The language of the poem preserves and describes that experience. It is like a window revealing the diversity of the world by its very nature of invisibility, of self-effacement. Clearly the language employed must be adequate to convey the particular quality of an experience. Even more, in preserving that experience, it cannot help but also create and shape it: "I felt for the first time I was speaking for myself. Thoughts, feelings, language cohered and jumped. They have to do that."[8]

However, Larkin's language is not radically self-referential. His medium tends to disappear in the act of reading as experiences, emotions and thoughts are presented. Wherever Larkin makes us aware of language, he wishes to emphasize the difference between truth and linguistic clichés representing illusions. In the short poem "Take One Home for the Kiddies" the advertisement slogan contrasts with the reality of children neglecting their pet animals. For Larkin the poetic function, defined by Jakobson as repetitive structures, does not suggest an identity between the world and the text, but rather that language is saturated with the experience of the world. The poetic strategies employed by the poet are meant to trigger off reflections on the problems of life. Unlike theorists of experimental poetry Larkin does not believe in an identity between the world and language, an identity which would indeed make of words, styles and quotations privileged witnesses of reality. "Rather than words comes the thought of high windows"[9] says the speaker of the poem "High Windows". There is, in other words, a "non-linguistic knowledge"[10] which does not coincide with the linguistic cognitive system and its rules. Against Helmut Heißenbüttel's attempt to base modern experimental practices in poetry on linguistic theory the following objection has been made by Bernd Scheffer: "Eine umfassende Semantik der Literatur, eine umfassende Theorie ihrer 'Bedeutungen' kann sich weder auf Texte noch auf Sprache allein beschränken [...]".[11] According to him, Whorf's theory of a *sprachliches Weltbild* is obsolete. Significantly, Paul Ricoeur's theory of narrative also emphasizes the central role of the term experience. In the light of theory, Larkin's alleged lack of modernity is, therefore, rather doubtful. But he is certainly an outspoken critic of modernist and post-modernist attempts to treat the world as a text. He opposes those "agglomeration of words" which in experimental texts like Joyce's *Finnegans Wake* displace experience and baffle a 'normal' perception and experience of the world:

> I write, or wrote, as everyone did till the mad lads [i.e. the modernists, H.U.S.] started, using words and syntax in the normal way to describe recognizable experience as memorably as possible. That doesn't seem to me a tradition. The other stuff, the mad stuff, is more an aberration.[12]

Larkin's traditionalism must be related to his Englishness and to the English tradition of empiricism. In his poetry it is not a matter of consciously harking back to and continuing certain themes, motifs and forms, but rather an accepted practice of dealing lyrically with the world. He ignores, of course, that 'mad', obscure and visionary modes are also part of the poetic tradition. And in a sense he is philosophically naive, not realizing that self-reflexivity is, as systems theory has pointed out, a distinguishing feature of any system.

(3) Larkin's poetry and critical statements exemplify the attitude of what literary historians call the Movement[13], which, beginning in the Fifties, was directed both against exuberant neo-romanticism (Dylan Thomas, and others) and against the destruction of logic and syntax by the modernist experimenters (Pound, Eliot, and others). If there is any manifesto of that move-

ment it is to be found in Robert Conquest's introductions to his anthologies *New Lines I* (1956) and *New Lines II* (1963).

"The Building"

Social knowledge gained through experience is shown in the poem as something that has to be acquired in a process of learning. The reader's interpretive activity is already triggered off by the *title*. It is provocatively vague. "The Building" needs to be identified. Accordingly, the anonymous observer and speaker does not merely describe but also explores and interprets. Only gradually do we become aware of the fact that the poem describes and interprets the behaviour of visitors and patients in a hospital. In other words, both title and description conceal to some extent what the description is referring to. We learn about shabby porters, about teacups in the waiting-room, "shopping bags" (l. 12), "a frightening smell" (l. 7), "steel chairs" (l. 10), "ripped mags" (l. 10) etc., but nothing about doctors, instruments, illnesses and the like. Twice a nurse is mentioned fetching someone away from the waiting-room, but even she is first called "a kind of nurse" (l. 14). Both the title and the description are part of a poetic estrangement, i.e. de-familiarization, forcing the reader to look at reality with heightened awareness. Unlike the implied reader of Henley's poem "The Hospital"[14], the implied reader of Larkin's poem is not encouraged to indulge in sentimental empathy. Rhetoric tells us that the figure used in the title is a synecdoche, i.e. in our case a wider, more abstract term than the one actually meant ("hospital"). All this implies that the reader is forced to engage in an act of decoding.

This idea of a cognitive process leading to a final insight is emphasized by the *visual and auditory shape of the poem*. In poetry in particular, form is meant to constitute meaning. Accordingly, Larkin constructs a complicated stanzaic structure which isolates a final line because eight rhymed, eight-line stanzas are split up into nine seven-line stanzas (cf. first stanza: abcbdca/d...). The isolated final line emphasizes the *theme* and the message of the poem. The hospital is ultimately a house of death, a final destination, not a place of recovery. Neither religion (significantly, the church near the hospital is "locked"), nor the heroic attempts of modern science, represented by the huge building, let alone the touching convention of giving flowers to the ill or dying, have been powerful enough to overcome the power of death. For Larkin death is a stark, ultimate reality not allowing of any solace. The final commentary of the speaker is unambiguous:

> [...] That is what it means,
> This clean-sliced cliff; a struggle to transcend
> The thought of dying, for unless its powers
> Outbuild cathedrals nothing contravenes

The coming dark, though crowds each evening try
With wasteful, weak, propitiatory flowers. (ll. 59-64)

Confronted with this ultimate reality of death, the world itself turns out to be "unreal" (l. 45), "a touching dream" (l. 46) made up of illusions which we need to endure life. The inexorable march of life and of consciousness toward this reality is marked and reflected by run-on lines and rhymes breaking down the borders between the stanzas. For purposes of emphasis, pauses considerably slow down the rhythm of the last line, thus turning it into a heavy, alliterating tread marking the finality of death. Characteristically, Larkin's invention conforms to the traditional idea of poetry in its use of rhymed stanzaic units. But within that framework he is also innovative. Furthermore, although he tries to reinstate poetry as a mode of comprehensible communication, his use of suggestive estrangements must not be underrated.

Among other things, this becomes apparent in his handling of the devices of *apostrophe*, *perspective* and *imagery*. Apostrophe basically means that the speaking and reflecting subject turns to the world, God, other people etc. and addresses them, thereby frequently giving them, sometimes with the help of metaphors, a name. "Other people" may simply be readers or listeners to whom the poet appeals without actually naming them. In Larkin's poem the apostrophe of the (implied) reader or listener is frequently expressed by the deictic gesture 'see', an imperative.

While encountering the 'other' the speaker or voice usually adopts various roles involving different perspectives. Functionally, these roles are closely linked with apostrophes, because they, too, are forms of interaction between the subject and the world. In "The Building" the implied speaker's attitude resembles that of an uninformed traveller and observer, who sees the building for the first time and tries to read its signs. By adopting the stance of someone who is exploring unknown territory, the speaker treats the familiar as if it were unfamiliar, thus giving it the appearance of something new and menacing requiring the closest observation. Let us consider the first stanza:

Higher than the handsomest hotel
The lucent comb shows up for miles, but see,
All round it close-ribbed streets rise and fall
Like a great sigh out of the last century.
The porters are scruffy; what keep drawing up
At the entrance are not taxis; and in the hall
As well as creepers hangs a frightening smell.

Acting as if he (she) were a moving camera the speaker gives us first a view of the spectacular building from a distance, then describes the entrance at close range and finally enters the building to present those waiting. As description and interpretation unfold, we are further drawn into the building:

For past these doors are rooms, and rooms past those,
And more rooms yet, each one further off

And harder to return from; and who knows
Which he will see, and when? For the moment, wait,
Look down at the yard. Outside seems old enough:
Red brick, lagged pipes, and someone walking by it
Out to the car park, free. Then, past the gate,
Traffic; a locked church; short terraced streets
[...] (ll. 34-41)

The reader is eventually made to view the outside world from the perspective of the inmates of the hospital. This complete reversal of perspectives does not merely serve the purpose of producing the illusion of the actual dynamic experience of visiting a hospital. It also introduces a re-interpretation of the world, which becomes unreal, whereas death, or rather Heidegger's "Dasein zum Tode", becomes real. This insight moves the speaker to a perfectly conventional, emotional apostrophe of the world reminiscent of preaching:

[...] - O world,
Your loves, your chances, are beyond the stretch
Of any hand from here! And so, unreal,
A touching dream to which we all are lulled
But wake from separately. In it, conceits
And self-protecting ignorance congeal
To carry life, collapsing only when
Called to these corridors [...] (ll. 43-50)

The poet's insight is the result of seeing, in the double sense of sensual and intellectual perception. Beginning with the apostrophe "but see, / All round it close-ribbed streets rise and fall" there are altogether three appeals to the reader or fictional companion of the traveller-observer to perceive and to interpret what he perceives (ll. 3, 24, 26). The visitors and the inmates of the hospital, too, are busy interpreting the meaning of the selection of individuals and of the spectacle of a patient being wheeled past.

We already know the answer given in the commentary by the speaker. However, the metaphors "the lucent comb" and "this clean-sliced cliff" hint at further possibilities of interpretation which the poet in his role of commentator does not explicate. A "comb" is an instrument to create order and tidiness. By means of such a 'technical device' hospitals and doctors try to restore the order of the body. As long as such a positive function is fulfilled by modern civilization, it can indeed be likened to a 'honeycomb' which "comb" also means. The bright lighted cells of the "comb" are signs of promise and of comfort, just like the many rooms of a hotel (cf. l. 1). Yet "comb" also means something more ancient and dangerous. It is a 'deep hollow', a natural phenomenon reminding one perhaps of death and the grave. Death is an inescapable fact of nature. Admittedly this connotation seems to be ruled out by the idea of height evoked in the first line unless one surmises that Larkin is engaging in a subtle act of ironic deconstruction. However that may be, it is clear that civilization's promise of the good life without fear is daily contradicted by the fact of death and the fear this fact inspires. However much people may use science and the hospital as substitutes for religion, where, as the religious imagery of the poem suggests, 'confession' ("confess", l. 22) is taken and "congregations" (l. 54) meet, it is almost certain that the modern, shining building will become just as old, ugly and inefficient as the civilization created by the nineteenth century, not to mention the fact that science is part of the *malaise*. For this old civilization surrounding it resembles a skeleton and the sigh of something dying (ll. 2-4). Larkin's comparison infuses the text with a dose of gothicism to establish a telling contrast between the modern present and the Victorian past which turns out to be a pseudo-contrast. Calculated changes of imagery, voice and tone, which constitute meaning, are part of his poetic repertoire. Larkin ranges in this poem from the colloquial ("hangs a frightening smell") to lofty and unusual combinations of the abstract and the concrete like "conceits [...] congeal".

The key-words of the text are linked by alliteration: "comb", "corridors", "congeal", "clean-sliced cliff", "cathedral", "coming", "crowds". The most suggestive of these seem to me to be "cliff" and "comb". Do we have to accept the poet's reading ("this is what it means") of the phrase "clean-sliced cliff" (l. 60)? Or does the metaphor, read in conjunction with the synecdoche "building", hide a poetological meaning, too? The poet's own commentary indicates that acts of decoding are required. Larkin's imagination sets a firm, ancient rock against the water of transitoriness, i.e. death. The rock is carefully carved by a maker, who could be God, nature or, in a transferred sense, the poet himself. If this self-reflexive implication of the poem is acceptable, the ominous title "The Building", which is unusually reticent for a Larkin poem, is not only a synecdoche for hospital, but also a metaphor for the timeless 'architecture' of poetry. For whereas the language of poetry overcomes time and death, science and religion apparently do not. Larkin himself points out that his poetry preserves experiences that would otherwise fall into oblivion: "I write poems to preserve things that I have seen/thought/felt (if I may indicate a composite and complex experience) both for myself and others, though I feel that my prime responsibility is to the experience itself."[15]

Conclusion

Poetic strategies, like the handling of verse, apostrophe, perspective, commentary and imagery transform a pragmatic social institution, i.e. the hospital, into an ambiguous symbol of death, of a final destination, of the efforts of civilization, and perhaps of poetry. Such a production of a host of suggestions, of connotations appealing to the memory and to the imagination of the reader, is really what poetic language is all about. Still, Larkin's poem explores the *reality* of death in the modern world. It recaptures the sense of that movement which we associate with experience. Its modest estrangements force the reader to face that experience rather than the verbal medium. The poem is thoroughly contemporary, but not experimental in a modernist or postmodernist sense, traditional, yet also innovative. It is a structure of words which, to use Umberto Eco's distinction[16], is "open" as any other work of art, but not radically or experimentally "open" as modernist creations. The fact that Larkin's poetry perceives the world largely in terms of sociography may account for its popularity. It also indicates, however, a certain limitation which Larkin himself tries to overcome in an attempt at a negative sublime ("The Window") or, in a more general way, in cautious attempts at delimiting and universalizing meanings ("The Building").

Notes:

1 Ph. Larkin: *High Windows.* London, 1974, pp. 24-26.

2 Due to recent revelations concerning his private life and opinions ("dirty old man") Larkin's reputation has suffered a setback. However, poems should be judged on their own merits and not with a view to possible moral or political defects of their maker.

3 On the epistemological and structural importance of *apostrophe* or *prosopopeia* for poetry cf. P. de Man: "Lyrical Voice in Contemporary Theory: Riffaterre and Jauss". – In C. Hosek, P. Parker (Eds.): *Lyric Poetry. Beyond New Criticism.* Ithaca, London, 1985, pp. 55-72.

4 T. Randolph: "From witty men and mad/All poetry conception had". Larkin rejects Platonic 'madness' as a source of poetry.

5 Quoted in W. Bernsdorf (Ed.): *Wörterbuch der Soziologie.* Bd. 3. Stuttgart, ^{2}1969, p. 1663. The following lecture by R. Steinmetz is particularly important: "Das Verhältnis von Soziographie und Soziologie". – In *Verhandlungen des 5. Deutschen Soziologentages vom 26.-29.9.1926 in Wien.* Tübingen, 1927.

6 Ph. Larkin: *The Whitsun Weddings.* London, 1964, p. 19.

7 Idem: *High Windows,* p. 17.

8 Idem: *Required Writing. Miscellaneous Pieces 1955-1982.* London, 1983, p. 68.

9 Idem: *High Windows,* p. 17.

10 N. Smith, D. Wilson: *Modern Linguistics. The Results of Chomsky's Revolution.* Harmondsworth, 1974, p. 32; cf. p. 34: "Linguistic knowledge can be distinguished from other types of knowledge, which depend on different intellectual endowment, and are acquired at different rates." Winfried Nöth, too, distinguishes between experience or knowledge and linguistic signs: "Das Objekt ist das Korrelat der Erfahrung. Seine Kenntnis ist Voraussetzung für das Verstehen eines

Zeichens. Ein Zeichen kann nicht die Kenntnis des Objektes vermitteln, es kann dieses nur darstellen." - In *Handbuch der Semiotik.* Stuttgart, 1985, p. 37.

11 B. Scheffer: "Moderne Literatur läßt sich nicht länger sprachtheoretisch begründen. Helmut Heißenbüttels Theorie als Beispiel". *Merkur* 40, 2, 1986, 565-577, 568.

12 Ph. Larkin: *Required Writing*, p. 75.

13 Cf. B. Morrison: *The Movement. English Poetry and Fiction of the 1950s.* Oxford, 1980.

14 W.F. Henley: *Poems.* Vol. 1. London, 1908, p. 3. A comparison between the two poems could show how Henley's late Victorian realism is still saturated with sentimental rhetoric, whereas Larkin's is not.

15 Quoted in D. Timms: *Philip Larkin.* New York, 1974, p. 66.

16 Cf. U. Eco: *Das offene Kunstwerk.* Frankfurt/M., 1993, p. 57.

Ingrid v. Rosenberg, Duisburg

De-Constructing a Poem Deconstructing a Myth: U. A. Fanthorpe's "Not My Best Side" (Uccello: *S. George and the Dragon*, The National Gallery)

I

Not my best side, I'm afraid.
The artist didn't give me a chance to
Pose properly, and as you can see,
Poor chap, he had this obsession with
Triangles, so he left off two of my
Feet. I didn't comment at the time
(What, after all, are two feet
To a monster?) but afterwards
I was sorry for the bad publicity.
Why, I said to myself, should my conqueror
Be so ostentatiously beardless, and ride
A horse with a deformed neck and square hoofs?
Why should my victim be so
Unattractive as to be inedible,
And why should she have me literally
On a string? I don't mind dying
Ritually, since I always rise again,
But I should have liked a little more blood
To show they were taking me seriously.

II

It's hard for a girl to be sure if
She wants to be rescued. I mean, I quite
Took to the dragon. It's nice to be
Liked, if you know what I mean. He was
So nicely physical, with his claws
And lovely green skin, and that sexy tail,
And the way he looked at me,
He made me feel he was all ready to
Eat me. And any girl enjoys that.
So when this boy turned up, wearing machinery,
On a really dangerous horse, to be honest,

I didn't much fancy him. I mean,
What was he like underneath the hardware?
He might have acne, blackheads or even
Bad breath for all I could tell, but the dragon –
Well, you could see all his equipment
At a glance. Still, what could I do?
The dragon got himself beaten by the boy,
And a girl's got to think of her future.

III

I have diplomas in Dragon
Management and Virgin Reclamation.
My horse is the latest model, with
Automatic transmission and built-in
Obsolescence. My spear is custom-built,
And my prototype armour
Still on the secret list. You can't
Do better than me at the moment.
I'm qualified and equipped to the
Eyebrow. So why be difficult?
Don't you want to be killed and/or rescued
In the most contemporary way? Don't
You want to carry out the roles
That sociology and myth have designed for you?
Don't you realize that, by being choosy,
You are endangering job-prospects
In the spear- and horse-building industries?
What, in any case, does it matter what
You want? You're in my way.

What a provoking version of a familiar old story U.A. Fanthorpe's poem presents to the reader! How she came to write it is a nice story, which at the same time points the way to an interpretation.

Ironically, "Not My Best Side" does show its writer from one of *her* best sides and represents a milestone in her career as a poet. It won Fanthorpe a prize that led to a close and fruitful relationship with the small publishing house Peterloo Press, based in Cornwall, that has lasted to the present day. Since 1978 Peterloo Press has brought out five volumes of Fanthorpe's poetry and even helped her get a selection published in Penguin.[1] Fanthorpe, like a remarkably large number of women poets born in the 1920s[2], turned to poetry rather late in life when she was well over forty. Having worked as a teacher of English for sixteen years, she decided to become – as she put it herself – "a middle-age drop-out". After various temporary jobs and brief periods on the dole, she found permanent employment as a receptionist in a small hospital. And there the great change in her life happened: as she wrote in a small autobiographical piece "Slow Learner", "poetry struck during her first month behind the desk".[3] Moved by what she saw going on in the hospital, the suffering, the patience and the bravery of the patients, Fanthorpe suddenly found herself writing poetry in her lunch-breaks. The hospital experiences have remained one of her central themes ever since, making her in spirit a distant relation of Gottfried Benn. Later her range widened, including other subjects such as memories of her childhood and family and of life in schools, little incidents of everyday experience, images of landscapes and townscapes (mostly London, once Rome), but also topics from history, literature and legend. When dealing with subjects from cultural tradition, Fanthorpe – just as with her contemporary topics – likes to present "unexpected voices, marginal voices", as a critic once put it[4], handling them with a characteristic ease and bridging the time gap by always keeping her language simple and close to contemporary everyday speech. Thus her figures of legend come across as people like you and me, as the poem to be discussed here may prove, though there are others more serious in tone. Whatever the context, Fanthorpe has remained true to a conviction she once confessed to in an interview: poetry ought not to be "difficult" but suited to reach a large audience.[5] Her first literary endeavours had already been published in magazines and newspapers when Fanthorpe decided to take part in a competition run by *Phoenix*, a poetry magazine published by Harry Chambers (who, luckily for her, also owns Peterloo Press). She won second prize with "Not My Best Side".

The task set was to write a poem about a picture, and as her subject Fanthorpe chose *Saint George and the Dragon*, a fifteenth century Italian painting by Paolo Uccello (1397-1475), which hangs in the National Gallery in London. The picture shows the climax of the legendary battle: Saint George, mounted on his white steed, is approaching in full gallop from the right, driving his lance into the dragon's eye. His opponent is positioned slightly left of centre, squaring his feet (of which there are actually only two as the dragon in Fanthorpe's poem complains (I, ll. 5-6) and bowing his head in defeat. He seems to have emerged from his cave in the background, whose opening forms one of many triangles in the picture: indeed, as Fanthorpe's dragon drily remarks, the painter, "poor chap", seems to have "had this obsession with triangles" (I, ll. 4-5). (Presumably he meant to underline the importance of the trinity of protagonists involved.) Apparently, the dragon is held by a maiden on a string, who, standing left of the dragon, completes the triangle of figures. It is certainly a striking picture for the brightness of its delicately chosen colours, the vividness with which the climax of the ritual fight is presented and – not least – for the odd posture of the maiden. This may strike modern observers as slightly comical: she is standing there bolt upright, seemingly unmoved by the dramatic events happening before her eyes and – as the poem puts it – leading the dragon "literally on a string"(I, ll. 15-16). It is a picture to inspire the imagination; yet even if this is so, there are certainly many others no less challenging as the rich tradition of European and American iconic poetry proves.[6] It remains an intriguing question why Fanthorpe should have picked this particular one.

In her book *Feminism and Poetry*, Jan Montefiore has recently written: "European myth and fairy tale fascinate women poets to the point of obsession."[7] She proves her remark with an impressive list of examples ranging from H.D.'s *Trilogy* (1944) to the more recent poetry of Liz Lochhead, Anne Sexton and Stevie Smith, not forgetting to mention also such writers of fiction as Angela Carter, all of whom have made use of, and recast, myths and fairy tale motifs, giving them a new female, more often than not a definitely feminist, twist. For explanation, Montefiore points to the narrative character of myth, arguing that storytelling has traditionally been a favourite pastime of women while assembled round the kitchen hearth. Therefore, the telling of revised well-known stories appears to her a particularly well-suited means of literary communication within the newly forming community of feminist-minded women. More convincing than this theory which claims storytelling as a predominantly female occupation – much can be said to the contrary – is an explanation some other feminist critics have offered: they stress the connection between myth and subjectivity. Alicia Ostriker, for example, drawing on Freudian and Jungian theories, reminds the reader how myth, handed down through the generations by cultural traditions, sinking into the subconscious and providing us with material for dreams and desires, essentially helps to form our consciousness and attitudes.[8] Thus it becomes understandable why feminist-oriented artists should feel challenged to reinterpret some of the innumerable stories in myth and folklore in which men perform heroic deeds while women are restricted to much less glamorous roles, figuring as victims, prizes, destructive femmes fatales or as mere admiring spectators (and, of course, as any possible combination of these roles). What must have been going on in all these women's and girls' heads is a question that has apparently puzzled many contemporary women poets. Among them is Fanthorpe as the brief introduction to four poems on figures from Shakespeare's tragedies shows in an exemplary way:

> I wrote these four poems because I was interested to see how the masculine world of Shakespeare's tragedies would look from the woman's angle. In fact, women exist in this world only to be killed, as sacrificial victims. So I imagined Gertrude (mother-in-law), Regan (king's daughter), Emilia (army wife) and the un-named waiting gentlewoman in *Macbeth* having a chat with some usual female confidante, like a hairdresser, or a telephone.[9]

A hope seems to have spurred these female reinterpreters of legend: that their fresh versions of the well-known stories might work on the readers' or hearers' consciousness along the same lines as the originals once did, thus subtly helping to alter attitudes to gender roles. It seems worth noting that most of these writers do not try to defuse the patriarchal myths by juxtaposing them with equally heavy-weight female versions, but rather by applying the lighter, nevertheless equally sobering (and definitely more pleasant) medicine of irony and ridicule. Fanthorpe, with some of her poetry, is part of this trend. And that is probably why, when it came to the *Phoenix* poetry competition, Uccello's picture suggested itself to her as a good subject: it deals with a relevant legend, and the manner of presentation – despite the delicacy of the painting – makes it appear slightly comical to the modern observer, perhaps even reminding him or her of the illustrations in a children's book. Uccello's picture was one to meet Fanthorpe's intentions half way.

As to the appropriate interpretation of her poem, Fanthorpe has given the reader a substantial eye-opener herself drawing the meta-level right into the poem when she lets the knight mention the very conceptual key-terms: "Don't / You want to carry out the *roles* / That *sociology* and *myth* have designed for you?"(III, ll. 13-14). This little *Verfremdungseffekt* leaves no doubt. (Gender)-roles are the subject of her poem in combination with "myth" and "sociology" as the two ideological forces that are decisive for their formation. To understand Fanthorpe's opinion on gender roles fully, the reader needs only to take the poet's hint and explore the particular myth at stake as well as analyse the poetical – i.e. linguistic and metrical – means by which she has worked her particular version.

In anthologies "Not My Best Side" is usually printed without the original subtitle mentioning Uccello's picture as the model. Of course, the poem is understandable and funny enough in itself. Yet, leaving out the indication of the source does not only mean denying the poem its place in the tradition of iconic poetry, but also suppressing a valuable clue to the way Fanthorpe has dealt with legend. For how does the story of Saint George that Uccello painted run? Since its origin in the 4th century the tale had undergone many variations until its fixation in the *Legenda Aurea*, a famous 13th century collection of saints' legends that spread all over Europe. According to this final version, Saint George saved the King of Lybia's daughter from a dragon, who had to be kept from destroying the country with his pestilential breath by the regular sacrifice of, first, two sheep, later a virgin. After his victory Saint George, however, did not marry the princess. He merely asked her to throw her (chastity?) belt round the monster's neck and lead it "tame as a pet dog" into the king's capital as a sign of God's strength (this then is the origin of the "string" in Fanthorpe's poem! [I, ll. 15-16]).[10] Thus Saint George won over the people of Lybia to Christianity, who were then baptised in their thousands. The fight with the dragon in this legend symbolizes the victory of Christian belief over heathendom and has nothing to do with a love story, though it may have had an influence on more romantic stories invented in later days.

What changes has Fanthorpe administered to this venerable legend? Slyly omitting the knight's name, she first of all has given such a twist to the story as to turn it into another type of fight, one that we in the Protestant north of Europe are much more familiar with and which I would like to call the "love-story type of dragon fight". Even at first glance the reader, whether German or British, immediately recognizes the essential features: knight rescues girl from monster and is rewarded by her hand; girl is supposed to be delighted. Dragon fights in a great variety of forms had indeed been one of the most wide-spread themes in international oral and written legend and literature ever since antiquity. The love-story version, of which the story of Perseus and Andromeda is an early example, became particularly popular in medieval Europe in the wake of the cult of courtly love. It was told in heroic songs and romances of chivalry as, for example, the German song of "Hürnen Seyfrid", as well as in many fairy tales told all over the world, notably the numerous international versions of the tale of "The Two Brothers", one of which was printed in and thus made known to a larger audience by the Grimm Brothers' collection of 1812.[11] Though the Grimm collection quickly became popular in Britain, too, after the first translation in 1823, Spenser's *Faerie Queene* (1596), in telling the adventures of the Knight of the Red Cross, may have done more to keep the memory of the story alive in this country. However the channels of tradition may have worked, the story in its essential outlines has become so well-known in Britain as well as in Germany that it was condensed to the proverbial "knight in shining armour" whom every girl is supposed to wait for. The saying is predominantly used to ridicule the secret wishes of adolescent girls frightened of planning their own lives and dreaming of being swept off their feet and taken care of by some powerful but nevertheless loveable man. Of course, this is the connotation of the dragon fight Fanthorpe is playing with in her poem. To drive home the fact that this myth is not simply an entertaining tale from the remote past, but still has a bearing on the present, Fanthorpe brings the story close to the modern reader's experience by employing a number of clever devices, a particularly striking one being the use of modern language.

Before going into the question of language, however, another of Fanthorpe's poetic devices needs to be discussed because it concerns the most basic feature of the poem: that is, its structure. One might have expected the poet to choose the ballad form – the medieval subject might have suggested it. Instead, Fanthorpe preferred a dramatic rendering. Rather than influencing the reader's perception by a lyrical "I"'s comment or the creation of a particular atmosphere, she chose the form which Gisbert Kranz calls the "monologuish iconic poem" letting her three protagonists speak for themselves.[12] This form seems specially suited to provoke readers to think for themselves. In three stanzas of nineteen lines each, all in free verse (the rhythm closest to everyday speech), each headed by a Roman number reminiscent of the acts of a drama, Fanthorpe has her protagonists speak their minds in monologues, the equal length of the stanzas symbolizing their equal importance. (Of course, the girl in her version carries no less weight than the combatants!) The dragon and the maiden speak asides, talking, almost chatting to the reader in a confidential manner, while the knight is apparently addressing the other two in a kind of public speech, not giving them a chance to respond.

Just as the painter was obsessed – as the dragon in Fanthorpe's poem rightly remarks – with the idea of the triangle, so each of the three figures in his or her soliloquy turns out to be obsessed with a fixed idea, an idea that runs quite contrary to, and stands in comical contrast to, their roles in tradition, thus casting a doubtful light on these. The dragon, instead of majestically representing the forces of untamed or even malign nature, is merely concerned about his image, resembling not so much a proper frightening monster as a film star acting one. The girl for her part, rather than in mortal fear of the beast and full of love and gratitude for her deliverer, is preoccupied with thoughts of her material future. Finally, the knight is the destroyer rather than the rescuer, and clearly obsessed by his desire for power. The reader, listening carefully to what the characters say, soon realizes that this is by no means the fixed triangle of legendary tradition; on the contrary, Fanthorpe's triangle is made up of a number of shifting binary oppositions. To be sure, just as in the traditional versions of the story, the maiden and the knight are humans, and to that extent the dragon is their common opponent; but then the dragon and the knight are also both males, and the girl is the woman between them (this aspect of the notorious "eternal triangle" treated in innumerable novels and films is stressed particularly by the girl); and finally, and perhaps most important, the dragon and the girl form a pair as they are both subject to the knight's desire for power – his victims. The two new oppositions implied by Fanthorpe contain dynamite enough to blow up the triangle of legendary tradition at any moment, which in her version appears as merely a very temporary and highly precarious one.

The form of monologues further allowed Fanthorpe to make use of dramatic irony, heightening the illusion-shattering effect: the dragon and the girl may be bluntly told the knight's intentions, but he does not know what they think nor do they read each other's minds. Only the reader is in on the full secret, and so the characters, though listlessly, still act out their "roles that sociology and myth have designed" for them. In this way, the distance between them – as well as the distance between all of them and their traditional counterparts –

is amusingly and effectively stressed: the girl feels desired by the dragon and rather fancies him, whereas he in reality finds her "unattractive" to the point of being "inedible" (I, l. 14); the knight expects the girl to jump at his offer of help, while she rather dislikes and mistrusts him; the knight feels superior to both, believing he has the power to "kill and/or rescue" whomever he wants (III, l. 11) while the dragon knows that all the militant boy's efforts will be in vain, as he himself is immortal and will "always rise again" (I, l. 17). The horse – actually the fourth figure in the picture and just as big as the dragon – in a clever little move is made into a special touchstone for the three protagonists' incompatible views: while the knight is so proud of it and praises it fulsomely, the girl, realizing that it is used as a weapon ("a really *dangerous* horse" [I, l. 11]), abhors it and the dragon complains of its "deformed neck and square hoofs" (I, l. 12), i.e. its ugliness which disgraces the dignity of the show.

Much of the comical effect of the poem is produced by the language of the protagonists, each of whom speaks an individual jargon which nicely underlines his or her character and role. The dragon and the girl use the most ordinary everyday speech, including any number of fillers and readymades ("I'm afraid" [I, l. 1], "after all" [I, l. 7], "I mean" [II, l. 1], "if you know what I mean" [II, l. 4], etc.). The dragon is moreover characterised by the fashionable jargon of show business ("to pose properly" [I, l. 3], "the bad publicity" [I, l. 9], "I should have liked a little more blood to show they were taking me seriously" [I, ll. 1-19]). The girl's speech is even simpler than his and the funniest, not only because of the overtly sexual overtones of her text. The extremely ordinary expressions of 20th century experience she uses clash in a particularly comical way with the traditional foil: for example, when she praises the dragon's "lovely green skin" and "sexy tail" (II, l. 6) and fears the boy might have "acne, blackheads or even bad breath" (II, ll. 14-15) or when she – with the proverbial female ignorance of technical matters and terms – calls the knight's splendid armour respectlessly "machinery" (II, l. 10) or even just "hardware" (II, l. 13). Furthermore she has a habit of opening her statements with an anaphorical "and" and preferably hides herself behind generalizing clichés such as "it's hard for a girl" (II, l. 1), "any girl enjoys that" (II, l. 9), "a girl has to think of her future" (II, l. 19). In short, her speech signals a conventional, lower class, not very bright girl. What a come-down from the fairy-tale princess! Nevertheless, the dragon and the girl in their chatty way come across as rather sympathetic, homely creatures – not so the knight. His language, which has a distinctly American ring, is an unholy mixture of the discourses of business ("diplomas in Dragon Management and Virgin Reclamation" [III, l. 1]), advertising and the automobile and arms industries ("my horse is the latest model with automatic transmission and built-in obsolescence" [II, ll. 3-5], "my spear is custom-built and my prototype armour still on the secret list" [III, l. 5-7], "you can't do better than me" [III, ll. 7-8]). The effect is chilling, and the reader's laughter may mix with a tinge of horror when he comes to the last stanza. If the dragon at the beginning of the poem is rather charmingly insecure about his image, the knight has no such doubts but is boldly boasting away of his competitive advantages, linking a series of self-confident "I's", "me's" and "my's" to superlatives such as "latest" and "best" until he finally rounds off his self-praise with the summing-up statement: "I'm qualified and equipped to the eyebrow" (III, l. 9). In the second half of his stanza he then openly shows his egotism and desire for power when he threatens not only the dragon, but the girl: "You are in my way" (III, l. 19).

This armoured man – armoured in the literal as well as in the symbolical sense described by Klaus Theweleit in his book on male fantasies – is a danger not only to nature (= the dragon), but to women as well and to mankind at large. This knight is only interested in his own progress; the girl's wishes count for nothing with him. (What a prospect for their "happy future" prescribed by tradition!) Of course, Fanthorpe's knight is a caricature, yet as in any caricature there is a kernel of truth. Fanthorpe is warning of that old-fashioned type of man, who is by no means an extinct species, the blind activist, in love with technology and the "most contemporary" arms (III, l. 12), the mindless destroyer without consideration either for his fellow human beings or for nature. That such attitudes are not just the anxious fantasies of an oversensitive mind, but still exist in the real world is deftly hinted at by the poet in that she lets the knight borrow the well-known job-preservation argument so popular with politicians who want to promote investments in the military (III, ll. 15-17). When the poem was written, at a time when the East-West conflict seemed permanent, this argument was in particularly frequent use, but has by no means become obsolete since. Indeed, ours is a time to be more afraid of man than of monsters.

So the knight in Fanthorpe's poem – quite in contrast to tradition – does not invite to identification. Although he may believe he has presented himself from his best side in his self-advertisement, this has turned out to be an illusion. And what of the other two? Ever since Kenneth Grahame's story of the "Reluctant Dragon" (1896), who became friends with a village boy and would only consent to a bloodless show-fight with Saint George, literature has become much more sympathetic to dragons than of old; friendly, even soft-hearted dragons have become quite the fashion.[13] Michael Ende's dragon Fuchur in his *Never Ending Story*, who serves the hero Bastian as friend, helper and vehicle, is a good example, and so is Steven Spielberg's E.T. In comparison with such sentimental versions of the species, U. A. Fanthorpe's dragon with his touchy concern for his public image comes across refreshingly ironically, though certainly not as a grand symbol of endangered nature either. Really, he is not shown from his best side either. And what of the maiden?

For a feminist poem she is rather a surprising heroine. For though she feels attracted to the dragon, she follows her materialistic instincts and succumbs to the knight with a sentence that reveals worldly wisdom: "a girl has to think of her future" (II, l. 19). No thought of venturing on her own way if she does not love him! The maiden's aphorism seems to echo Marilyn Monroe's unforgettable song "Diamonds are a girl's best friends". And, indeed, the girl's attitude represents basically the same mixture of naiveté and calculation Anita Loos had satirized already in 1925 in the figure of the men-and-money hunting New York girl Loreley, heroine of her short novel *Gentlemen Prefer Blondes*, on which Howard Hawk's famous film comedy of 1953 was based. The heroine's name, with its hint at yet another well-known medieval myth with significance for gender roles, seems to further underline the kinship between the two figures; yet while Loos' and Fanthorpe's satire is equally sharp, in the film Monroe's charm takes much of the sting out of the criticism.[14]

Thus it turns out that Fanthorpe, showing none of the three characters from their best side (though she certainly blames the knight most), rejects the myth as a whole. Her reason for this has become apparent: the myth exalts aggressive man at the expense of woman and beast, reducing the one to a silly, passive little opportunist and the other to a somewhat ridiculous show-star, robbed of any real power. Fanthorpe's view stands in marked contrast to another recent interpretation of the "dream of the knight" offered by the German essayist Barbara Sichtermann.[15] Sichtermann argued that girls do well in dreaming of being carried away by the "knight in shining armour", as the knight, in her view, represents the power of sexuality itself. However, if one adds the dragon to the picture, Sichtermann's interpretation cannot stand unchallenged. If anybody symbolizes sexuality here, it is certainly the dragon as the girl in our poem clearly senses. Fanthorpe in her marvellously funny poem shows that the times for maidens to dream of being rescued by knights should indeed be over unless men and women want to be reduced to their worst sides.

Notes

1 The volumes of U.A. Fanthorpe's poetry published by Peterloo Press are: *Side Effects* (1978), *Standing To* (1982), *Voices Off* (1984), *A Watching Brief* (1987) and *Neck-Verse* (1992). Her *Selected Poems* were published by Peterloo Press and as paperback in the Penguin Poets series, both in 1986. "Not My Best Side" first appeared in *Side Effects*, then in *Selected Poems* and also in various anthologies of contemporary poetry.

2 F. Adcock in her "Introduction" to idem (Ed.): *The Faber Book of 20th Century Women's Poetry*. London, 1987, offers an explanation for this phenomenon,

namely that a climate unresponsive to women's poetry had put them off when they were still young: "women seem particularly unwilling to be discouraged from writing, however late it might be getting" (p. 10). Today, she notices, women feel encouraged to start publishing their poetry at a much earlier age.

3 Information about Fanthorpe's biography can be found in a short autobiographical piece "Slow Learner". *Poetry Matters. Journal of Peterloo Poets* 5, Winter 1987, 34-35; in S. Davies: "A First-Division Look". *Arts West.* Sept. 1988, 26-27; or in R.A.W.: "Behind the Poetry". *Arts North.* Nov./Dec. 1987, 15.

4 Ibid.

5 About the state of modern poetry she said to the interviewer Sara Davies: "Where it went wrong was with a tendency to write for other poets, or in particular to write for university departments. Obviously departments of English are interested in teaching poetry and therefore it's got to be difficult or else there's nothing to teach. This has nothing to do with what poetry ought to be doing – it has a much bigger audience than that." (Cf. note 3)

6 The tradition of iconic poetry reaches back to Greek and Roman antiquity. In England, poems inspired by pictures or statues were particularly popular in the Romantic period and later among the Preraphaelites. Examples are P. Shelley: "Ozymandias", "On the Medusa of Leonardo da Vinci in the Florentine Gallery"; J. Keats: "On Seeing the Elgin Marbles", "Ode to a Grecian Urn"; W. Wordsworth: "The Last Supper, by Leonardo da Vinci, in the Convent of Maria della Grazia", "On a Portrait of the Duke of Wellington upon the Field of Waterloo, by Haycon"; D.G. Rossetti: "For Spring by Sandro Botticelli", "For Our Lady of the Rocks by Leonardo da Vinci". Rossetti also composed poems to go with his own paintings like "Astarte Syriaca" – written on the frame of his own picture with the same title. In this century T. S. Eliot ("La Figlia Che Piange"), W.H. Auden ("Museé des Beaux Arts"), W.B. Yeats ("Leda and the Swan", "On a Picture of a Black Centaur by Edmund Dulac"), W.C. Williams ("Pictures from Breughel") turned their attention to the sister art. For a first overview of the large field see G. Kranz: *Das Bildgedicht in Europa.* Paderborn, 1973, and U. Bachteler: *Die Darstellung von Werken der Malerei in der amerikanischen Lyrik des 20. Jahrhunderts.* Darmstadt, 1979. – Fanthorpe's poem differs in intention from the bulk of such poems, i.e. their usually reverential attitude towards old masters, and resembles more the ironical stance, aiming at disenchantment, of the dadaists, Warhol or Tucholsky ("Das Lächeln der Mona Lisa"). Fanthorpe's irony, however, does not, like theirs, aim at the worn-off charm of the all too famous, mass-reproduced classical works (after all, Uccello's picture is not as famous as the Mona Lisa), but goes in a different direction.

7 J. Montefiore: *Feminism and Poetry.* London, 1987, p. 39.

8 A. Ostriker: "The Thieves of Language. Woman Poets and Revisionist Mythmaking". *Signs* 8, i, 1982.

9 U.A. Fanthorpe: *Selected Poems* (Penguin ed.), p. 50.

10 *Die Legenda aurea des Jacobus de Voraigne.* Aus dem Lateinischen übers. von R. Benz. Heidelberg, 1979, p. 301ff.

11 For the various versions of the legend and their history see, for instance, the comprehensive article "Drache" by L. Röhrich in K. Ranke et.al. (Eds.): *Enzyklopädie des Märchens. Handwörterbuch zur historischen und vergleichenden Erzählforschung* 3, Berlin, New York, 1981, Sp. 787-820; J. Simpson: "Fifty British Dragon Tales. An Analysis". *Folklore* 89, 1978, 79-93; U. Steffen: *Drachenkampf. Der Mythos*

vom Bösen. Stuttgart, 1984. – For the influence of the Grimm Brothers' collection in Britain see J. Zipes: "Introduction" to his edition of *Victorian Fairy Tales. The Revolt of the Fairies and Elves.* New York, London, 1987, pp. XIII-XXIX. – The title of the fairy tale in question in the Grimm collection is "Johannes Wassersprung und Caspar Wassersprung" (Nr. 74). As one of the few British versions Simpson quotes "Assipattle and the Mester Stoor Worm" told on the Orkneys (Simpson, p. 83 and 92). Of course, many other tales about dragons are told in Britain as elsewhere.

12 G. Kranz (*Das Bildgedicht in Europa*) attempts a categorization of iconic poetry according to form.

13 Grahame's fairy tale was originally published in his book *Dream Boys*, 1898. Reprint in J. Zipes (Ed.): *Victorian Fairy Tales*, pp. 327-349. An equally friendly dragon made his appearance about the same time in Edith Nesbit's story "The Last of the Dragons" (c. 1900) though the story was published only much later (posthumously in *Five of Us – and Madeleine* (1925), reprint ibid, pp. 353-358), while Nesbit's dragons in her more famous *Book of Dragons* (1900) are still sinister creatures.

14 A. Loos: *Gentlemen Prefer Blondes*, 1925. The sequel *But Gentlemen Marry Brunettes* (1928), tells the contrasting story of Loreley's friend Dorothy, who falls in love only with penniless men but ends up in luck nonetheless (Both novels in one vol. publ. by Viking Penguin: New York, 1989). – The more serious aspects of Loos' criticism were taken up in W. Empson's poem "Reflection from Anita Loos" in which he muses about the cruel consequences of social ambition (W. Empson: *Collected Poems.* New York, 1956, p. 66). Empson quotes a sentence uttered by Dorothy in which she, for her part, rejects the necessary submission: "A girl can't go on laughing all the time". This line, in its parallel construction, answers and contradicts the statement of Fanthorpe's maiden in an almost uncanny way. – I owe the hints to Empson's poem and to Loos' novels to Manfred Pfister.

15 B. Sichtermann: "Der Rittertraum". – In idem: *Weiblichkeit. Zur Politik des Privaten.* Berlin, 1991 (1983), pp. 81-89.

Evelyne Keitel, Chemnitz-Zwickau

Reading Michèle Roberts' Poem "Rite de Passage" through Psychoanalysis and Feminism

rite de passage
(for Joan of Arc)

it is always the quiet ones
whom the whirlwind picks:
Joan, thrust from dumb worship
of forests, God's fist at her back
the saints articulating
her bones to an iron
syntax, the ringing logic of mail

once she danced in wordless circles
of girls, hands linked, once she hung
leaf-loops, flowers in knots
on trees, her invocation
a green twist, a perfect O

then the vision plucked her away
and sentenced her: the voices
insisted she marry, and name
the new part of herself: war's
rhetorician, she stammered
embracing the angel, faint in his angular grip

Joan, after that meeting
returned to broken places: compatriots hurt
by her eyes'
pure androgynous glare; turning
her face from family, she forswore
silence and mother-tongues

yet, in the end, after victories
after the failed leap from the tower
she was trapped: ecclesiastical
grammar, the rope of deft priests, tied
and tripped her; she conjugated
their only available verb: I confess
to heresy; I am unnatural

they pitied her: duped
peasant, illiterate girl
and duly they sent her back
to the smoking green wood, the sharp tree
– lashed to it, burning, a human garland
poor freak (born too soon) she carried on
crying out messages they could not hear (1986)

This poem[1] is dedicated to Joan of Arc, the French peasant girl who led the French army against the English during the Hundred Years' War. Her troops won a momentous victory at Orléans, repulsing the English's attempt to conquer all of northern France. Captured a year later, Joan was accused of heresy and burned at the stake. Michèle Roberts'[2] poem is not only dedicated to Joan of Arc, it is also about the Maid of Orléans. On a surface level, the poem construes her deeds as both historical and legendary.

In my interpretation of Roberts' poem, I will call this first level, the one that comes to mind immediately (even when reading the poem for the very first time), the level of fact vs. fiction. I will subsequently argue that there are two more levels to this poem. They are less obvious, because they abstract from the historical figure, exploring instead realms of more general relevance. Yet, like the first level, these two further levels are also characterized by specific structural oppositions. Through a close reading, I will show that, on a second level of interpretation, the use of language in this prose poem without rhyme or meter contrasts silence and language. My third level of interpretation, in turn, will introduce a psychoanalytic reading which is based on the tensions between the pre-oedipal and the oedipal as they prevail in this poem. In a final, spiral-like move, I will use Julia Kristeva's distinction between historical and monumental time to link the third level of interpretation back to the first, so that my readings will come full circle.

1. Fact vs. Fiction

Already during her life-time, Joan's character, her heroic feats, and her final downfall were invested with an auspicious quality. Myths and legends have abounded, tainting our vision of the legendary saint.

Joan was born in a small village on the Meuse in 1412. Throughout her life, she remained illiterate, but she is said to have had a shrewd and acute common sense. And she must have been exceptionally pious: At 13 Joan began to have visions of angels and saints, St. Michael, St. Catherine, and St. Margaret (the patron saints of her country) among them. The legends have it that their voices guided Joan all her life.

The crown of France at the time was in dispute between the *dauphin* Charles, the son and heir of Charles VI, and the English king Henry VI, whose armies, in alliance with the Burgundians, were occupying the country. In 1427, the *dauphin*'s cause seemed hopeless: five years after his father's death, he had still not been crowned at Reims, the traditional place for the investiture of French kings, because Reims was well within the territory held by the English. As long as the *dauphin* remained unconsecrated, however, the rightfulness of his claim to be king was open to question in the minds of his people.

Intending to participate in the warfare and dressed in men's clothes, Joan joined the *dauphin*. She succeeded in convincing both him and the ecclesiastical authorities whom he asked for advice – the fear of heresy was ever-present – that she was neither a witch nor feeble-minded. Subsequently, the *dauphin* gave her an army of several hundreds of men.

Eventually, after having raised the siege of Orléans in May 1429 and won several more battles at towns along the Loire River, Joan was captured. Determined to escape from the castle in which she had been imprisoned, she jumped from a tower into the moat; she fell unconscious but was not seriously hurt.

Joan was brought to trial before the inquisition at Rouen, because the English could not simply do away with so popular a figure. They had to undermine the French people's faith in her and, through her, in the recently crowned King: The purpose of the trial was to show that Charles VII was nothing but a fool in the hands of a scheming and evil witch.

Joan was burnt in 1431. One of the more colourful legends that have cropped up has it that the executioner who had led Joan to the stake and lit the pyre declared afterwards that he had found her heart – which would not burn – intact among the ashes: a sure sign of her saintliness. Joan was beatified in 1909, and canonized in 1920.

The structural opposition of fact vs. fiction – always a precarious one – does not work at all for as colourful a person as Joan of Arc. It collapses, because every form of discourse about her, even a paragraph in a history textbook or an entry in an encyclopedia, can only ever present her through the thick lens of accumulated legends.

By introducing the saint and some of the deeds attributed to her (the "victories" – l. 25, the "failed leap from the tower" – l. 26), Roberts' poem perpetuates the legends surrounding Joan. At the same time, however, Roberts recreates the myth anew. It presents Joan in a new light, in a specifically literary language.

2. Silence vs. Language

"Rite de Passage" tells Joan's story in terms of a battle of words against silence. It is a poem about war. And it is a poem about language. Its vocabulary is one indigenous to grammar textbooks, their nouns ("syntax"- l. 7, "grammar" - l. 28, "verb" - l. 30, "messages" - l. 38) and verbs ("articulating" - l. 5, to "name" - l. 15, to "conjugate" - l. 29), as well as the semantic opposites of this vocabulary, adjectives that designate non-language ("quiet" - l. 1, "dumb" - l. 3, "wordless" - l. 8, "illiterate" - l. 33). In this poem, language equals warfare, silence equals bliss.

It is significant that the notions of armed hostilities on the one hand and, on the other, linguistics, are repeatedly condensed into one phrase: "an iron syntax" (ll. 5-6) is one case in point, "the ringing logic of mail" (l. 7) another. While logic, in antiquity, was a branch of rhetoric, mail denotes a suit of armor made of metal links or plates and connotes postal services, that system of human communication which relies on the exchange of letters. "To sentence" is ambivalent in and by itself: a sentence being both a punishment pronounced by a court and a grammatically self-contained speech unit consisting of syntactically related groups of words. Thus, when "the vision plucked [Joan] away and sentenced her" (ll. 13-14), she was condemned as well as thrust into language.

The poem describes an initiation.[3] It is an initiation into language, a *rite de passage* from an enchanted state of silence and harmony, with "girls", "danc-[ing] in wordless circles", "hands linked", braiding "leaf-loops" out of "flowers in knots", an aspirated "perfect O" (ll. 8-12) being the only sound discernible in their idyllic "forests", to the cruel realities of language, war, and a ruined country with "broken places" (l. 20). The initiation entails proceeding from a state of charmed innocence to a state of painful knowledge. The process itself is chaotic (instigated by a "whirlwind"- l. 2). And it is violent. Joan is forced into the ordeal by feeling "God's fist at her back" (l. 4). She is pushed into a marriage of sorts. Through an "embrace" that resembles a wedding ritual and consists in violence, sexual violence, maybe even a rape (the embrace, "an angular grip", leaves her "faint" - l. 18), Joan enters a new stage in her life, dominated by novel (masculine) activities. Her altered status is marked by a change of names (marriage, for women, conventionally means taking on a new name). And when Joan is coerced into naming herself or, to be more precise, into naming this "new", this knowing "part of herself", she "stammer[s]": "war's rhetorician" (ll. 15-17). Now, after the initiation (the rape), after having left the company of girls, the blissful state of harmony and innocence, Joan knows how to speak.

By way of an initiation, Joan suddenly knows. Moreover, she has immediately become adept. She has complete and absolute mastery over her field.

She is a "rhetorician". She knows how to speak to perfection. And she knows how to win monumental victories. Her name is "war's rhetorician" (ll. 16-17), and rightfully so. Joan excels in the art of rhetorics, just as she excels in the art of warfare.

3. *The Pre-Oedipal vs. the Oedipal*

Psychoanalytically speaking, the poem construes a *rite de passage* from the pre-oedipal to the oedipal. The pre-oedipal is a stage in ontogenetic development characterized by joyfulness and exhilaration, by intermittent fusions with the mother's body, and immediate gratifications of all physiological and psychic needs, whereas the oedipal is defined by conflicting drives, problematic and discordant social relationships and, last not least, language acquisition.

According to Sigmund Freud, every human being has to emerge from the pre-oedipal. In order for individuation to become possible, it is inevitable that we leave this near-paradisiacal, enchanted state and enter the oedipal with all its brutal realities. The crucial cross-over is both instigated and marked by our learning how to speak: It is only through language that we begin to have an inkling of who we are and what the world around us consists of.

This initiation process is both liberating – we might eventually become an independent self – and severely constricting: Assimilating the properties of language means accepting its peculiar tendency to posit boundaries and limits through systems of syntactic inflections, functions, and relations. Language originates in and depends on binary oppositions: black and white, day and night, man and woman. Through language acquisition, we internalize the laws underlying language which also contain the (patriarchal) laws of our society, its symbolic order.[4] Language acquisition entails becoming aware of our respective gender and of sexual difference. Joan, on the crucial crossroad between blissful ignorance and linguistic knowledge, between the pre-oedipal and the oedipal, meets with physical abuse; it is only apt that in this poem the abuse takes on the form of *sexual* violence.

Language acquisition is a precarious and an essentially painful process, the cost of individuation high. Both boys and girls have to give up the state of divine merging with the maternal for good. According to psychoanalysis, individuation is instigated through the oedipal conflict[5] and an overpowering threat of castration.[6] Castration provokes anxiety. But it also allows for total reassurance, signifying, as it does, masculinity, patriarchy, stasis, law, and order. In Freudian theory, the little boy can overcome the pitfalls of the oedipus complex by renouncing the incestuous desire for his mother and, instead, identifying with his father's position of patriarchal power. The female child, however, has to achieve a double renunciation: She must give up the amorous impulses toward her mother and, subsequently, displace the desire for her father. She has, in effect, to restructure her entire psychic organisation without getting the chance of turning this process into a positive venture: On account of her gender, the little girl is barred from identifying with a position of patriarchal power.

Joan, however, is an exception: By assimilating the symbolic order of her society, she actively enters into the essentially male world of warfare. She learns how to play the male power game. And she excels. She marches from victory to victory, in fact liberating her country from English occupation. In surmounting the pre-oedipal, which is metonymically related to the mother's body, the maternal, and the female (with "wordless circles of girls, hands linked" – ll. 8-9), Joan had to forswear "silence and mother-tongues" (l. 24). Within the realm of the oedipal (dominated by the father's threat of castration, the paternal, and the patriarchal), however, she steps outside the place traditionally assigned to women which, of course, entails "turning her face from family" (ll. 22-23) and neglecting social conventions.

But Joan does not abandon the pre-oedipal completely. After all, it is only one "part of herself" which is "new" (l. 16) and therefore has to be named. There is another, silent, hidden part which continues to live, which goes unquestioned, and does not need to be renamed. Joan achieves the feat of fending for herself in the masculine war business, and yet drawing strength and energy from the feminine pre-oedipal. For her, the masculine and the feminine, the oedipal and the pre-oedipal, converge into a realm beyond gender-difference: They give rise to "androgyn[y]" (l. 22).

Joan's "compatriots" (l. 20) can sense this strange and disquieting androgynous quality in her. They are "hurt by her eyes' pure androgynous glare" (ll. 21-22). They conceive her to be "unnatural" (l. 31). Having achieved the impossible, Joan becomes a "freak" (l. 37). This is her true "heresy" (l. 31), one that the "deft priests" (l. 28) cannot even begin to understand. Even if she "cr[ies] out her messages", they "[can] not hear" (l. 38). They send her back to the forests of her pre-oedipal, to "smoking green woods" (l. 35), which makes her end meet her beginning, but which also, by necessity, extinguishes her. There is no going back to the pre-oedipal. The intersection between the pre-oedipal and the oedipal, once crossed, remains barred for good. Any attempt of going back will cost one's life.

Roberts' poem alludes to and is informed by the secrets of the pre-oedipal. Freud was not very interested in the pre-oedipal.[7] Neither was his most famous successor, Jacques Lacan.[8] Both remained in deep ignorance of what woman wants.[9] Feminists working within the psychoanalytic tradition have begun to revise some of their more misogynist theories. Infuriated by the

Freudian equation of anatomy and destiny, they have initiated a fundamental reformulation of certain key terms of psychoanalysis. Although their approaches are many and diverse, they all share in common a strong interest in the pre-oedipal. Their work is based on the philosophical assumption that the pre-oedipal, because of its close connection with the mother's body, constitutes a genuinely female realm.[10] Thus, psychoanalytically oriented American feminists reevaluate the female in relation to the maternal[11], whereas French feminists, by way of Lacanian poststructuralism, put forth a linguistic theory of sexual difference.[12]

4. Monumental Time vs. Historical Time

Kristeva, in her article "Women's Time", elaborates on the pre-oedipal by drawing a distinction between two different conceptions of time, "time as project, teleology, linear and prospective unfolding: time as departure, progression and arrival – in other words, the time of history"[13] which belongs to the oedipal on the one hand and, on the other, "a monumental temporality, without cleavage or escape, which has so little to do with linear time (which passes) that the word 'temporality' hardly fits: all-encompassing and infinite like imaginary space"[14], in short: the pre-oedipal's eternity.

"Rite de Passage" recaptures this very rift. There is linear time, the time of war, history, and Joan's heroic (if legendary) deeds. But there is also the infinite time of imaginary space, evoked at the beginning of the poem and, again, at its end: Joan passes from monumental time through historical time back into monumental time. Yet, as opposed to the warriors and priests surrounding her, Joan retains some of her pre-oedipal, female wisdom. She knows how to fuse the male and the female, a feat well beyond comprehension (not only) for her compatriots. They had to turn her into a martyr and a saint. She was, indeed, "born too soon".

Notes

1 M. Roberts: *The Mirror of the Mother.* London, 1986, pp. 86-87.

2 Roberts has also written six novels. *Daughters of the House* was shortlisted for the 1992 Booker Prize and won the W. H. Smith Literary Award for 1993. The novel is, as one reviewer has it, "at once a ghost story, a tale of visions and miracles, a painful physical remembering of female adolescence, and a specific local reconstruction of post-war France" (*Independent on Sunday*, 13. 9. 94). Her other novels are *A Piece of the Night, The Visitation, The Wild Girl* (translated into German as *Die Freundin des Herrn*), *The Book of Mrs. Noah, In the Red Kitchen.* Roberts has taught creative writing in schools, colleges, and on BBC radio. She has

been a writer-in-residence for two London boroughs, Essex University, and the University of East Anglia. Having lived and worked in Italy and the U.S., she is now dividing her time between London and northern France.

3 Generally speaking, an initiation consists of the rites, ceremonies, ordeals, or instructions with which one is made a member of a sect or society (often a secret society) or is invested with a particular function or status. Anthropology has conducted extensive studies of initiation rites. It might well be worthwhile to interpret the poem through the lens of anthropology's sustained interest in initiation. For an application of anthropological insights to the interpretation of literary plots cf. J. Campbell: *The Hero with a Thousand Faces.* Princeton, 1972. Another possible approach to this poem, again one that I will not pursue in the course of my threefold interpretation, is provided by Catholicism: Distinct parallels between the Maid of Orléans and the Virgin Mary can be construed.

4 According to the French psychoanalyst and poststructuralist Jacques Lacan, the symbolic order embraces all social, cultural, and kin relations that determine the human subject. The symbolic order is mediated in and through language. The infant is born into this linguistically structured, symbolic universe and has to submit to it in order for language acquisition and individuation to become possible.

5 Martin Stanton defines it as follows: "The oedipus complex [...] is supposed to account for the infant's negotiation of incestuous desires for its parents, which includes both erotic and destructive components, as well as concomitant guilt and fear of reprisal. [...] In traditional formulations, the infant is portrayed as discovering, exploring and passing through the complex during a specific phase of development called the 'oedipal phase', that is, between three and five years old. The complex therefore serves to further the child's psychic growth and consolidate its ego and superego functions, as well as help orient its sexual proclivities. During this phase, each individual is supposed to acquire some effective relation through knowledge to the law that governs the child/mother/father triad, and thus opt for the one prescribed route out of the complex: renunciation of incestuous desire and identification with the parent of the same sex." ("Oedipus Complex". - In E. Wright [Ed.]: *Feminism and Psychoanalysis. A Critical Dictionary.* Oxford, 1992, pp. 290-291)

6 Elisabeth Bronfen writes: "The castration complex [...] occurs during the preoedipal [...] stage of infantile development and is inextricably connected to the oedipus complex. [...] In its most literal sense this means that the girl must accept her definition as inferior, because she is anatomically castrated, lacking a penis, while the boy must accept the father's castrating 'no' to his incestuous wish for the mother, i.e. must accept that he is temporarily inferior to the phallically more powerful father." ("Castration Complex". - In E. Wright [Ed.]: *Feminism and Psychoanalysis,* p. 41)

7 Sigmund Freud limited his account of the pre-oedipal to a discussion of the male child's development. With respect to the female child, Freud was lost: "Die Einsicht in die präödipale Vorzeit des Mädchens wirkt als Überraschung, ähnlich wie auf anderem Gebiet die Aufdeckung der minoisch-mykenischen Kultur hinter der griechischen. Alles auf dem Gebiet dieser ersten Mutterbindung erschien mir [...] schwer analytisch zu erfassen, [...] altersgrau, schattenhaft, kaum wiederbelebbar." ("Über die weibliche Sexualität". *Sexualleben.* Frankfurt/M., 1982, 276.) This is the reason why, throughout his life, Freud was riddled by the mysteries of femininity: "Über das Rätsel der Weiblichkeit haben die Menschen zu allen Zeiten

gegrübelt. [...] Auch Sie werden sich von diesem Grübeln nicht ausgeschlossen haben, insoferne Sie Männer sind; von den Frauen unter Ihnen erwartet man es nicht, sie sind selbst dieses Rätsel." (*Vorlesungen zur Einführung in die Psychoanalyse. Und Neue Folge.* Frankfurt, 1969, p. 545)

8 For an explication of Lacan's theories, cf. my "Weiblichkeit und Poststrukturalismus - Perspektiven einer feministischen Literaturwissenschaft". *Amerikastudien/American Studies* 33, 1988, 149-66.

9 Cf. Lacan's notorious statement: "Die Frau ist ausgeschlossen von der Natur der Dinge, die die Natur der Wörter ist - darüber beklagen sich die Frauen gegenwärtig genug. Sie wissen einfach nicht, was sie sagen; das ist der ganze Unterschied zwischen ihnen und mir." *Alternative* 108/109, 1976, 161.

10 Harry Brod writes: "'Pre-' is woman's time. Just as in the phylogenetic story of 'mankind,' 'prehistory' refers to a more matrifocal era, before the linguistic law of the written record inscribed history as male by forgetting women's oral history, so in psychoanalysis's ontogenetic tale the 'pre-oedipal' designation obscures the central matrifocality of the early years of development, considering them as mere prelude to the ostensibly more crucial patrifocal period of gender formation." ("Masculinity". - In E. Wright [Ed.]: *Feminism and Psychoanalysis,* p. 238)

11 N. Chodorow: *The Reproduction of Mothering: Psychoanalysis and the Sociology of Gender.* Berkeley, 1978; D. Dinnerstein: *The Mermaid and the Minotaur. Sexual Arrangements and Human Malaise.* New York, 1976.

12 L. Irigary: *Speculum of the Other Woman.* Ithaca, 1985; H. Cixous: "The Laugh of the Medusa". *Signs. Journal of Women in Culture and Society 1,* 1976, 875–893; J. Kristeva: *The Kristeva Reader.* Ed. T. Moi. Oxford, 1986. For a short, concise and comprehensive account of these theories, cf. T. Moi: *Sexual/Textual Politics. Feminist Literary Theory.* London, 1985.

13 J. Kristeva: "Women's Time". - In *The Kristeva Reader.* Oxford, 1986, p. 192.

14 Ibid., p. 191.

Klaus Ensslen, München

Plain Living and Plain Talk in Langston Hughes' "Mother to Son": A Poetics of the Black Folk Voice

Mother to Son

Well, son, I'll tell you:
Life for me ain't been no crystal stair.
It's had tacks in it,
And splinters,
And boards torn up,
And places with no carpet on the floor –
Bare.
But all the time
I'se been a-climbin' on,
And reachin' landin's,
And turnin' corners,
And sometimes goin' in the dark
Where there ain't been no light.
So, boy, don't you turn back.
Don't you set down on the steps
'Cause you finds it's kinder hard.
Don't you fall now –
For I'se still goin', honey,
I'se still climbin',
And life for me ain't been no crystal stair.

Langston Hughes' poem "Mother to Son" was written in or before 1922[1], i.e. at the very beginning of the long, productive career of a writer who was to tenaciously voice the concerns of ordinary African Americans in poetry, prose and drama. Stimulated by the opening of national cultural interest for black artists during the Harlem (or New Negro) Renaissance of the 1920s, Hughes in his own work gave a decidedly non-elitist, grass-roots impetus to the literature of that decade. In the 1930s Hughes increasingly politicized his view from street level by taking up stances of proletarian literature while continuing to cling to African American folklore and oral tradition. After World War II he broadened his original and editing work (often in cooperation with others) and became one of the pioneering propagators of black literature, folklore and culture. Born in 1902, Hughes grew up in a geographically and socially unstable family. At the age of twenty he decided against the option offered by his father (who had left the United States in protest against racial discrimination to become a fairly successful businessman in Mexico) and for the precarious hand-to-mouth existence of his mother. After erratic academic and professional starts and extended rovings, by sea and by land, through Europe and Africa (which at one point took him deep into the Soviet Union and some of its Asian republics), Hughes in 1932 definitely settled for the professional life of a writer and editor in various cities of the USA, eventually gravitating towards Harlem and New York where he lived from 1942 until his death in 1967.[2]

From his earliest publications, Hughes found himself involved in the discussion about the literary convention of black dialect. An inheritance from the post-Civil-War adaptation of black culture by white Southern writers indebted to the Plantation tradition and to minstrel theater, black dialect had first been tested as an instrument of poetic self-articulation by Paul Laurence Dunbar around the turn of the century.[3] Dunbar managed to infuse black dialect with an impressive performative energy, fending off some of its denigrating and caricaturing elements at the expense, however, of reducing its expressive range to humor and pathos. As late as 1922 James Weldon Johnson in his groundbreaking preface to *The Book of American Negro Poetry* would deplore the continuing sway of this hampering literary convention, and he would try to break its spell by salvaging the imagery and rhythm of the black sermon in some of his own poetry (cf. *God's Trombones* of 1927), while giving up the vernacular for literary English. In contrast to Jean Toomer, Countee Cullen and Claude McKay who in their poetry chose the same high road to literary recognition, it remained the merit of Hughes, and in his steps also of Sterling Brown (cf. his seminal *Southern Road* of 1932) to reestablish the expressive potential of dialect as a true vernacular in African American poetry, initiating a process of incorporating the living spoken idiom which has born its full harvest only in the Second Black Renaissance from the 1960s up into our own time (in the work of poets such as Sonia Sanchez, June Jordan, Ted Joans, Carolyn Rodgers, Kalamu ya Salaam and others, with one line leading directly to the merging of music and poetry in the performances of rap and hiphop artists of the 1980s and 1990s).

Hughes' early poetry exemplifies much of the tension between an exotic literary appreciation of black folklore and speech and a direct performance-oriented adaptation of vernacular. In his first published volume of verse, *The Weary Blues* of 1926, the bulk of poems (written between 1921 and 1925) still dramatize an exotic perception of the world of black musicians by some more or less participating observer (cf. "Jazzonia"), and it took Hughes some years to go from a mediated presentation to the unbroken identification with the folk voice and blues form in a poem like "Bound No'th Blues".[4] The perception of music and other forms of African American culture apparently were still channeled by the fashionable cultural climate of the time which marked the Harlem Renaissance as an occasion to go slumming for members of the dominant culture. While the stereotyping pressure of this pattern (prurient observer/audience vs. exotic performer) seemed hard to escape in certain thematic contexts (music, dance, even religion)[5], the unspectacular, everyday situation and subject matter of the poem "Mother to Son" apparently facilitated empathy and identification with the black voice, and with the situation and perception of the person behind that voice.

Hughes very radically places us as readers right next to the speaking voice and persona of his poem, almost under that person's elbow, or in the very position of the son addressed. This sharpens the poetic convention of dramatic monologue into a scenic dialogue, with the son cast in the role of a mute scenic presence. How radical a break with literary convention this choice of eye-level position represents, might be judged from a glance at one of the exemplary texts of the period written by the leading white critic, photographer, stimulator and sympathizer of the Harlem Renaissance: In Carl Van Vechten's novel *Nigger Heaven* (1925) the programmatic call for a literary recording of everyday black life is kept in neutralizing balance by the invisibility of ordinary black people in the text, and by the total blindness of the black protagonist (an aspiring young writer) for this mode of life. The dramatic situation suggested by the poem "Mother to Son", on the other hand, contains a whole sociology of black urban life in a nutshell: The mother is not an abstract moral preceptor, or a categorical voice from a higher normative level; she embodies the experience of a lifetime and addresses her son with empathy as a peer, and in terms of growing emotional identification ("son" – l. 1, "boy" – l. 14, "honey" – l. 18). Her taking on the burden of practical and moral advice to her son points to the absence of a father as a role model, thereby suggesting the topoi of the single-headed family, the matriarchal strong black woman, and the black male adolescent threatened by discouragement ("don't you turn back" – l. 14), immobilization ("don't you set down" – l. 15) or even criminalization ("don't you fall now" – l. 17). The concrete dramatic location refers to a run-down Harlem tenement or apartment house (as details of the imagery will show), and the act of painstakingly climbing the many-storeyed staircase implies the return of the exhausted mother from work, or from shopping after work. The image of the "crystal stair" (ll. 2, 20), by contrast, is a reference to the world of luxury, illusion, and more specifically to the dream factory of urban media (theater, musical stage, film – by extension anticipating TV as a unifying stage for these dream images), and it marks the material distance of a work- and poverty-stricken urban black existence to the dream world of Broadway and Hollywood. Given the linguistic anchoring of this larger social situation in black vernacular, it is striking how carefully the poem avoids any suggestion of racially specific forms of discrimination. While gaining the aura of a possible extension of its symbolic energy to the condition of poor and depressed people of any group or color, this centrifugal aura of signification still rests on highly concretized sociographic details. Hughes in later years would often prefer to charge poems of a similar sociographic potential with more historical or political data (as the poems "The Negro Mother" and "Ballad of the Landlord" can illustrate).[6]

1. Textual Analysis of "Mother to Son"

1.1 Imagery as Structural Device

The dramatized situation of the poem basically rests on two contrasting images introduced as oppositional signifiers for "life" (in the sense of individual biography): the image of the "crystal stair" (ll. 2, 20), given as a succinct, cliché-like topos with contextual innuendoes of a highly expansive kind; and the image of a Harlem apartment house made tangible and concrete by a number of details. The first image is compact, isolated and condensed, the second image is atomized, interconnected and expanding: one (repeated) line of the text for the "crystal stair" image is set against the bulk of the text articulating the Harlem image comprising 18 lines (or 17, if we subtract the first verse containing no reference to the apartment house). The first image brackets the text and forms a deliberate contrast to the many lines devoted to the second image on more than one level: The isolated "crystal stair" image functions like a prelude, or pre-text, or prefacing motto to the mother's extended improvised exhortation; it is nostalgic and dream-like when set against the tangible and mimetic (or 'realistic') image of the Harlem staircase. Its contrasting function is further emphasized by its occurring in the two longest lines of the poem, while the counterimage is articulated by lines of strikingly uneven length (from one syllable in line 7 to ten syllables in line 6), and also by containing a clearly iambic rhythmic pattern (revealed more strikingly in the regular pentameter of line 20, while line 2 is one syllable short at the beginning of the line). Given the overall irregular appearance of a poem that clearly aspires to the status of free verse (and which in its total effect might even be called 'prosaic'), one should, however, hesitate in applying terms like pentameter or iambic, or preferably see them merely as echoes from metrically structured verse.[7]

The contrasting nature of the oppositional images, however, also extends into the way in which they invite to processes of symbolic signification. The "crystal stair" image functions as a succinct topos with high symbolic proliferation: It refers to the dream factory of Hollywood or Broadway (vaudeville, musical, theater, melodrama), to the promises of Christian religion ("crystal stair" as the approach to a heavenly Jerusalem), and to the oneiric realm of fairytale fictions (Cinderella, stairs as equivalent of marriage and release from suffering). The common semantic denominator of these topical references is easily definable in terms like 'wealth', 'splendor', 'success', 'release from, and rewards for, suffering and poverty'.

The counterimage of the Harlem apartment house staircase, on the other hand, is presented in discrete sensual detail ("tacks" – l. 3, "splinters" – l. 4, "torn up" "boards" – l. 5, "no carpet" – l. 6, "landin's" – l. 10, "corners" – l. 11, "no light" – l. 13) and as a situational dramatized scene: The onerous climbing of a tired woman towards her apartment is filtered through her telling which implies another equally tangible dramatized situation – her advising a possibly dejected or even threatened son, most likely of grown-up age and apparently lacking the guidance of paternal authority. This image articulates a process rather than a frozen topos, and it triggers metonymic complementation and situational fleshing out by the reader, rather than the metaphoric substitutions we are invited to produce for the "crystal stair" topos. (This would also confirm the impression of the prosaic character of the bulk of the text, metonymy being a privileged principle of text formation in prose, buttressed by syntactical and narrative space.) The anchoring of the apartment house image in Harlem and African American culture is provided in this context by way of an admirable economy of linguistic and sociographic signals: just three vernacular forms ("I'se" – l. 9, "you finds" – l. 16, "a-climbin'" – l. 9) effectively evoke the specific regulations of Black English; the mentioning of landings, lighting and carpet imply (even where now absent) the former splendor and presently run-down condition of urban houses typical for Harlem. In a subtly ironic reversal (or sardonic echoing), Hughes' text in this way also undermines the cliché of the crystal stair by reminding the reader of the fleeting and illusionary nature of splendor and success. On a covert, non-explicit level of meaning, the poem thus adumbrates the interpenetration and mutual critical mirroring of its cliché-oriented and its mimetic-realistic imagery. The subversive undercurrent of this correspondence, however, is not balanced or neutral, but clearly works towards the partisan enhancement of the mother's lived norms of persistence, and towards the authoritative debunking of dream factory clichés.[8]

1.2 Prosodic and Phonological Articulation

The deliberate contrasting and echoing of positions (or norms) on the level of imagery is carefully supported by prosodic and sound elements. The poem retains some elements of formal verse (typography, capitalization of line openings, iambic pattern of stresses, vestiges of rhyming), but veils and camouflages them effectively (sometimes paradoxically). The tendency of the text to fall into an iambic pattern haunts the poem like a vexatious ghost, but always falls short of materializing. The first two lines, e.g., read consecutively, would constitute a perfectly iambic sequence of alternate stressed and unstressed syllables; but both the emphatic opening and closing of the first line ("Well, son" and the final colon) prevent the establishment of such a reading. The colloquial "Well" is given unusual weight and status as the first word of the text; the colon introduces an emphatic didactic and declarative pause (thus setting the stage for the mother's admonition). They both disrupt the option of reading the first two lines as one unit (with the second line as a run-on line). – In lines 3 to 18 the pauses at the ends of lines are usually similarly pronounced, and even in lines 8 and 9 (which taken together might be read as a blank verse line) the syntactic parallelisms with lines 10 and 11 exert a stronger regulative force and tend to distract from the possible rhythmic shape of lines 8 plus 9. The same holds true of the hidden combined blank-verse pattern of lines 18 and 19 where the slight shift in position within the lines of syntactically parallel word groups ("I'se still goin'", "I'se still climbin'") serve to articulate difference rather than metric similarity – even though these two lines also prepare for the closing line in a subtle way, by anticipating its blankverse structure. In general, however, iambic zones within the poem are so jagged at the edges that they will remind the reader more of the natural alternating speech-rhythm of English than of any deliberate metric pattern.

The rhyme principle of formal verse is treated even more radically in both retaining and veiling strikingly isolated instances. The whole poem contains only one clear rhyme pair ("stair" – "bare"), and these words are not only spatially separated by four intervening lines; their relation is also obscured by their occurring in the most contrasting lines of the poem as far as length of line is concerned (line 2 with nine syllables, line 7 with only one syllable, the rhyme word "bare"), and in addition to that, by line 7 being tied to line 6 (again a very long line with ten iambic syllables) through a weakened consonance ("floor" – "bare"). "Floor" and "bare" plus the dash between them (marking a pause) form an energetic node with its own explosive aura on the semantic level – a bare floor being a subtly congruent contrast to the counter-image of "crystal stair". (The oppositional nature of these images is further underlined on the lexical level if we realize that "crystal" is the only strikingly elevated or precious word in the whole poem, and almost the only word of recognizably Latin, non-Saxon derivation – with carpet as a possible contender.) The only other vestige of the formal principle of rhyming would be the assonance of "dark" and "hard" (at the ends of lines 12 and 16) – two words that contain a strong semantic affinity with "bare" and thus articulate the central thematic thrust of lines 3 to 18. "Bare", "dark" and "hard" form the semantic backbone of the extensive realistic image of the poem, minus the dramatized situational signals of 'climbing' and 'going'.

As to other phonological data, the poem excels in largely avoiding phonemic equivalences (sound repetitions) – with one telling exception: "crystal stair" contains a veiled alliteration of the 'st'-sound combination which might be said to cause a slight slowing down of speed when sounding the line, a subtle air cushion or rhythmic jamming (retardation), with emphatic effect for the topological image. Other sound equivalences (as in "b*oa*rds t*o*rn up" or the 't' and 'p' phonemes in lines 3 to 6) are well masked by their unpredictably occurring within the highly irregular verse lines. Phonologically the poem is as quiet, prosaic, unsounding as possible, and it actually chooses a high recurrence of words or word forms only for phonologically inconspicuous material. Foremost among these semantically and phonologically 'light' words is the conjunction 'and': Anaphorically opening two groups of three consecutive lines each, it constitutes the most striking syntactic parallelism of the poem. In the first triad of lines (lines 4 to 6), the anapher correlates with three nouns (all of them concrete sensual details for the delapidated staircase – "splinters", "boards", "places" – with lengthening linguistic qualifiers added to the second and third noun). In the second triad (lines 10 to 12), the "and"-parallelism carries over into the participles "reachin'", "turnin'" and "goin'", all articulating the continuing strenuous process of ascending for the dramatized voice of the text. Both triads subtly represent the cumulative, open-ended and painstaking nature of that process and the concept of life symbolized by it. In other words, one of the most inconspicuous, semantically 'empty' words of the lexicon in this poem is given a central thematic and representational function. The capitalization of the word "And" at the beginning of 7 lines (the last line resumes the anapher, by way of a quiet echo which gains new reverberations by here being joined to, and introducing, a slight variation of the "crystal stair" image line) paradoxically gives this semantically light word a privileged prosodic position and status. With only slight exaggeration, one could claim that the whole poem, while debunking the word "crystal", poetically enhances and elevates the word "And" by making it the silent linguistic pivot of its imagery and prosodic structure.

2. *Sociocultural and Didactic Conclusions*

Hughes' poem "Mother to Son" is a quiet but radical example of how to subvert, circumvent or replace poetic conventions in the service of giving voice to a view from below in the unconstrained idiom of the street. It introduces colloquial Black English unapologetically as a poetical peer to Standard English: There is no framing of the vernacular in this text by an implicit or explicit textual norm derived from the standard poetical practice of the time, and there is no ghettoization of the vernacular by making it appear exotic or primitive. There are only relaxed transitions from the title and the first line of the poem (which could be taken as Standard English) to the more expressive, dramatically enhanced forms of an easy-flowing spoken idiom. The expressive power of this idiom comes through in its economic handling of imagery, verse and sound structure, in its unabashed use of repetition, cumulation and parallelism, and in its ability to evoke a dramatic situation with rich pragmatic and symbolic implications. Far from any temptation to use poetic diction or metaphorical overarticulation, the poem boldly engages an increasingly ubiquitous popular culture and its dream images to confront them with a mimetically authenticated slice of everyday life.

The presence of socioeconomic conditions, such as poverty, exploitation and racism, can be felt in this poem although they are not referred to explicitly (racism for one being practically invisible). Yet the situational, contextually suggestive nature of the dominant metonymic figure of the poem allows a high measure of inference by the reader; it stimulates his social and contextual imagination to fill in the rhetorical reticence of the text. Hughes' poetry more often than not is characterized (and sometimes threatened) by a tendency to verbally minimize and foreshorten its intended communication. Thus the energy for resistance, for keeping on under discouraging and sometimes murderous conditions required for the survival and moral health of African Americans in American society even today, is articulated in "Mother to Son" mainly through insistent parallelisms in the text, and if we look for any protesting or militating overtones in the voice of the poem, then we come closest to such elements in the emphatic didactic appeal of the parallelisms of the last 6 lines ("don't you turn back", "Don't you set down", "Don't you fall now" plus "I'se still goin'" – "I'se still climbin'"). The emphatic energy of the words "you" and "still" adumbrate the potential for moral and pragmatic survival and progress the mother of the text is trying to inculcate in her son – yet these words are far from granting even a slim base for a critical, let alone a political assessment of American society. To draw conclusions of such a nature is a burden left entirely to the reader of the poem, inclusive of any pertinent information the reader may be able to activate in order to fill out the bare outlines of the symptomatic situation of the dramatic voice of the poem.[9]

In this sense, Hughes' poem challenges the reader's appetite for external circumstantial evidence and points far beyond the information provided in the text. This can be seen as a didactic asset of the poem – that it opens vistas and invites curiosity, or makes the reader aware of his or her deficits in factual knowledge. Part of this curiosity, it seems, would be directed to the vernacular and would presuppose the acknowledgement of its communicative and expressive power. Hughes' poem shows that the barest, most ordinary, even toned down language of the street can be a poetic and dramatic vehicle of high quality. Just as Mark Twain's *Huck Finn* made a non-specific vernacular a respected literary vehicle and opened up the publishing world to a flood of local color idioms and voices, Hughes may be said to have broken through most of the hampering restrictions of the conventions for black dialect before his time and to have opened literary production for the untamed voices of African American folk as we find them in the poetical work of Sterling Brown and the fiction of Rudolph Fisher and Zora Neale Hurston shortly after the publication of "Mother to Son".

In choosing an everyday situation and an ordinary spoken idiom, Hughes' poem goes against the conventional expectations of readers faced with poetry. There is nothing of the elevated and hieratic status of traditional poetry in this text, and as a consequence the unconscionable resistance of many potential readers against the presumably elitist, linguistically demanding, or even hermetic tendencies particularly in modernist poetry (as represented by the work of Hughes' contemporaries Ezra Pound, T.S.Eliot, Hart Crane or Wallace Stevens) is circumvented and opens the readers' attention to the subtle handling of structural devices not overshadowed by the cramping aura of an intimidating, awe-inspiring linguistic and formal coding. Hughes' "Mother to Son" embodies a refreshing and in some ways liberating dramatization of the expressive potential of colloquial speech and the perspective of poor people, and it accomplishes this not by offering a wide and comprehensive view of the full range of this mode of perception and articulation, but by concentrating on a clearly delimited, deceptively simple, and sparingly articulated situation as *sujet* of the text, furnishing it, however, with a broad aura of symbolic extension and showing no fear of claiming common ground with the so-called popular arts in this regard. In combining simplicity of imagery and diction with subtlety of lexical and prosodic organization as well as boldness of proliferating signification, Hughes' poem "Mother to Son" presents a radical re-examination and an experimental exploration of the possibilities of poetic discourse.

Notes

1 "Mother to Son" was first published in *The Crisis,* Dec. 1922, 87. It was one of the poems of Hughes' first volume of poetry (*The Weary Blues*, 1926, p.107), and it proved its popularity early by being included in Countee Cullen's anthology *Caroling Dusk* (1927) as well as in A. Locke's *Four Negro Poets* (1927). The poem was to remain one of the best known from the poet's pen: after "The Negro Speaks of Rivers" (with 39 entries) and "I, Too" (33 entries) it was the most often reprinted poem by Hughes (with 27 entries; cf. D.C. Dickinson: *A Bio-Bibliography of Langston Hughes 1902-1967.* Hamden, 1967, pp. 217-218). See *Selected Poems,* New York, 1959, p. 187.

2 For extensive information on Hughes' biography consult A. Rampersad: *The Life of Langston Hughes.* Vols. I and II, New York, 1986 and 1988. For a short survey and listed dates, cf. J.A. Emanuel: *Langston Hughes.* New York, 1967.

3 Cf. K. Ensslen: "The Status of Black Poetry from 1865 to 1914". - In R. Hagenbüchle (Ed.): *American Poetry. Between Tradition and Modernism 1865-1914.* Regensburg, 1984, pp. 136-168.

4 The poem "Jazzonia". - In *The Weary Blues.* New York, 1926, p. 25; "Bound No'th Blues". - In *Fine Clothes to the Jew.* New York, 1927, p. 87; *Selected Poems,* p. 174.

5 A late reaction to this stereotyped view of black culture and music can be found in Toni Morrison's latest novel *Jazz* (New York, 1992) - a book which tries to countervail the traditional exotic view of the period (according to Morrison's own statements at a reading in Munich, Summer 1993).

6 "The Negro Mother". - In *The Negro Mother and Other Dramatic Recitations.* New York, 1931, pp. 16-18; *Selected Poems,* pp. 288-289; "Ballad of the Landlord". - In *Jim Crow's Last Stand.* Atlanta, 1943, p. 20; *Selected Poems,* pp. 238-39.

7 R.B. Miller in *The Art and Imagination of Langston Hughes* (Lexington, 1989), after claiming that "the individual lines skillfully blend anapestic, iambic, and trochaic cadences" (p. 35), finally concedes a more informal view (p. 36): "Although the last line is iambic, the meter of the poem depends more on the noted simulation of Black rhetoric, the actual cadences of folk speech, than on metric form." ('Meter' here should probably be replaced by 'rhythm'.)

8 Because of this implicit valuation of contrasting norms, it would seem highly unlikely that Hughes intended the mother's ascent to be read as a "Christian metaphor of travel" or as "racial quest" (ibid., p. 39). Both these readings, as well as seeing the mother as a "Black Madonna" (O. Jemie: *Langston Hughes.* New York, 1976, p. 31), seem to result from conflations of the poem with other Hughes texts (esp. with "The Negro Mother"), or from an unwarranted broadening and diffusing down of symbolic connotations.

9 Relevant complementations of contextual information for the dramatic situation presented by the poem might be found - on the linguistic and literary level - in J. L. Dillard: *Black English. It's History and Usage in the United States.* New York, 1972; and in E. B. Redmond: *Drumvoices. The Mission of Afro-American Poetry. A Critical History.* New York, 1976; or - on the historical and sociocultural level - in J. Anderson: *This Was Harlem. A Cultural Portrait.* New York, 1982; and in C. D. Wintz: *Black Culture and the Harlem Renaissance.* Houston, 1988.

Peter O. Stummer, München

Poetry as Contextualized Communication: Derek Walcott's "The Sea Is History"

The Sea Is History

Where are your monuments, your battles, martyrs?
Where is your tribal memory? Sirs,
in that grey vault. The sea. The sea
has locked them up. The sea is History.

First, there was the heaving oil,
heavy as chaos;
then, like a light at the end of a tunnel,

the lantern of a caravel,
and that was Genesis.
Then there were the packed cries,
the shit, the moaning:

Exodus.
Bone soldered by coral to bone,
mosaics
mantled by the benediction of the shark's shadow,

that was the Ark of the Covenant.
Then came from the plucked wires
of sunlight on the sea floor

the plangent harps of the Babylonian bondage,
as the white cowries clustered like manacles
on the drowned women,

and those were the ivory bracelets
of the Song of Solomon,
but the ocean kept turning blank pages

looking for History.
Then came the men with eyes heavy as anchors
who sank without tombs,

brigands who barbecued cattle,
leaving their charred ribs like palm leaves on the shore,
then the foaming, rabid maw

of the tidal wave swallowing Port Royal,
and that was Jonah,
but where is your Renaissance?

Sir, it is locked in them sea-sands
out there past the reef's moiling shelf,
where the men-o'-war floated down;

strop on these goggles, I'll guide you there myself.
It's all subtle and submarine,
through colonnades of coral,

past the gothic windows of sea-fans
to where the crusty grouper, onyx-eyed,
blinks, weighted by its jewels, like a bald queen;

and these groined caves with barnacles
pitted like stone
are our cathedrals,

and the furnace before the hurricanes:
Gomorrah. Bones ground by windmills
into marl and cornmeal,

and that was Lamentations –
that was just Lamentations,
it was not History;

then came, like scum on the river's drying lip,
the brown reeds of villages
mantling and congealing into towns,

and at evening, the midges' choirs,
and above them, the spires
lancing the side of God

as His son set, and that was the New Testament.

Then came the white sisters clapping
to the waves' progress,
and that was Emancipation –

jubilation, O jubilation –
vanishing swiftly
as the sea's lace dries in the sun,

but that was not History,
that was only faith,
and then each rock broke into its own nation;

then came the synod of flies,
then came the secretarial heron,
then came the bullfrog bellowing for a vote,

fireflies with bright ideas
and bats like jetting ambassadors
and the mantis, like khaki police,

and the furred caterpillars of judges
examining each case closely,
and then in the dark ears of ferns

and in the salt chuckle of rocks
with their sea pools, there was the sound
like a rumour without any echo

of History, really beginning.

I done
Converted God
To a father and a friend
So He could see
The trouble "we" is in.[1]

To know the pain of history
words contain.[2]

1. Accessibility

When Rachel Salamander and August Everding succeeded in persuading Derek Walcott to participate in their cycle of invited speakers in Munich entitled 'The End of the Century', they were surprised to hear that the turn of their phrase came in for some criticism by the poet. He was not in favour, he said, of the notion of the measured sequentiality of time, nor did he like the pessimistic streak that went with the concept of the millennium. Where he comes from, the Caribbean, the seasonal cycle was unknown, he maintained. Therefore the invention of centuries did not take place, the flux of time in the change between night and day was sufficient. The division into centuries, he feared, had something imperialistic to it, very much akin to caesars and popes.[3]

Walcott thus places himself squarely in the non-metropolitan non-European periphery of the Caribbean island world, but confidently uses concepts of the European past as well, and, of course, avails himself of the English tongue. One way of approaching him is, then, the context of the New Literatures in English, formerly referred to as Post-colonial Literatures or, further back still, as Commonwealth Literature. Consequently, his theoretical outlook is dealt with in this framework. In his “Adamic celebration of language”, he recreates his world against the backcloth of the bitter memory of a colonial past. He creatively articulates difference and alterity in his English, while preserving the recognizable mould of English “which allows it to be understood”.[4] It is revealing to compare the changes which have occurred in this field over the last thirty years, when one looks at what one of the founding fathers of “Commonwealth Literature”, Norman Jeffares, had to say about Walcott in 1964, and to put this alongside the remarks made by Eberhard Kreutzer, in his survey which bears the same title. Under the heading “Die Commonwealth-Literaturen”, Jeffares provides about ten pages of overview and devotes eighteen lines to the literature of the West Indies, of which the last two read:

> In der Lyrik wäre Derek Walcott (geb. 1930) zu erwähnen, der Elendsverhältnisse darstellt und, wie die Prosaerzähler, sich um die Klärung der westindischen Lebenseinstellung bemüht.[5]

Whereas Kreutzer, in 1991, attributes forty-four pages to the subject and reserves slightly more than two pages for the Caribbean. With “Commonwealth-Literature”, he, interestingly enough, not only uses the singular, but evidently does not regard the fact that this is a politically loaded term as an unsurmountable hindrance to its further usage. He uses George Lamming as a paradigm and diagnoses ‘insularity’ and ‘migratory impetus’ as overriding patterns in Caribbean writing. He contrasts Brathwaite with Walcott, without going into the details of this cultural conflict between African roots and ‘nation language’ on the one side and a more syncretistic tendency, with an outspoken reticence as far as the use of patois and creole is concerned, on the other. Kreutzer explicitly mentions the poem “The Schooner *Flight*” from the collection *The Star-Apple Kingdom* (1979), and the epic *Omeros* (1990), to prove his generalizing point. He concludes with a reference to the all-pervasiveness of the sea in the works of Walcott:

> Die Insel-, Schiffbruchs- und Strandungsmetaphorik, die raumsymbolische Ausrichtung auf eine mit Fluchtmöglichkeiten wie Bedrohlichkeit ambivalent besetzte, allseits umgebende See kehren in vielen Spielarten der Suggestion persönlicher, milieuspezifischer und universaler Probleme in seinen Gedichten wieder.[6]

The contextualizing of Walcott’s theoretical stance with reference to two of his fellow Caribbeans, French-speaking philosopher Edouard Glissant, and novelist Wilson Harris, who writes in English, though desirable really transcends the reading of one poem, but the context of the Nobel Prize, which Walcott was awarded in 1992, might well provide an additional line of approach, especially when one keeps in mind predecessors such as Rabindranath Tagore, Patrick White and Wole Soyinka, and uses Burnett and Mölter[7] as introductions to the author.[8]

In the autobiographical "Another Life"[9] we learn that the motto of St Lucia, half-way between French Martinique and 'Little England' Barbados, where Walcott was born in 1930 together with his twin brother, is *statio haud malefida carinis* (literally: not a useless place for ships, to ride at anchor that is), and the pupil persona renders this slyly as "a safe anchorage for sheeps". Later it is characterized as "Sancta Lucia / an island brittle / as a Lenten biscuit".[10] Even in these short quotations, the intertwining of the classics, of christianity, of language facility and verbal wit, in unison with a man-in-the-street perspective, becomes immediately apparent. His puns are never self-indulgent, as evinced in the title of his widely anthologized "A Far Cry from Africa"[11] and often playfully insist on language reflexivity, as in the rumination on *omeros*, with *o* being the "conch-shell's invocation", with *mer* standing for "mother and sea in our Antillean patois", with *os* signifying "a grey bone".[12] Walcott's is a mixed heritage in more than one sense. He was educated in a Roman Catholic school, highly influenced by rebel Irish brothers, yet his mother was a staunch Methodist; in the streets of St Lucia the *lingua franca* was French Creole, but at home Standard English was strictly adhered to[13], thus recalling the vicissitudinous fate of the island throughout the period of seafaring colonial enterprises, where the embattled isle often changed hands and, in this way, mirrored the course of global politics in the 18th century.[14] Walcott's grandparents were half white and half black, with a Dutch element on his mother's side. This is why the 'red nigger' Shabine, pivotal persona of "The Schooner *Flight*", mentions his sound "colonial education" and says about himself:

> I have Dutch, nigger, and English in me,
> and either I'm nobody, or I'm a nation.[15]

Similarly, in a poem called "Names"[16] from the collection *Sea Grapes* (1976), and appropriately dedicated to Edward Brathwaite, we find the musing on the island's cultural multiplicity:

> Have we melted into a mirror,
> leaving our souls behind?
> The goldsmith from Benares,
> the stonecutter from Canton,
> the bronzesmith from Benin.[17]

In a poem by the name of "The Spoiler's Return", which also turns up in many anthologies, we perceive the fusion of cultures on a higher plane. For on the one hand we have the deceased famous calypsonian, Spoiler, of the title, who, having come back from the dead, castigates grievances in the local way and tongue, whereas on the other hand the author refers the reader to the classic satirical tradition from Juvenal and Martial to Dryden, Pope, Swift and Byron. Incidentally, the poem contains quite a characteristic gibe at V.S. Naipaul: "I see these islands and I feel to bawl, 'area of darkness' with V.S.

Nightfall." The scathing twist of the name disavows the sham approval of Naipaul's definitely European stance vis-a-vis the India of his forebears and his native Trinidad. Walcott published his first poem when he was fourteen and his first collection of poetry at the age of nineteen. What should not be forgotten, however, is the fact that he is also very much a man of the theatre. He is the author of over thirty plays and worked with the Trinidad Theatre Workshop for almost two decades between 1959 and 1976.

It needed the exile Joseph Brodsky, who he conducted creative writing classes with in the States, to point an accusing finger at the fact that until quite recently the anglophone critical establishment was unwilling to recognize "that the great poet of the English language is a blackman". How high Walcott himself is wont to put his stakes, we can doubtlessly derive from this statement in the poem "Forest of Europe", which is dedicated to the very same Brodsky:

> The tourist archipelagos of my South
> are prisons too, corruptible, and though
> there is no harder prison than writing verse,
> what's poetry, if it is worth its salt,
> but a phrase men can pass from hand to mouth?[18]

2. *Formal Aesthetics*

In a sense, Shabine, the author's *alter ego*, already mentioned, is rather disillusioned; on his trip through the Caribbean, he spurns the notion of progress, when he argues, "progress is something to ask Caribs about", or "Progress is history's dirty joke".[19] The author has widened his perspective since the days of "Ruins of a Great House"[20], where the rhetoric of decay in the description of the slave-owner's mansion conjures up echoes of Kipling with the rush of the wind sounding the knell of the empire, but smacks of the declamatory with the programmatic "abuse of ignorance by Bible and by sword". Yet the more felicitous the coinages become, the more effortlessly the poet seems to have found his voice, the more serious is the widened awareness. For it was not for nothing that the angry Shabine had threatened the Vincentian sailor, who dared to make fun of his poetry, with a dead-serious, no-nonsense knife, and wounding him, assured, from then on, that "none of them go fuck with my poetry again". Sea-centred as "The Schooner *Flight*" is, the last line consequently reads, "Shabine sang to you from the depths of the sea."

It is certainly no accident that the title of the poem under closer scrutiny, "The Sea is History", looks vaguely reminiscent of the unaccented end rhymes which we find in several of Shakespeare's sonnets, just as the dominant three-line stanza tends to recall Dante's *terza rima*. However, 'history' pronounced as a trisyllabic, with the primary stress on the last syllable, also fits quite nicely the groove which was originally established by rastafari poets with their adherence to oral traditions and later popularized by DJs and dub poets. The European audience became familiarized with this rhythmical reggae pattern through the likes of Bob Marley, Peter Tosh, Mutabaruka, and later in England by Linton Kwesi Johnson and Benjamin Zephaniah, who, for instance, uses this device with considerable effect in his explanatory poem "Dis Poetry":

> I pass thru University
> I pass thru Sociology
> An den I got a Dread degree
> In dreadful Ghettology.[21]

In *Sea Grapes* Walcott began to develop the use of the tercet, then let it be the exception more than the rule in *The Star-Apple Kingdom*, only to lead it to epic perfection in the 325 pages of *Omeros*, a book which has repeatedly been placed alongside of Joyce's *Ulysses*, in its scope as well as in its intricate structure and masterly handling of language. Yet, for all its ingenious weaving of epic textures, Walcott has shied away from the closely-knit interlacing of the genuine *terza rima* through the use of end rhyme. In "The Sea is History" the three-line stanza does not fully persist. On the contrary, there is a conspicuous movement in the poem from the use of quatrains at the beginning towards the prevailing three-liner, and twice, to the climactic one-liner near the end, which both sum up stages of the argument in a fashion that resembles the punch-line of the well-made American short story of the 19th century. End rhyme is also scarce and shows a parallel tendency. In the first stanza we encounter a massive concentration of rhyme as an additional marker of the affirmative assertion of the poem's thesis. Line 3 contains the identical rhyme by the repetition of "The sea. The sea [...]", and in addition line 3 is linked to line 4 by the bracket of the end rhyme "sea" / "History". The central proposition is thus phonologically underscored in a threefold manner, as identical rhyme, as inner rhyme and as end rhyme. And end rhyme recurs only in stanza 16 and 18, first, again identical in "Lamentations –/ Lamentations", and second in "choirs / spires". These rhymes signal the general religious undercurrent and the ever-present biblical sub-text. Specifically "Lamentations" evokes the five chapters of Jeremiah's lament in the Old Testament, where he bewails the fate of Zion in the wrath of the Lord, "hear, I pray you, all people, and behold my sorrow: my virgins and my young men are gone into captivity"[22].

3. *Imagery and Argument*

What constitutes the persuasive impetus of the poem is the dynamic cross-current of a self-centred recalcitrant Caribbean sea-scape confronted by a concrete-oriented consciousness insisting on reification and linear 'development'. The dialogical verve of what is basically a didactic apologue foregrounds the tension between First World condescension ("where are your monuments?" – l. 2; "where is your Renaissance?" – l. 33) inquiring after objectified cultural achievements and a Third World defensive collective awareness which confronts the European self-asserted inquisitiveness by giving the male ("Sirs", "Sir" – ll. 3, 34) master-narratives of the North, such as the Bible and Architecture, a debunking ironical twist. What transcends a mere polemical diatribe is, although well hidden behind the metaphorical mode, the paradoxical employment of a rational deductive procedure, from tenet to furnished proof in true 18th century fashion (the use of capital letters included), to disenchant colonialism as part of the enlightenment project ("light at the end of the tunnel" – l. 7). It was solely the bottom of the sea which recorded for a long time the fatal impact of explorers' caravels, of buccaneers' brigs, of slavers' 'cargo', of belligerent men-of-war. Port Royal is not the austere Cistercian convent of Jansenism, but the old harbour of Jamaica that was destroyed by an earthquake in 1692. The coming of Christ was not the dawn of sunrise, but the dusk of sunset ("son set" – l. 58). Tribal memory began, of sorts, with Abolition, yet Emancipation could not, for a long time, redeem its inherent promise.

The Caribbean consciousness grudgingly concedes the beginning of history in stanza 22, and, full of resigned disillusionment, states the falling apart into isolated islets, when so-called flag independence came in the sixties and seventies and immediately led to the aping of British or American statal attitudes. We encounter no more animals of the sea, but mostly flies and beetles, 'blind' bats and 'stiff' herons. We need only recall that fireflies produce their light by oxidation of luciferin to appreciate the sarcastic adumbration of the total lack of any real warmth and intellectual brightness among the self-styled leadership. Walcott wasn't entirely without hope though, when, in "The Star-Apple Kingdom", he wrote much more explicitly about Michael Manley's Jamaica and the "history-orphaned islands" of the Caribbean:

> What was the Caribbean? A green pond mantling
> behind the Great House columns of Whitehall,
> behind the Greek facades of Washington,
> with bloated frogs squatting on lily pads
> like islands, islands that coupled as sadly as turtles
> engendering islets.[23]

On the whole though, the reader cannot avoid the impression that on the face of it the poem seems to signal the Caribbean might well have come to terms with the First World view of linear history, whereas deep down there remains a feeling that, in the long run, the primordial seascape perspective could prevail after all.

Notes

1 A poem entitled "God" by Ja A. Jahannes in *African American Review* 27, i, 1993, 138.
2 From Walcott's poem "The Schooner *Flight*" in *The Star-Apple Kingdom.* London, 1980, p. 12.
3 Cf. Walcott in *Focus.* 29.5.1993, 94. The textual basis for our deliberation are the following texts: "The Sea is History" as fourth out of ten poems in *The Star-Apple Kingdom.* London, 1980 (1979), pp. 25-28, which also exists in a German translation by K. Martens: *Das Königreich des Sternapfels*, published by Hanser (Munich); *Collected Poems 1948-1984.* New York, [3]1990 (1986), which also contains the poem, pp. 364-367; *Omeros.* New York, 1990.
4 B. Ashcroft, G. Griffith, H. Tiffin: *The Empire Writes Back. Theory and Practice in Post-Colonial Literatures.* London, 1989, p. 51.
5 *Kindlers Literatur Lexikon.* Vol. I: *Essays.* Weinheim, 1982; pp. 332-341; here p. 340 (undoubtedly an influential work of reference in Germany).
6 *Englische Literaturgeschichte.* Ed. H.U. Seeber. Stuttgart, 1991, pp. 394-438; here p. 423 (one of the more recent histories of English Literature written in Germany).
7 See their portrait and interview in P. Burnett: "The Empire Writes Back". *New Statesman & Society*, 16.10.1992, 35; and V. Mölter: "Ich gehöre zu keiner Rasse". *Abendzeitung* (Munich), 17./18.10.1992, 8.
8 Shorter portraits are to be found in: *Contemporary Poets.* Ed. J. Vinson. London, 1970; and *Fifty Caribbean Writers.* Ed. D.C. Dance. London, 1986. For background presentation see F. Gewecke: *Die Karibik.* Fankfurt, [2]1988; J. Michener: *Caribbean.* London, 1990, in particular the treatment of slaves and the involvement of various European nations in chapter VII, entitled "The Sugar Interest". For a general historical survey see E. Williams: *From Columbus to Castro. The History of the Caribbean 1492-1969.* New York, 1970. For comparison with other West Indian writers see S. Brown (Ed.): *Caribbean Poetry.* London, [2]1992 (1984), a book intended for work in English schools. The monographs by E. Baugh (1978), R.D. Hamner (1981) and S. Brown (1991) will soon be superseded by the one about to be published by J. Figueroa. Of assistance would also be the essay by fellow Caribbean poet Fred D'Aguiar: "Adam's Other Garden. Derek Walcott's Explorations of the Creative Imagination". – In *Declaration of Cultural Independence in the English-Speaking World.* Ed. L. Sampietro. Novara, 1989; and, of course, Walcott's own essay "The Muse of History". – In *Is Massa Day Dead. Black Moods in the Caribbean.* Ed. O. Coombs. New York, 1974.
9 *Collected Poems*, p. 172.
10 Ibid., p. 177.
11 *The Penguin Book of Caribbean Verse.* Ed. P. Burnett. London, [3]1988, p. 243; from: "In a Green Night" [1962], *Collected Poems*, p. 17.
12 *Omeros*, p. 14.

13 See J. Figueroa: "Derek Walcott – A Personal Memoir". *Kunapipi*, 24, ii, 1992, 82-89.

14 Cf. P. Ismond: "By the time it was finally settled on the British (1814), it had passed hands between them fourteen times. The French, however, in addition to their early start, had held the island during its longest spell of peacetime development. They were therefore responsible for the most formative influences. St. Lucia thus emerged as a special type of anomaly: Officially British, but essentially French in cultural influence." ("West Indian Literature as an Expression of National Culture: The Literature of St. Lucia". *World Literature Written in English*, 29, ii, 1989, 104-115, here: 105-106).

15 *The Star-Apple Kingdom*, p. 4.

16 *Collected Poems*, pp. 305-308.

17 Ibid., p. 306.

18 *The Star-Apple Kingdom*, pp. 40.

19 Ibid., p. 14.

20 *Collected Poems*, pp. 19-21.

21 "Dis Poetry". – In *City Psalms*. Newcastle-upon-Tyne, 1992, p. 13.

22 *Lamentations*, 1, 18.

23 *The Star-Apple Kingdom*, p. 56.

Barbara Korte, Chemnitz-Zwickau

Sista Rootz's "Dictionary Black (Trap)" and the Politics of Language

Dictionary Black (Trap)

I was looking through mi dictionary
just the other day
An' in front of mi eyes
Tho' I was not surprised
Was a list
as long as mi back
Stating literal form and fact
Of all those words containing 'Black'

The first thing it say
is 'opposite to white'
I say to miself
Mmhm alright
It say 'persons with dark skin'
'Blackhearted – Dismal – Grim'
'Angry – Threatening – Black looks'
'Black Marks – Black lists'
and 'Black books'
'Deadly – Sinister – Wicked – Hateful'
All these words
to make us grateful

A kidnapped so-called Negro
on a slave ship
Is a 'Blackbird'
I thought they did have wing
Eat worm an' sing an' ting
'Blackbirding'
is the trade itself
That brought these people
enormous wealth
'Black-Cap'
One gets when
'Sentenced to death'
'Black maria – Blackmail – Black Death'

Hold on a sec
Mek mi tek a breath.
I haven't finished yet

So just for the lark of it
I check out the 'Dark' of it
Well guess what it says
It says 'Black more or less'

A 'Darky',
Is a 'negro'
'Not fair – atrocious – evil'
And the 'Prince of Darkness' is
(you've guessed)
'The Devil'

Of course
Africa is that 'continent dark'
where all us 'Blackbirds' disembark
along their shore
we had arrived
To 'darken their door'

I knew next what to sight
So I turned to 'White'
All sweetness and light
not a Black word in sight

This 'White race member'
Whose 'burden is leading'
Characterised by his
'civilised good breeding'
Benefitting mankind
with 'white-witch'-power
'Superior' in their 'ivory tower'

There is no Whitey
Nothing distasteful
'Coz only us Darkies
are disgraceful

So due to their fear, greed and hatred
They have on purpose created
A language deceiving
The whole world's believing
This Oxford-Concise

with its ism and schism
and outright **RACISM**
While we pay the price
we pay the price
Like the Black Madonna
And Jesus The Christ

Dictionary Black - Trap - **CRAP**[1]

Over the last few decades, writers of non-European origin have made a considerable contribution to the literature of Britain.[2] Sista Rootz, of African Caribbean descent, is a most versatile member of Britain's Black artistic community. She has been writing and performing her poetry since the mid-seventies and works voluntarily with young people, using her poetry and visual art in an attempt to "dispel any stereotypical negativity and racism".[3] "Dictionary Black (Trap)" deals with an experience that must affect her most deeply as an artist whose medium is language: the way in which the words at her disposal transmit a discriminating ideology. Specifically, the poem focusses on colour terms applied to human beings. Such terms do not mirror an empirical reality but signify, in the words of a prominent African American critic, "the difference between cultures and their possession of power, spelling out the distance between [...] bondsman and lord in terms of their 'race'."[4]

Most members of ethnic minorities in the UK (almost five per cent of the total population) originate from former and the last still extant British colonies. Today, almost half of the UK's non-white population are British-born, with Caribbean and Indian or Pakistani parentage prevailing. The post-war years, which saw the decline and fall of the British Empire, have been hailed as a period of de-colonization, the mother country itself now waving the fashionable flag of multi-culturalism. However, the spirit of Empire has not dried up, as Margaret Thatcher demonstrated in her notorious Falklands victory speech.[5] In a polemical essay, Salman Rushdie emphasizes that non-white Britons have little reason to consider themselves de-colonized: "Four hundred years of conquest and looting, four centuries of being told that you are superior to the Fuzzy-Wuzzies and the wogs, leave their stain."[6]

"Dictionary Black (Trap)" examines how the English spoken in Britain today is stained by a racism which may, at least in parts, be considered a legacy of the British imperial enterprise.[7] Racist language may not be immediately life-threatening, but it is nevertheless pernicious because a language determines its speakers' opinion of the world. "It is a key instrument in socialization, and the means whereby society forms and permeates the individual's consciousness."[8] One of the central arguments of discourse theory is that language as uttered in social contexts invariably carries the power structures operative under a given ideology: it reflects who is in possession of authority and who is subjected to this authority.[9]

English as spoken at the imperial centre became the 'received' standard throughout the British Empire. During the heyday of British imperialism, in the second half of the 19th century, the vocabulary of this 'master' idiom was inscribed in what has since become one of the major institutions of the English language: James Murray's *New English Dictionary* (*NED*), or, as it is known today, the *Oxford English Dictionary* (*OED*). Murray was aware of the fact that the vocabulary of a language is constantly developing.[10] However, a dictionary is necessarily an inventory of words made at a certain 'stage' in this development and preserves this stage at least until its next revision. With vocabulary the prime component of a language to preserve the social and cultural knowledge of its speakers, dictionaries therefore contribute to the stabilization of world views and ideologies. Furthermore, they endow their word/world inventory with the authority of the written text and the reputation of the scholarly work. "Dictionary Black (Trap)" alludes to this authority in line 7, which states that a dictionary gives "literal form and fact" to a specific use of words. A dictionary which sanctions only or primarily one world view is, in Bakhtinian terms, monological. Sista Rootz exposes the monologism of a particular dictionary: the *Concise Oxford Dictionary of Current English* (*COD*).

In Britain, the *OED* and its less comprehensive offshoots come closest to representing a quasi-official dictionary, not least due to their association with Oxford University, the most prestigious stronghold of British education and culture. Of the Oxford dictionaries, the *COD* is arguably the most influential one because of its wide distribution, for example in schools and universities: "The whole world's believing / This Oxford-Concise" (ll. 71f.). In a process easily re-enactable for readers with their own *COD* at hand, "Dictionary Black (Trap)" scrutinizes this dictionary's entries for *black*, *dark* and *white*.[11] This scrutiny involves a growing awareness of the ideology underlying these entries – a monological "ism" promoting *apartheid*, the "schism" of races (l. 73).

For the poem's persona, the process starts accidentally: she is "looking through" her dictionary (l. 1) when her attention is caught by the entry for "black". The long list of definitions for this word starts with a seemingly objective description, "'opposite to white'" (l. 10), with which the persona can hesitatingly agree: "Mmhm alright" (l. 12). The description "'persons with dark skin'" (l. 13), too, at first appears fairly neutral. However, it cannot be neutral as the opposition of *black* and *white* refers not only to skin colour, but, more fundamentally, to values traditionally attached to the respective colours in Eurocentric culture(s). *Black* is associated with a list of negatives (starting in l. 14) so long that the persona is almost overwhelmed: "Hold on a sec / Mek mi tek a breath" (ll. 34f.). If black is a colour charged with negative associations, how can a person denominated as *black* be at all seen in a 'bright' light?

Prepared by what the persona has found under *black*, the entry for *dark*, exhibiting the same ideology, does not surprise her: "Well guess what it says" (l. 39), "you've guessed" (l. 45), "of course" (l. 47). In a world perceived through a racist screen, the opposite, positive values for *white* are equally predictable: "I knew next what to sight / [...] /not a Black word in sight" (ll. 53/56). Significantly, the pejorative equivalent to *Darky*, *Whitey*, is not listed in the dictionary (l. 64) – at least in the edition which the persona has at hand (it is included in the *COD* of 1982). The poem suggests that the word was omitted because it is incompatible with a world view in which the white race is in possession of power and only those who *lack* authority are conceivable in the diminutive.

The *COD*'s 1982 edition introduced new markings for "deprecated usage", one of them being "R" for "racially offensive". *Darky* is marked with an "R", but another word, which must be equally insulting to people of African descent, is not: the word *blackbird* meaning "a kidnapped so-called Negro / on a slave ship" (ll. 21f.).[12] The nonchalantly contemptuous metaphor coined by white slavers catches the essence of slavery: people were deprived of their freedom as thoughtlessly as some people catch and cage birds – those creatures which, with their capacity to fly, are proverbially linked with freedom and in relation to whom captivity is perceived as particularly cruel. For people of African Caribbean origin, the voyage of slave ships from Africa to the Caribbean islands is still a communal trauma; *blackbird* with its special meaning must offend them. However, the *COD* notes only the most common and most obviously discriminatory expressions. For less common words, racist implications go unnoticed.

The *COD*'s entry for *blackbird* raises yet other questions. For most speakers of English today, the only meaning of *blackbird* is a particular kind of bird. Most readers of the poem will therefore share the persona's commonsensical reaction: "I thought they did have wing / Eat worm an' sing an' ting" (ll. 24f.). Considering that slavery in the British Empire was (nominally) abolished as early as 1833, the word *blackbird* referencing to slavery should primarily be of historical interest. The entry in the *COD*'s 1982 edition is, indeed, marked "Hist." for "historical; history" (it was not in earlier editions). However, should a word with a specialized, historical meaning be at all included in a dictionary explicitly devoted to the rendering of 'current' English? The editor of the 1982 edition specifies as part of his editorial policy:

> The words, phrases, and meanings given are those current in the English of the present day – either in living use, or familiar through their occurrence *in frequently quoted literature of the past.*[13] [my emphasis]

Does *blackbird* with its historical meaning really meet this criterion? One might argue that the dictionary entry keeps a word alive for speakers of English who would not, without the *COD*, come across it. Or does the word's inclusion in the *COD* imply that there still are people to whom it can be applied? The British no longer capture slaves, but an imperial attitude which views non-white people as inferior has undoubtedly survived.

Blackbird is not the only relic of the discourse of Empire in the *COD*. As "Dictionary Black (Trap)" goes on to expose, such relics are scattered all over the entries for *dark* and *white*. The notion of Africa as the dark continent (l. 48), for example, was popularized in the second half of the 19th century, when British interest in Africa resurged and released a stream of explorers and missionaries[14] – most of whom displayed a condescending attitude towards the continent's autochthonous population.

> Africa grew 'dark' as Victorian explorers, missionaries, and scientists flooded it with light, because the light was refracted through an imperialist ideology that urged the abolition of 'savage customs' in the name of civilization.[15]

For the alleged blessings of this civilization the enlightened were expected to be "grateful", as line 20 of "Dictionary Black (Trap)" emphasizes.

The poem introduces the word *light* in connection with a phrase that is one of the most famous catchwords in Victorian cultural studies: "sweetness and light" (l. 55). For Matthew Arnold, in *Culture and Anarchy* (1869), sweetness and light epitomize a culture's harmonious perfection – with Arnold's notion of culture firmly based on the alleged superiority of European culture. Arnold can hardly be considered a direct advocate of Empire, but his work contributed to the ideological underpinning of British cultural imperialism.[16]

Line 63 of Sista Rootz's poem, "'Superior' in their 'ivory tower'", refers to a conventional emblem of cultural elitism. The line thus links up with the earlier reference to the assumed preeminence of European culture – a culture whose importation was intended to supersede indigenous cultural expression in the colonies. As contextualized in the poem, however, the ivory *tower*, with its suggestion of elevation and its phallic implication, also connotes (white) authority in a more general sense. Through 'ivory', it evokes the exploitation and subjection on which this authority was built: ivory, in its literal sense, was a prime object of colonial greed; 'black' ivory, in the 19th century, was a common synonym for African slaves.

One of the most notorious watchwords of British imperialism is evoked in lines 57f.: "This 'White race member' / Whose 'burden is leading'". Rudyard Kipling's poem, "The White Man's Burden" (1899)[17] disguises subjugation of the colonies as the white man's beneficial duty. "'White-witch'-power" in

Sista Rootz's poem (l. 62) refers to this lie of the munificent Empire, white witches, according to the *COD* (1982), "using power for beneficent purposes only". Sista Rootz's allusion to "the white man's burden", with *leading* in a position of emphasis at the end of a line, draws attention to the true desire behind the imperial enterprise: the desire to exert power, out of conviction of white superiority.

Sista Rootz's poem shows how the English language, not least through cultural institutions like dictionaries, preserves racial stereotypes that were part of a discourse of British imperialism. Without its imperial past, contemporary Britain would not be free of racism. However, the perpetuation of the ideology of Empire may have provided a fertile breeding ground for new forms of racism. Quite obviously, language as encoded in the *COD* maintains a segregation of people into white and black, dominating and subjugated. Up to and including the 1982 edition, the *COD* does not contain a single entry for *black* which would refer to race in unambiguously positive terms. Until the very recent past, a counter-discourse to the white man's ideology of colour was banned from the dictionary.

As "Dictionary Black (Trap)" progresses and the opposite values attached to colour terms become increasingly obvious, the persona gets more and more agitated. What starts out in a rather calm mood ends in a downright *j'accuse* of white language policy: "They have on purpose created / A language deceiving" (ll. 69f.). This language may be "crap", as goes the poem's final word, but it is powerful enough to capture Black people in a "trap" of prejudice. Ultimately, the schism implicit in white colour terms reflects on the persona's own language, specifically her use of personal pronouns. The poem's second half in particular features a clear division between 'us' and 'them' (ll. 49-52, 66-76) – those who have moulded language to support their desire to rule, and those who "pay the price" (l. 75) for this policy. What at the beginning is a dictionary with which the persona identifies ("mi dictionary" – l. 1), finally emerges as a dictionary in which others have institutionalized *their* language. In the end, white language forces the persona to develop a group identity defined against the whites, segregation thus being further aggravated. While initially the persona is presented as an individual ("I was looking [...]" – l. 1), the use of the first person plural at the end indicates her identification with the group of all people victimized and betrayed, "like [...] Jesus The Christ" (l. 78), by a monologically white dictionary.

Ending on a communal note suits the politically activist character of Sista Rootz's poem, a character shared by much of contemporary Black British poetry. This poetry is frequently performance poetry, most prominently in the work of *dub* poets like Linton Kwesi Johnson, who speak their poetry to the rhythm of reggae music. "Dictionary Black (Trap)", too, is a poem whose impact is best achieved when read aloud: it becomes obvious then how rhythm (in fact polyrhythm), rhyme, repetition and the poem's non-stanzaic division support its argument.[18] A note of performance is not least achieved through the poem's formal dialogism: the way in which it repeatedly establishes rapport with an audience (ll. 34-36, 39, 45). Its clear and direct style forces the listener to understand. Considering its features of orality, "Dictionary Black (Trap)" can be said to participate in a dominant line of contemporary Black British poetry, much of which is not composed in standard English.

In the version of "Dictionary Black" printed in this volume, features of Black English stand in explicit contrast to an English which is ideologically white. Throughout the poem, this white discourse is put in inverted commas, indicating that it is a language which the persona quotes but does not speak herself. Black discourse forms a counter-discourse to white people's stereotypes, most obviously in the following lines: "I thought they did have wing / Eat worm an' sing an' ting" (ll. 24-25). What is expressed here in Black English is an understanding of the word *blackbird* untainted by imperialist lingo. After all, the creole languages which African slaves and their descendants developed in the Caribbean allowed them to establish and maintain a new identity and culture of their own, against the colonizer's suppression of their original African languages and cultures.[19] In Britain today, these varieties of English provide Black poets with an alternative to the British standard – an alternative employed in different degrees and to different purposes, from complete rejection of the standard variety[20] to a free shifting between languages.

Sista Rootz's poem could be studied in conjunction with poems entirely written in Black English. The anthology in which "Dictionary Black" was first published contains a range of examples. "No Dialects Please", by Grenada-born Merle Collins[21], is a particularly suitable companion piece as it also directly addresses the issue of language: specifically, how an authoritative 'British' voice tries to silence poetry composed in non-standard English. Collins points out that the cultural superiority implied in this restriction is founded on an illusion: considered historically, standard English is as 'impure' as are Caribbean creoles: "de dialect of de Normans and de Saxons / dat combine an reformulate / to create a language-elect" (ll. 13-15). Another reason for the suppression of non-standard English is fear of its subversive power, its potential to question the validity of the master discourse: "so frighten o we power / dat dey have to hide behind a language" (ll. 63-64). Like "Dictionary Black (Trap)", Collins's poem thus postulates a them / us division; standard English is the white man's idiom. More emphatically than Sista Rootz, Collins conveys an impression of the power of Black English. Efforts to protect the hegemony of the old master idiom and the ideology it carries are doomed to fail; a Black counter-discourse can no longer be silenced.

1 The poem first appeared in R. Cobham, M. Collins (Eds.): *Watchers and Seekers. Creative Writing by Black Women in Britain.* London, 1987. Sista Rootz now considers this version of the poem "tired" (personal communication) and prefers the one printed here, which makes heavier use of Caribbean English grammar and spellings. It might be worth while comparing the two versions for teaching purposes. The main dialect spellings and meanings used are: *mi* (my), *ting* (things), *sec* (second), *mek* (let), *tek* (take), *'coz* (because). For general characteristics of Caribbean-derived, Black varieties of English as spoken in Britain see D. Sutcliffe: *British Black English.* Oxford, 1982, p. 176.

2 See P. Guptara (Ed.): *Black British Literature. An Annotated Bibliography.* Sydney, 1986; D. Dabydeen (Ed.): *The Black Presence in English Literature.* Manchester, 1985; J. Berry: "The Literature of the Black Experience". – In D. Sutcliffe, A. Wong (Eds.): *The Language of the Black Experience. Cultural Expression Through Word and Sound in the Caribbean and Black Britain.* Oxford, 1986, pp. 69-106.

3 Personal communication.

4 H.L. Gates Jr.: "Writing 'Race' and the Difference It Makes". – In idem (Ed.): *'Race', Writing, and Difference.* Chicago, London, 1986, pp. 120, here: p. 6.

5 For an extract see D. Dabydeen (Ed.): *The Black Presence in English Literature.* "Preface", p. ix.

6 "The New Empire Within Britain" (1982). – In *Imaginary Homelands: Essays and Criticism 1981-1991.* London, 1991, pp. 129-138, here: p. 130. For background reading on Black people in Britain see, amongst many other publications: C. Husband (Ed.): *'Race' in Britain: Continuity and Change.* London, Melbourne, 1982; T. Kushner, K. Lunn (Eds.): *The Politics of Marginality. Race, the Radical Right and Minorities in Twentieth Century Britain.* London, 1990; J. Donald, A. Rattansi (Eds.): *'Race', Culture and Difference.* London, 1992. A government view is given in a publication by Her Majesty's Stationery Office: *Ethnic Minorities.* London, 1991. For a bibliography with earlier material see P. Stummer: "Die Rassenfrage im zeitgenössischen England. Realität und narrative Reflexion". *anglistik & englischunterricht* 16: *Race and Literature*, 1982, 9-30.

7 The link between racist language and imperialism is central in the Rastafarians' critique of standard English, in which skin colour denominations are also a prime target. See J. Bones: "Language and Rastafari". – In D. Sutcliffe, A. Wong (Eds.): *The Language of the Black Experience*, pp. 37-51.

8 G. Kress, R. Hodge: *Language as Ideology.* London, 1979, p. 1.

9 Central arguments of discourse theory are summarized in the introductory chapter of T. Crowley: *The Politics of Discourse. The Standard Language Question in British Cultural Debates.* Houndmills, 1989.

10 "General Explanations". *NED* 1, Oxford, 1888, p. xviii.

11 The version of the *COD* currently on the market is the eighth edition published in 1990. In contrast to its antecedents, this edition is distinguished by a comparatively high sensitivity to 'politically correct' language. Sista Rootz refers to an older edition. Most of the definitions and annotations in the entries under consideration remained unchanged up to and including the seventh edition (1982).

12 Note that "so-called" is added to the original dictionary entry because the term *Negro* is now considered offensive by many Black people.

13 J.B. Sykes (Ed.): *COD.* Oxford, [7]1982, p. viii.

14 Henry Morton Stanley's bestselling *Through the Dark Continent* was published in 1878.

15 P. Brantlinger: "Victorians and Africans. The Genealogy of the Myth of the Dark Continent". *Critical Inquiry* 12, 1985, 166-203, here: 166.

16 The following quotation from *Culture and Anarchy*, for example, could be easily used to legitimize the Empire's civilizing mission: "[culture] knows that the sweetness and light of the few must be imperfect until the raw and unkindled masses of humanity are touched with sweetness and light." *The Complete Prose Works of Matthew Arnold* V. Ed. R.H. Super. Ann Arbor, 1965, p. 112.

17 *Rudyard Kipling's Verse. Inclusive Edition 1885-1918.* London, n. y., pp. 371f.

18 A recording of Sista Rootz performing the poem is available; please contact me for further information.

19 See A. Wong: "Creole as a Language of Power and Solidarity". – In D. Sutcliffe, A. Wong (Eds.): *The Language of the Black Experience*, pp. 110-122.

20 One of the most prominent Caribbean critics of English language imperialism is Edward Kamau Brathwaite. See an interview in C. Searle (Ed.): *Words Unchained. Language and Revolution in Grenada.* London, 1984, pp. 232-239, and Brathwaite's lecture "English in the Caribbean. Notes on Nation Language and Poetry". – In L. Fiedler, H.A. Baker (Eds.): *English Literature. Opening Up the Canon.* Baltimore, London, 1981, pp. 15-53. For an extensive discussion of the language issue in post-colonial literatures also see B. Ashcroft, G. Griffiths, H. Tiffin: *The Empire Writes Back. Theory and Practice in Post-Colonial Literatures.* London, 1989.

21 R. Cobham, M. Collins (Eds.): *Watchers and Seekers*, pp. 118f.

Elfi Bettinger, München

Grace Nichols' "Sugar Cane": A Post-Colonial and Feminist Perspective

Sugar Cane

1

There is something
about sugar cane

he isn't what
he seem –

indifferent hard
and sheathed in blades

his waving arms
is a sign for help

his skin thick
only to protect
the juice inside
himself

2

His colour
is the aura
of jaundice
when he ripe

he shiver
like ague
when it rain

he suffer
from bellywork
burning fever
and delirium
just before
the hurricane
strike
smashing him to pieces

3

Growing up
is an art

he don't have
any control of

it is us
who groom and
weed him

who stick him
in the earth
in the first place

and when he
growing tall

with the help
of the sun
and rain

we feel the
need to strangle
the life

out of him

But either way he can't survive

4

Slowly
pain-
fully
sugar
cane
pushes
his
knotted

joints
upwards
from
the
earth
slowly
pain-
fully
he
comes
to learn
the
truth
about
himself
the
crimes
committed
in
his
name

5

He cast his shadow
to the earth

the wind is
his only mistress

I hear them
moving
in rustling tones

she shakes
his hard reserve

smoothing
stroking
caressing
all his length
shamelessly

I crouch
below them
quietly

1. Opening Remarks

There is something about this poem[1] – it isn't what it seems. Its extraordinary arrangement, its liberal use of space on the page in the original, immediately strikes the eye. Written only on the left margin, the string of words dangling down over four pages visually conjures up the silhouette of a sugar cane. Indeed, the poem's short lines, consisting of anything from one to five words, form a pattern on the page that resembles a long, slim cane with irregularly knotted joints. But this eye-catching first impression is at the same time the first pitfall: it tempts us into a mimetic reading whereby we see only one side of the cane since it is not arranged in the middle of the page but aligned on the left.

What's in a name? The compound 'sugar cane' carries with it rich connotations, bringing together the sweet and the bitter, pleasure and pain, gratification and punishment. However, we are about to fall into the second seductive trap: the discovery of supposedly essential meanings 'inscribed' in the words which seem to embody 'nature' authentically. Thus, a metaphoric reading is produced which easily assumes a universalist posture and in so doing ignores how language bears the burden of cultural experience. Post-colonial and feminist readings, however, insist on the cultural specificity of texts. Insofar as they emphasize that identity and difference are always constructed, they draw attention to the gap between language and lived experience. Instead of being naturalized, language and text must be contextualized to trace how they "bear the imprint of the material forces of politics, economics, and culture which act upon them within the imperial [and patriarchal] framework."[2] Such a metonymic reading, as it is termed by the critic Homi Bhabha, highlights the extent to which the text is symptomatic of the post-colonial condition.[3] In reading through its features the social, cultural, and political forces which traverse the text can be made visible. The gap which enfolds the space "between the simultaneous abrogation of language as normative standard and the appropriation of language as cultural mode in the post-colonial text"[4] functions as an important reminder, a warning that the text, the shared site of discourse, is not the site of shared experience. Here lies the danger of expropriation for

> critical discourse is in itself 'imperialist' and the literary text is often not seen as speaking for itself. Furthermore it is critical language that serves to homogenise creative discourse in a way that denies each creative text and literatures its own specificity and social and cultural context.[5]

While bearing this warning in mind, "Sugar Cane" by the Guyanese poet Grace Nichols can open up issues of language and place, origin and destination, past and future for poetic exploration, topics already provocatively raised by the collection's title, *The Fat Black Woman's Poems.*[6]

2. *Unfolding the Text*

The distinctive vertical structure of the poem "Sugar Cane" presents five numbered, irregularly long segments which are themselves broken into short syntactic units, arranged in couplets, triplets and quartets, uninterrupted by punctuation. When mentioned for the first time in the opening stanza, sugar cane is not identified by an article, either definite or indefinite, thereby implying a generic use. By contrast, the second couplet starts with "he": sugar cane is personified. As the poem proceeds, the noun acquires the grammatical properties of a name. 'He' – and the male pronoun seems most appropriate for the phallic form – is then nevertheless characterized by a trait that is normally attributed to femininity: 'he' is an enigma. The poem sets in with a riddle – a popular device in oral traditions: Sugar cane is not what 'he' seems.

How does this riddle function? At first, oppositions are constructed: outer – inner, solid – fluid ("indifferent hard" – "sheathed in blades" – "the juice inside" – ll. 5, 6, 11), their sexual connotations being rather explicit. However, contrary to the conventional metaphysical dichotomy of appearance and reality, the binary oppositions in this case operate not so much within a framework of essence or truth. No particular value is attached to the inner, being traditionally the site of truth, no promise made for a kernel to hold a 'real' self. Instead, the oppositions articulate a general sense of insecurity. Though armoured and protected by 'his' sheath, threat and danger linger over the existence of sugar cane. 'He' is in need of help and protection. Effectively oscillating between the generic noun and the personal name, sugar cane, even though personified, is individualized at the same time as 'he' but stands as a member of a communal lot.

All of the following segments derive their dynamics from the introductory riddle. Sugar cane's destiny is circumscribed, explored from different points of view. Rather than the unfolding of a linear narrative with a beginning and an end, each one of the segments addresses a different aspect of 'his' existence. The second segment features nature and climate: both have dangers in store for 'him'. Sugar cane is threatened by various diseases and disasters. The poem evokes specifically those connected to the tropics, such as jaundice, ague, burning fever, delirium and the hurricane. The grammatical tense, the unmarked simple present in conjunction with the deletion of the copula[7], adds an element of timelessness. Together with an unmarked third person singular, these linguistic features disrupt the 'English' surface of the text, point to the tension between marginality and the linguistic centre of Received Standard English. In making its presence felt, the linguistic variant insists on the gap and resists reabsorption and domestication. Eventually, sugar cane's fate culminates in destruction: "just before / the hurricane / strike / smashing him to pieces" (ll. 24-27).

Just as life and death are not absolutes so far, so too subject and object can interchange places. The third segment shifts sugar cane from the subject position to that of the subjugated object: "Growing up / is an art // he don't have / any control of" (ll. 28-31). Instead of the singular "he" an unspecified plural "we" enters into the subject position as the agent of 'his' life and death: "it is us / who groom and / weed him // who stick him / in the earth / in the first place" (ll. 33-38). The care taken is described in agricultural terms, "groom" and "weed". Both activities are inherently ambivalent: benign and helpful yet at the same time exercises of control, power and domination, governed by self-interest. Inevitably, in the process of harvesting they aim at sugar cane's destruction. In the third segment as in the second, death awaits 'him', this time not by the force of nature but constructed in distinctively human terms, as a killing or even murder: "we feel the / need to strangle / the life // out of him" (ll. 43-46). Within this constellation no escape seems possible. Sugar cane is a victim, doomed to a certain death, as is laconically stated in the concluding line: "But either way he can't survive" (l. 47).

It is in the fourth segment that the visual arrangement makes itself felt most impressively: every single word, even down to the morphemes, gets a line of its own. As a result, the rhythm assumes an incantatory quality which corresponds to the slow process of both growing up and discovering the truth. Through the repetition of their attributes "slowly / pain- / fully" (ll. 48-50, 61-63), a parallel between both developments, the physical and the mental, is both established and syntactically encoded. The "truth" (l. 68) 'he' learns is painful. It does not consist in some abstract metaphysical principle. The truth is something in which sugar cane is deeply implicated: "the / crimes / committed / in / his / name" (ll. 67-76).

Now it is out in the open: we are at the scene of crime. And sugar cane is involved in it. Even the clear-cut distinction implied by the binary opposition of victim and oppressor collapses. The dark mood is carried over into the fifth segment's opening lines, where grief still prevails: "He cast his shadow / to the earth" (ll. 77-78). But slowly guilt and repentance fade, the initial erotic tone resurfaces: "the wind is / his only mistress" (ll. 79-80). Pain starts giving way to pleasure.

In the very last segment, yet another agent enters the scene of action, a sort of lyrical first person voice, an "I" which is less a centering consciousness than a witness, or rather a voyeur. It overhears and 'over-sees' what is going on: "I hear them / moving / in rustling tones" (ll. 81-83). An erotically charged atmosphere is created in which the term "rustling" connotes secretive movements and falling garments. The wind is constructed as sugar cane's feminine counterpart. It is 'she' who plays the active part in this scene of seduction: "she shakes / his hard reserve" (ll. 84-85). The latent sexual connotations from the very first segment ("hard", "sheathed", "juice") reemerge and are openly celebrated, linking beginning and end. In the last stanza, the reader is to some extent implicated in this act of love-making. The up-and-down motion within the poem, which replicates the eye's movement over four pages, accelerates and intensifies: "smoothing / stroking / caressing / all his length". Furthermore, the touching is done "shamelessly". This characterizes the act as openly transgressing the prevailing moral norms, whilst at the same time insisting on the establishment of its own standard of behaviour. But then the movement of, and in, the poem comes to a halt. The reader has arrived at the bottom of the page, the first-person narrator crouches on the ground. Below 'him' and 'her', below sugar cane and the wind engaged in shameless caresses, the narrator stops still and falls silent: "I crouch / below them / quietly" (ll. 91-93). There is amazement, wonder and acceptance in this final stillness: there is nothing more to be said.

3. The Post-Colonial Condition

Circling back to the beginning by imitating the move of the poem's non-linear narrative, we arrive again at our starting point: the riddle. The end of the poem gives us neither an answer nor a solution, rather it 'merely' presents scenes of life and death. In thwarting our expectations the poem questions the assumptions about the genre 'riddle' itself and calls for the reader's active participation in the construction of possible meanings. However, the poem does offer some clues: there is the structure of pain and pleasure, of death and sexuality. And most strikingly, there is a change of mood after the fourth segment, after the acknowledgement of "the crimes committed in his name". Might this not be a key to the riddle?

If "symptomatic" readings of texts are not concerned "with 'discovering' their essential metaphoric meaning but rather with identifying and articulating the symptomatic and distinctive features of their post-coloniality"[8], the role of sugar for the imperialist project in the Caribbean has to be examined. What cotton meant for the exploitation of the Afro-American slaves in the Southern States, sugar meant to the indigenous and slave population in the Caribbean.[9] The pervasive oxymoron 'bitter cane' highlights what Ellis calls "the curse of sugar, the original sin of popular Caribbean experience". For as he continues:

> Sugar cane in the region was the prompter of slavery and the diaspora, the raison d'être of colonialism, the inspiration for cupidity and for the capitalist exploitation of labour, and the inciter of rage against those who would not submit meekly to this exploitation.[10]

The extremely hard and dangerous labour in the sugar cane fields took a high and bloody toll for work that offered only seasonal employment. Little wonder that sugar hardly featured as sweetener, as gainful employment, or the source of national wealth in Caribbean texts.[11] Through the metaphorical personification of sugar cane, Nichols' poem links its ('his') fate metonymically with the lives of those who actually plant and harvest the crop. The historical memory of enslavement, transportation, and cultural denigration, still deeply affecting the cultures and literatures of post-colonial societies is thus kept alive.

4. *The Intertexual Dimension*

The empire has been writing back for some time, creating a tradition of its own, wresting language and power from the dominating European culture. From 1950 onwards, the struggle for liberation from the yoke of colonialism has also resulted in a liberation of the imagination. In the 1960s, the Caribbean Artists' Movement was formed in London, stimulating the exploration of post-coloniality, anti-imperialism, nationalism and migration. When Nichols started to write in the later 1970s she could insert herself into an already rich tradition, echoes of which traverse her poem "Sugar Cane". Born in 1950 in

Guyana, where she grew up, Nichols worked as a teacher, journalist and reporter before she came to Britain in 1977.[12] At that time, the community of established black writers with reputation still consisted mostly of men.[13] Important voices among them were Edward Kamau Braithwaite from Barbados and Wilson Harris from Guyana. Both had developed their influential views on how to conceptualize post-colonial culture. Braithwaite emphasizes the link with African and Amerindian ancestors in his model of Creolization, invoking a cross-cultural time-space dynamic. Harris, however, insists on the release of energies through the breakdown of traditions. Antagonistic energies, through crisis and catastrophe, transform into a creative syncretism, unavailable to monocultural societies.[14]

Since no discourse is ever a monologue, reverberations of her predecessors' and contemporaries' texts are woven into Nichols' "Sugar Cane", unsurprisingly so, being part of a cycle entitled *i is a long memoried woman.* The poem's intertextual dialogue can be traced in its generic and rhetorical elements. Not only the 'armour' referred to in the title of Wilson Harris's novel *The Whole Armour* (1962) is echoed in her poem.[15] The central male character of that novel, Abram, shares the enigmatic quality of 'sugar cane': "No one knew his true name – or from whence he had come." He is a "bewildered man who wanted to rediscover an innocence at all costs" but in the end he comes to realize that "nobody [is] innocent." Furthermore, the young character Cristo has to pay for a crime he did not commit.[16] Like in Harris's other novels, "death or sacrifice is part of the tragedy of renewal in a world of process, [...] sacrifice is necessary to social and cultural transformation."[17] The view of regeneration through catastrophe leaves its trace in the two deaths which occur in "Sugar Cane" only to be followed by an erotic awakening.

Echoes of Braithwaite's work are audible throughout "Sugar Cane". When he celebrates his African roots rediscovered during his stay in Ghana he uses the same devices of syntactical repetition and parallelism:

> Slowly, slowly, ever so slowly; obscurely, slowly but surely, during the eight years that I lived there, I was coming to an awareness and understanding of community, of cultural wholeness, of the place of the individual within the tribe, in society. Slowly, slowly, ever so slowly I came to a sense of identification of myself with these people [...]. [18]

Furthermore, Braithwaite also made the oxymoronic expression 'bitter sugar' into a poem. His "Labourer" is a portrait of a sugar worker. Here, repetition, alliteration and enjambement together produce a strong incantatory effect:

> and the shame, the shame, the shame-
> lessness of it all, the name-
> less days in the burnt cane-
> fields without love; [...].[19]

The "shamelessness" and the "canefields without love" reemerge in Nichols' poem. There are also remarkable links to "Sugar Cane", the poem by Faustin Charles in the same collection: "Cane is sweet sweat slain; / cane is labour, unrecognised, lost / and unrecovered; / sugar is the sweet swollen pain of the years; / sugar is slavery's immovable stain".[20] By means of its elaborately constructed web of intertextual echoes, Nichols' "Sugar Cane", comments, deconstructs and reorders the positions traversing her text.

5. *Feminism and Post-Colonialism*

Black Feminists have analyzed how colonized women are oppressed by racism, sexism and imperialism. Even though their subjection is produced by the same operation of "othering" as through patriarchy[21], this mechanism of marginalisation is often unthinkingly reproduced by white liberal feminists when they ignore the extent to which they themselves are implicated in the structure of white power.[22] The struggle of the silenced subject for a voice, the dilemma of finding a language, is expressed by the writer Jamaica Kincaid, emphasizing once again that the colonial past, – the crime –, cannot be ignored. For as she says: "Isn't it odd that the only language I have in which to speak of this crime is the language of the criminal who committed the crime?"[23] In this struggle the post-colonial woman writer has to face several obstacles:

> The post-colonial woman writer is not only involved in making herself heard, in changing the architecture of male-centred ideologies and languages, or in discovering new forms and language to express her experience, she has also to subvert and demythologise indigenous male writings and traditions which seek to label her.[24]

Two of the prevailing stereotypes which affect black women are the mulatto figure, often portrayed as an exotic, luscious fruit, and secondly the powerful matriarch, the fertile earth mother.[25] Nichols effectively subverts them both: in her 'fruit poems', like "Mango", "Star-apple" and "Guenips", she appropriates the fruit image. Instead of turning it into a metaphor for woman, fruit is redefined as her means of seduction. At the same time, the matriarch is refuted: many of her poems display a considerable ambivalence towards the role of motherhood.[26]

Likewise, the first-person narrator in "Sugar Cane" assumes an erotic role rather than that of an all-encompassing motherly protector for a 'filial' sugar cane. The poem's multiple subject (we, I) rejects not only the function of an 'earth mother' but also avoids that which Braithwaite terms "the arrogance of the individualist ego". The poem's ending without judgment insists on an acceptance of difference on equal terms. The self-distancing installs that gulf of "post-colonial silence which cannot be overwhelmed by any interpretation" and which can only be "traversed when authors write and readers read in order to engage in communication."[27]

Thus, the mode of communication is a never-ending dialogue. It never produces a final text but obtains its meaning in conflict and contradiction. "Sugar Cane" resists appropriation and insists on difference, on dialogue, on cross-fertilization. Its up-and-down motion connects it with Harris's theory of regeneration through catastrophe by subverting, or in his own terms, "comsuming its own bias". The very same effect is produced in Nichols' poem "Skin-teeth":[28]

Know that I smile
know that I bend

only the better
to rise and strike
again

Here, 'up' and 'down' - both literally and figuratively - change places bewilderingly. In so doing, they capture and confront the discursive history of this topographical metaphor, the history of dominance and subservience, and show at the same time how the imagination can supply the key to the riddle: a present struggling out of a past, an attempt to construct a future. Or perhaps better still, an attempt to construct a multiplicity of futures. Or in the words of Grace Nichols: "the power to be what I am / a woman / charting my own futures".[29]

Notes

1 The poem "Sugar Cane" is taken from the collection *i is a long memoried woman* by Grace Nichols, printed with the permission of the publishers. Copyright: 1983, 1990 Karnak House. For this cycle Nichols was awarded the Commonwealth Poetry Prize in 1983. It is partly reprinted in G. Nichols: *The Fat Black Woman's Poems.* London, 1984. For reasons of space, the poem's one column layout could not be reproduced.
2 B. Ashcroft, G. Griffiths, H. Tiffin: *The Empire Writes Back. Theory and Practice in Post-Colonial Literatures.* London, 1989, p. 29. The addition in brackets is mine.
3 H.K. Bhabha: "Representation and the Colonial Text: A Critical Exploration of Some Forms of Mimeticisms". - In F. Gloversmith (Ed.): *The Theory of Reading.* Brighton, 1984, pp. 93-122.
4 B. Ashcroft, G. Griffiths, H. Tiffin: *The Empire Writes Back*, p. 55.
5 S. Nasta (Ed.): *Motherlands. Black Women's Writing from Africa, the Caribbean and South Asia.* London, 1991, p. xxii.
6 Indeed, the title already anticipates the interrelated concepts of race, gender and

sexuality. Nichols' second collection of poems is called *Lazy Thoughts of a Lazy Woman* (1989), a title that questions again specific constructions of femininity.

7 For the features of Creole see M. Hellinger: *Englisch-orientierte Pidgin- und Kreolsprachen. Entstehung, Geschichte und sprachlicher Wandel.* Darmstadt, 1985.

8 B. Ashcroft, G. Griffiths, H. Tiffin: *The Empire Writes Back*, p. 115.

9 Even though Guyana, Nichols' place of origin, is strictly speaking in the northeast of South America and not in the Caribbean, my essay follows the practice which refers to this whole multi-cultural region as either Caribbean or West Indies. This critical practice seems legitimized by the fact that the writers and poets themselves often unite under these labels in journals and anthologies.

10 K. Ellis: "Images of Sugar in English and Spanish Caribbean Poetry". *Ariel* 24, i, 1993, pp. 149-159, here: p. 151. A stimulating account of the importance of sugar for Caribbean culture is provided by F. Ortiz: *Tabak und Zucker. Ein kubanischer Disput.* Aus dem kubanischen Spanisch von M. Meyer-Minnemann. Frankfurt/M., 1987. I am grateful to Manfred Pfister for bringing this to my attention.

11 Ellis mentions as the only exception the Cuban poet Nicols Guillén who, because of the common ownership in socialist Cuba, could go beyond desperation.

12 Besides poetry, Nichols has written a number of children's books and a novel, *Whole of a Morning Sky* (1989). Her work is widely anthologized which evoked the following somewhat peculiar comment: "She is regarded as one of the best poets in Britain who also happens to be black and female." (*The Cambridge Guide to Literature in English.* Ed. I. Ousby. Cambridge, 1988)

13 Dabydeen and Wilson-Tagore note in 1988: "It is really only in writers like Merle Hodge, Jean Rhys, Erna Brodber and recently Grace Nichols that a certain particularised consciousness of West Indian woman begins to emerge." D. Dabydeen, N. Wilson-Tagore: *A Reader's Guide to West Indian and Black Literature.* London, 1988, p. 45.

14 See B. Ashcroft, G. Griffiths, H. Tiffin: *The Empire Writes Back*, pp. 146-154.

15 Harris's *Guyana Quartet* includes *Palace of the Peacock* (1960), *The Far Journey of Oudin* (1962), *The Whole Armour* (1962) and *The Secret Ladder* (1963), all published in one volume, *The Guyana Quartet*, London, 1985.

16 W. Harris: *The Whole Armour.* – In idem: *The Guyana Quartet*, pp. 244–250. The biblical references are pointed out by B. King: *The New English Literatures – Cultural Nationalism in a Changing World.* London, 1980, p. 112ff. The possibility of an allusion in "Sugar Cane" to the biblical Cain cannot be ruled out either.

17 Ibid., p. 113.

18 Braithwaite continues: "When I turned to leave, I was no longer a lonely individual talent; there was something wider, more subtle, more tentative: the self without ego, without I, without arrogance." E.K. Braithwaite: "Timehri". *Savacou* 2, Sept. 1970, 35-44, here: 38.

19 Idem: "Labourer". – In *Breaklight. An Anthology of Caribbean Poetry.* Chosen, ed. and introd. by A. Salkey. London, 1971, p. 240. This early anthology, characteristic of its time, presents almost exclusively male poets. It contains a number of 'sugar-cane poems': Milton Williams: "Iron Punts Laden With Cane"; Faustin Charles: "Sugar Cane Man" and "Sugar Cane".

20 F. Charles: "Sugar Cane". – In A. Salkey (Ed.): *Breaklight*, p. 185.

21 See G.C. Spivak: "Three Women's Texts and a Critique of Imperialism". – In C. Belsey, J. Moore (Eds.): *The Feminist Reader. Essays in Gender and the Politics of Literary Criticism.* London, 1989, pp. 175-195.

22 See B. Smith: "Toward a Black Feminist Criticism". - In E. Showalter (Ed.): *The New Feminist Criticism.* London, 1986, pp. 168-185; D.E. McDowell: "New Directions for Black Feminist Criticism". - Ibid., pp. 186-199; S. Willis: "Black Women Writers: Taking a Critical Perspective". - In G. Greene, C. Kahn (Eds.): *Making a Difference. Feminist Literary Criticism.* London, 1985, pp. 211-237.

23 J. Kincaid: *A Small Place.* London, 1988, pp. 31-32. Nichols' poem "Epilogue" addresses this dialectic: "I have crossed an ocean / I have lost my tongue / from the root of the old one / a new one has sprung" (*The Fat Black Woman's Poems,* p. 64).

24 S. Nasta (Ed.): *Motherlands,* p. xv.

25 Ibid., p. xiv. Dabydeen and Wilson-Tagore point out the historical dimension not without eventually reinforcing the image: "Historically the woman was central to the continuation of the slave system as a necessary part of the plantation system, her essential value resting on her ability to produce the labour force. This utilitarian and commercial view of her was only the planter's view however. In reality the slave woman was a mother in an almost spiritual sense. For her, the bond between mother and child was as sacred as the bond between the earth and creativity, and it was generally in her role as creator, protector and matriarch that early West Indian writers saw their spiritual survival." (D. Dabydeen, N. Wilson-Tagore: *A Reader's Guide,* p. 43)

26 See especially her "Heavy with Child" from *i is a long memoried woman.*

27 B. Ashcroft, G. Griffiths, H. Tiffin: *The Empire Writes Back,* p. 187.

28 *The Fat Black Woman's Poems,* p. 55.

29 From "Holding My Beads" - In *The Fat Black Woman's Poems,* p. 63.

I am grateful to Séan Allan (Reading University) and Peter H. Marsden (RWTH Aachen) for their helpful comments. I would also like to thank the British Council Cologne for their bibliographical services.

Gisela Ecker, Paderborn

Irena Klepfisz's "Fradel Schtok" and the Language of Hyphenated Identity

Fradel Schtok

Yiddish writer. B.1890 in Skale, Galicia. Emigrated to New York in 1907. Became known when she introduced the sonnet form into Yiddish poetry. Author of *Erzeylungen* (Stories) in 1919, a collection in Yiddish. Switched to English and published *For Musicians Only* in 1927. Institutionalized and died in a sanitarium around 1930.

Language is the only homeland.
- Czeslow Milosz

They make it sound easy: some disjointed
sentences   a few allusions   to
mankind.   But for me   it was not
so simple   more like   trying
to cover the distance   from here
to the corner or between two sounds.

Think of it: *heym*   and   *home*   the meaning
the same   of course   exactly
but the shift   in vowel   was the ocean
in which I drowned.

I tried.   I did   try.
First held with Yiddish   but you
know   it's hard.   You write   *gas*
and   *street*   echoes back
No resonance.   And – let's face it-
memory falters.
You try to keep track of the difference
like *got* and *god*   or *hoyz* and *house*
but they blur   and you start using
alley   when you mean *gesele*   or *avenue*
when it's a *bulevar*.

And before you know it
you're on   some alien path

standing before a brick house
the doorframe slightly familiar.
Still you can't place it
exactly. Passers-by stop.
Concerned they speak but you've
heard all this before the vowels
shifting up and down the subtle
change in the guttural sounds

and now it's nothing more
nothing more than babble.
And so you accept it.
You're lost. This time you really
don't know where you are.

Land or sea the house floats before you.
Perhaps you once sat at that window
and it was home and looked out
on that *street* or *gesele*. Perhaps
it was a dead end perhaps a short cut.
Perhaps not.
A movement by the door. They stand there
beckoning mouths open and close:
Come in! Come in! I understood it was
a welcome. *A dank! A dank!*
I said till I heard the lock
snap behind me.

1. Fradel Schtok, the Speaking Poetic Voice

This poem[1] speaks to us about language and place through the poetic voice and persona of a forgotten Yiddish writer. It uses simple words in two languages, English and Yiddish. Before the poem begins, the writer provides us with some information about Fradel Schtok. She was one of the two million Jewish immigrants who came from Eastern Europe to the United States between 1890 and 1925, driven from their homes because of murderous pogroms against the Jews in the *shtetl*, the raping of Jewish women, restrictions placed on trade and geographic mobility, and the expulsion of Jews from schools and universities. In the United States the Jewish immigrants settled in the big cities, mainly in New York, in extremely crowded areas yet in the neighbourhood of each other, and they worked mostly in the textile industries.[2] One of the traditions the Jewish immigrants brought with them was their high esteem for education, something which is tied up with Jewish religious beliefs and practices. In the course of the secularization and cultural adaptation which took place in the new surroundings, education, which had earlier been reserved primarily for men, became increasingly available to Jewish women. This resulted in an increasing number of women writers like Mary Antin[3] and Anzia Yezierska.[4] Most of them wrote in English, but some women writers like Fradel Schtok started out in Yiddish. At the beginning of the century, Yiddish was widely spoken in the streets of the densely populated Jewish districts; it was also the language of several daily newspapers like the *Forwerts* and of a popular tradition of Yiddish theatre. Pressures towards assimilation to an all-American norm, however, led to a rapid decline of the use of Yiddish and of familiar religious practices. On all cultural levels we can observe the effects of cultural displacement, in geographic, linguistic, religious terms, but also in terms of class affiliation and gender norms.[5]

The Fradel Schtok of the poem speaks about the experience of dislocation in many ways. She is clearly identified as the central speaking subject, not only through her use of the personal pronoun "I" but also by her use of colloquial expressions (e.g. "let's face it" - l. 15, "you know it's hard" - ll. 12-13), through her use of simple words and of the inclusive "you" through which she both addresses a listener and generalizes beyond her personal experience. One of the most prominent features of the poem, its specific rhythm, also refers directly back to a reflecting central persona. It is a slow, persistent rhythm, typographically marked by the enlarged spacing between words and phrases, and it is a probing rhythm which halts and listens to the reverberations of words. This rhythm underlines the search for sounds and meanings, but also for something else, a hint of which is already given in the epigraph of the poem.

The kind of dislocation that is most explicitly addressed is that of language. The speaker uses a Yiddish word, and an English one echoes it. The familiar becomes unfamiliar. It is less the exact reference of the word than first of all the sound which brings about a sense of estrangement, which leads the speaker on "some alien path" (l. 23) and into a language which does not produce the same sounds when spoken. The very difference between "*heym*" and "home" (l. 7), which only lies in the vowel, carries the weight of the dislocation of the speaker and of the necessary relocation in another cultural surrounding. Their difference is articulated in spatial terms, cast into the image of an ocean in which Fradel drowns. Another Jewish immigrant to North America, Eva Hoffman, reflects the same feeling when she titles her autobiography *Lost in Translation.*[6]

What is it that gets lost in translation? The persona first speaks of differentiations of meanings, the subtle distinctions each language makes like those between "*gas*" (l. 13), "*gesele*" (l. 20), and "*bulevar*" (l. 21) and between "*heym*" (l. 7) and "*hoyz*" (l. 18), a network of distinctions within which the speaking subject situates herself and which makes it impossible to translate one single term neatly into another one in the other language. Which correct term would there be for "*gesele*" for example? Would the American "*alley*" (l. 20) do? Moreover, by insisting on the value of sounds, the speaker addresses something beyond the search for the correct meaning. She alludes to the importance of the pre-verbal in a spoken language. Before the child is able to form words, he or she is deeply affected by the very sounds of a language, the reassuring, caressing, imposing sounds of the first intimate relationships. Many Jewish American literary texts from the beginning of the 20th century deal with the sounds of Yiddish in the tenement streets.[7] On a collective level it is the reassurance of being rooted in a surrounding culture. In the situation of exile, emigration and immigration, both the echo of intimacy and a preconscious certainty and hope[8] that one is able to express oneself and will be understood become disturbed or get lost.

2. *Language and Space*

If we look at the very words that are chosen to explain the speaker's feelings of loss and disorientation we realize that except for *"got"* and *"god"* (l. 18) all the terms are spatial ones: *heym*/home, *gas*/street, *hoyz*/house, *gesele*/alley, *bulevar*/avenue. They unfold a topography of home and the ways to and from it. Another topographical dimension is introduced by the analogies and images the speaker tries to find for her searching. "[T]o cover the distance from here / to the corner" (ll. 5-6), to "keep track" (l. 17), to be "on some alien path" (l. 23) and "you're lost" (l. 35) refer to actions in space which are used in a metaphorical way but still very close to everyday speech which has 'normalized' these metaphors by frequent use. The poem continually wanders from language to space and back again, opposing home and familiarity to unfamiliar territory and sound, making concrete in the speaker's movements what is said in the epigraph from Czeslow Milosz: "Language is the only homeland."

For the speaker, who has to situate herself in a new homeland, the distinctions she set up initially are increasingly blurred. The movements and oscillations between language and topography quicken in the fourth stanza, the house is no longer the image of something firm and fixed but "floats" as the persona drifts away into the new language. At the very point when she can no longer hear anything but babble she is completely lost in the landscape. Her memory fails ("perhaps" is repeated four times), and we can no longer be sure if it is still the old Eastern European *shtetl* that is evoked by the Yiddish words. As readers, we too become lost in the geography of emigration and immigration. In the end we do not exactly know who is meant by "they" either: are "they" the inhabitants of the country of immigration, those that speak the strange language and maybe also those that lured the historical Fradel into the mental institution? The speaker herself is confused and responds to the invitation from "them", even thanks them in her own language until the door shuts behind her. "[S]nap" (l. 48), though, indicates that it is less a homecoming than an imprisonment.

3. *The Author Irena Klepfisz*

This poem, which tells about the complicated and painful process of forced transition from one culture to another and which refers to a 'real' historical persona, has been printed and reprinted several times in the United States;[9] it has been presented at readings and often commented upon. Thus we can assume that there is an agreement between the author and her public which goes beyond that of just recounting a historical personality's fate. When we search for the specific cultural meanings of this text, we have to consider the author's cultural position and the roles she assumes and through which she speaks to her public.

Irena Klepfisz is a Jewish-American poet and essayist, university teacher of English and Yiddish, and political activist engaged in the struggle against anti-Semitism, and who has taken a stand against the Israeli occupation of Gaza and the West Bank, against homophobia and against patriarchal power. She was born in Poland in 1941. Her father was active in the Jewish Labor Bund[10], a socialist organization which was mainly responsible for the Jewish resistance during World War II. He was killed by the Nazis in the Warsaw Ghetto Uprising in April 1943 when he tried to prevent the use of a machine gun by a German officer; and most of her family was murdered in Treblinka. She and her mother survived by hiding and 'passing' as non-Jews, under hardly bearable conditions. They emigrated via Sweden to the United States when Irena Klepfisz was eight years old. Both her poetry and her essays reflect this history of loss and emigration and the finding of a place for herself in a new country. This she shares both with many other survivors of the holocaust and partially with those who came with the first wave of immigration after the turn of the century.

4. *Keeper of Accounts*

"A Klepfisz poem lives amid complex tensions, even when its texture may appear transparent", writes Adrienne Rich.[11] The roles Klepfisz assumes as a poet and essayist have grown out of her biography and historical awareness. They reflect the tasks of mourning, of keeping memory alive, of warning and of preserving and recuperating what can still be found of a destroyed heritage, and of the search for new cultural space. We can identify these authorial commitments behind the speaking voice of our poem. Klepfisz writes of her childhood:

> As a child, my first conscious feeling about being Jewish was that it was dangerous, something to be hidden. [...] My sense of danger was rooted in a total physical and emotional knowledge of the war.[12]

In one of her poems she calls herself a "keeper of accounts", re-appropriating an old anti-Semitic stereotype by turning it into a task she has to perform as legacy and responsibility of the survivor: "Like these, my despised ancestors / I have become a keeper of accounts", she says in a stance that runs like a refrain through her prose-poem "Bashert".[13] In poems like "Searching for My Father's Body", "The Widow and Daughter", "*Di rayze aheym*/The Journey Home", "Warsaw, 1988: Umschlagplatz" and "death camp"[14] she searches for information about her father's death and the location of his grave, she re-visits the places of her childhood and those associated with her murdered family, and their hiding places when neither she nor her mother could speak openly or reveal their identity to anyone:

> [...] During this time   she learned survival
> depends on complete distrust. Even today   she is still
> fierce   in her refusal to rely on others. Some would call
> it alienation. Others pride. I think   it's only
> the necessary stance   of any survivor.[15]

This is exactly the lesson Fradel Schtok of our poem has not learned and realizes it only too late, after the lock has snapped shut. Yet the poet keeps account of Fradel's fate.

5. *Geographies and Identities: the 'Point of Equidistance'*

There is another refrain-like line in "Bashert" which reads like a commentary on our poem: "I am almost equidistant from two continents". Again, as in the poem, Klepfisz uses geographic terms to signify something else. She speaks of "heritages", "histories", "legacies"[16] of two cultures ("two vast land masses touch") which she has to balance and which make up her present identity, for she not only lives in the past and in the old geographic and cultural space but also in the present and in a new country. As for many other Americans, her sense of self is based upon a composite identity, one which implies balancing acts and constant re-definitions which are reflected in the use of two languages and the references to two territories. Repeatedly Klepfisz refers to the Chicana writer, Gloria Anzaldúa, who writes in a mixture of Spanish and English. Only since the eighties has it become possible to articulate the duplicities, the differences within, the complexity of what has been called the "hyphenated identity" of American minority groups, yet one no longer considers this merely as an exception to the hegemonic norm. The earlier US-American model of a unified, consolidated, all-American identity that incorporates differences but merges them together, has increasingly been questioned. For Fradel Schtok, the pressures from this model of assimilation were much harder than for the author; Americanization and the giving up of her cultural differences were the only way out for Schtok, but she 'drowned' in the ocean of difference.

Clearly, Klepfisz's 'point of equidistance' does not refer to this model; her position acknowledges difference. Warsaw, Brooklyn and Chicago are recurring placenames in her poems. "There have been many plots of ground / that formed me", she writes in "Solitary Acts"[17], and although the question of what 'home' means remains a troubled one in her search through playgrounds, cemeteries, death camps, the *shtetl*, New York tenements and the Chicago university library, it is at the same time something which has to be worked out in a lifelong process. Images of dislocation and re-location abound in her work, yet there is no nostalgic search for one coherent identity or for one single geographic locale. Given this point of view, which was typical of the eighties, it is no longer necessary to "conflate geographies and identities and link both to a historical determination of the homogeneous, collective and shared nature of cultural enterprise"[18], and she can then venture back and present a historical persona for whom identity and geography were still inseparably tied together. Of herself and her group Klepfisz says: "We are in transition. Most of us are not trying to preserve traditions; rather, we are trying to discover and learn them and also reinterpret them from a contemporary perspective."[19]

6. mame-loshn: *its Poetics and Politics*

For Fradel Schtok Yiddish was the language she grew up with and which she had also used in her early writing. For the author of the poem her relationship to the Yiddish language is more complicated because she also had to learn to speak Polish in order not to give away her Jewish identity. She later grew up in a mixture of Yiddish and English, where, as she says, "a very large number of the *lebn geblibene*, survivors, lived in the same cooperative houses in which my mother and I lived, all within a few blocks of each other – a small, tight group in the midst of a Jewish, American-born, working class neighborhood".[20] Yiddish has both a symbolic and a concrete value: For her

> Yiddish is *mame-loshn*, mother tongue, the language of the Jews, the medium through which Jewish culture and politics are to be transmitted. *Mame-loshn* was the language that gave all the tenets which I'd been taught form and substance.[21]

For those, like Klepfisz, who see themselves as secular Jews and declared Anti-Zionists, the political dimension of language becomes more acute, because neither orthodox religion[22] nor territory can serve as a basis for group identity. Fradel Schtok's and Ceslow Milosz' sense of language as "the only homeland" has implications which we cannot find for any other group.

In her essays, Klepfisz writes about the rapid decline in the use of Yiddish and of a once living culture. Torn between mourning and determination she makes up her mind to revive this language, which is not just vanishing because it goes somehow out of use but because it has been violently disrupted by the extinction of the Eastern European Jewish culture in World War II. Among her projects is the translation of Yiddish women writers into English, one of these being Fradel Schtok[23], thus making accessible their work to an audience who does no longer understand the language. Another aim that runs parallel to this is to use Yiddish in her own writing. Her audience responds positively to this: "The intensity and emotionalism of that response takes me aback. Just a few Yiddish words, the very sound of the language evokes very strong feelings and memories"[24], she writes. In these poems Klepfisz is not just speaking for herself, but in the name and on behalf of others who can no longer speak. Fradel Schtok is used as a medium for this recuperative act, a poetic voice that remembers and reminds and admonishes. At the same time, because of her political engagement, Klepfisz uses Yiddish as "a symbol of resistance to assimilation".[25]

A contextualized reading like the one I have been trying to produce here cannot stop at this point. My attempt has been to make accessible a poem that speaks of a specific culture and of specific historical moments, those of a Jewish immigrant in the United States at the beginning of this century and of a Jewish-American writer who is concerned with the composite identity of US-American ethnic groups, of migrants and exiled people. Yet where are the readers? Here in this text, the actual readers are myself and the group of German students of English and American cultures this book aims to reach, and we construct our own meanings of what we read, meanings which are necessarily influenced by our own cultural heritage. As Germans, our position with respect to the contents of this poem is tied up with our own historical legacy, a legacy which imposes specific demands on the postwar generations, and we must be ready to deal with texts that evoke this past. Moreover, against the background of those who, despite of this historical legacy, are still trying to preserve, or construct, a unified, undisrupted 'German' identity, it may well be worth dealing with the writings of those who have multiple cultural affiliations[26], who have no single mother tongue, who see themselves, by necessity or choice, as migrants with identities that may be called hyphenated and who situate themselves within complexities that do not lead to one single position.

Notes

1 I. Klepfisz: "Fradel Schtok". – In idem: *A Few Words in the Mother Tongue. Poems Selected and New (1971-1990).* Portland, 1990, pp. 228-229.
2 See, for example, M. Rischin: *The Promised City. New York's Jews 1870-1914.* Cambridge/Mass., 1962; and I. Howe, K. Libo: *How We Lived. A Documentary History of Immigrant Jews in America. 1880-1930.* New York, 1979.
3 See, for example, M. Antin: *From Plotzk to Boston.* New York, 1985 (1899); and *The Promised Land.* Princeton, 1985 (1912).
4 See, for example, A. Yezierska: *Hungry Hearts and Other Stories.* New York, 1985 (1920).
5 While most of the accounts of immigrant life are focussed on Jewish men, a few more recent books look into the complicated situation of Jewish women immigrants. See C. Baum, P. Hyman, S. Michel: *The Jewish Woman in America.* New York, 1977; E. Ewen: *Immigrant Women in the Land of Dollars. Life and Culture on the Lower East Side, 1890-1925.* New York, 1985; see also my articles: "Einzug in das *Promised Land* oder *Lost in Translation*? Osteuropäische Jüdinnen auf dem Weg vom Schtetl zum American Dream". – In S. Schilling et al. (Eds.): *Jüdische Kultur und Weiblichkeit in der Moderne.* Köln, 1993; and "'No One Could Have Told Her Race'. Assimilation, Dissimulation and Memory in Jewish-American Women's Texts". *Annales du CRAA* 18, 1993, Special Issue: "*écrire la différence. Interculturalism and the Writing of Difference*", 149-160.
6 E. Hoffman: *Lost in Translation. A Life in a New Language.* New York, 1989.
7 For a description of Jewish life in the American cities see, for example, I. Howe: *The World of Our Fathers.* New York, 1976; and S.A. Glenn: *Daughters of the Shtetl. Life and Labor in the Immigrant Generation.* Ithaca, 1990.
8 We rather have to speak of 'hope' than of certainty, because philosophic and psychoanalytic theories of language have made quite clear that the intention of the speaking subject and the linguistic expression never come together. The problem then becomes exaggerated in the case of a 'foreign' language.
9 In M. Kaye-Kantrowitz, I. Klepfisz (Eds.): *The Tribe of Dina. A Jewish Women's Anthology.* Boston, 1989, pp. 160-161; also in *Moment.*
10 The Jewish Labor Bund was founded in 1897; it was a socialist movement whose members predominantly came from the urban Jewish working class in Eastern Europe.
11 I. Klepfisz: *Poems,* p. 25.
12 Idem: *Dreams of An Insomniac. Jewish Feminist Essays, Speeches and Diatribes.* Portland, 1990, p. 61.
13 Idem: *Poems,* pp. 183-200. In her introduction to this volume, Adrienne Rich writes: "'*Bashert*' is a poem unlike any other I can think of in American, including Jewish-American, poetry, in its delineations not only of survivor experience [...] but of what happens after survival" (ibid., p. 19).
14 All the poems are printed in I. Klepfisz: *Poems.*
15 "A Visit". – Ibid., pp. 173-174.
16 Ibid., pp. 196-197.
17 Ibid., p. 206.
18 I. Rogoff: "Geographien und Identitäten. Zum Diskurs des Exils". *Babylon* 10/11, 1992, p. 25. I am quoting from the original paper upon which this article is based.

19 I. Klepfisz: "*Khaloymes*/Dreams in Progress: Culture, Politics, and Jewish Identity". - In idem: *Dreams of An Insomniac*, p. 206.
20 Idem: "Secular Jewish Identity". - In ibid., p. 145.
21 Ibid., p. 143.
22 Much has been written about Jewish secularism; perhaps here it is only necessary to say that it does not mean giving up all Jewish rituals although they are based on religion or the commemorative days and the festivities.
23 See F. Schtok: "*Opgeshnitene hor*/The shorn head". Transl. I. Klepfisz. - In M. Kaye-Kantrowitz, I. Klepfisz: *Tribe of Dina*, pp. 190-193. Another woman writer whose Yiddish literature she translates is Kadja Molodowsky.
24 I. Klepfisz: "Forging a Woman's Link in *di goldene keyt*: Some Possibilities for Jewish American Poetry". - In idem: *Dreams of An Insomniac*, p. 173.
25 Idem: "Secular Jewish Identity", p. 155.
26 Further reading may be found in volumes like R. Ferguson et al. (Eds.): *Out There. Marginalization and Contemporary Cultures.* New York, 1990.

Christoph Bode, Bamberg

"Look on my Works, ye Mighty, and despair!": Notes on the Non-teachability of Poetry

Ozymandias

I met a traveller from an antique land,
Who said--"Two vast and trunkless legs of stone
Stand in the desart. ... Near them, on the sand,
Half sunk a shattered visage lies, whose frown,
and wrinkled lip, and sneer of cold command,
Tell that its sculptor well those passions read
Which yet survive, stamped on these lifeless things,
The hand that mocked them, and the heart that fed;
And on the pedestal, these words appear:
My name is Ozymandias, King of Kings,
Look on my Works, ye Mighty, and despair!
Nothing beside remains. Round the decay
Of that colossal wreck, boundless and bare
The lone and level sands stretch far away."

A: There's one thing that has always struck me about Shelley's "Ozymandias"[1] and that is the disparity between the popularity of the poem and the almost complete lack of critical debate about it. It is certainly one of the most widely anthologized pieces of the Romantic age, you can find it in innumerous school textbooks – it's a "classroom staple", as Anne Janowitz says –, and yet the major Shelley studies mention it only in passing, if at all, and most of the dozen or so articles about it – a ludicrously low number in the first place, considering the output of our critical industry – are not really about the poem itself but rather about its supposed "sources". Ironically, around this monument of Romantic achievement, there is a roaring critical silence.

B: Could it be that what strikes you as a conspicuous disparity is only natural? After all, "Ozymandias" does have a clear, straightforward, unequivocal message, doesn't it? As I see it, no two sane readers could possibly disagree as to what it means. It speaks for itself, needs no intermediaries. And that's the reason why, I think, it's included in textbooks.[2] It's eminently "teachable" in the sense that it can be used to dispel notions like "poetry is fuzzy", "the meaning of a poem isn't palpable", "poetry is subjective, emotional", or, for advanced students, "the sonnet form doesn't lend itself to progressive politics". In her contribution to the MLA volume, *Approaches to Teaching Shelley's Poetry*, Gyde Christine Martin (A *squirms uneasily in his chair*) starts off with remarking that "[m]any students feel that poetry is not a very efficient way of expressing ideas. To help them overcome their prejudice and impatience, I like to introduce 'Ozymandias' at the beginning of undergraduate courses for non-English majors."[3] See what I mean? But you don't seem to like that approach.

A: It confirms my deepest preconceptions about the whole series, which encompasses both the best and the worst that literature teaching in the States has to offer. Nothing could surpass the excellence of the parts on editions and recommended readings – the bibliographies alone are worth the price –, but in between, when these teachers tell you how they "do" their favourites in class ... (*exasperated*) poetry as an efficient way of expressing ideas, I mean, how prosaic can you get? It comes as no surprise, does it, that her students end up discussing, of all things, "Shelley's intention", which leads, the teacher amiably admits, to a certain "impasse".[4]

B (*reservedly*): I think your sweeping condemnation is grossly unfair and I am beginning to feel that our ideas of poetry and consequently of the teaching of poetry and therefore of what one could or should do with "Ozymandias" in class might possibly differ considerably.

A: No two sane readers...?

B (*deliberately controlled*): Let's see, let's begin at the beginning, let's start with the facts and then see where the disagreement comes in. Shelley wrote his poem late in 1817 in competition with his friend Horace Smith, who produced a sonnet under the same title, later clumsily renamed "On a Stupendous Leg of Granite, Discovered Standing by Itself in the Deserts of Egypt, with the Inscription Inserted Below".

A: Not exactly the most catchy title, eh? I hope the poem expresses Smith's "idea" more efficiently...

B (*ignoring* A): Shelley's was published in Leigh Hunt's radical weekly *The Examiner* on January 11, 1818, Smith's three weeks later in the same journal. 'Ozymandias' is the Greek name for the Egyptian pharaoh Ramses II, the Great, third king of the 19th dynasty (all pharaohs of the following 20th called themselves Ramses after him), whose reign – 1304 to 1237 BC – is the second longest in Egyptian history and is especially renowned for its prosperity, its ambitious building programmes and the many colossal statues of its ruler.

A: It was most probably during his reign that the Exodus took place.

B: Right. Now, in the wake of Napoleon's Egyptian expedition there was a great craze for things Egyptian at the time, but particularly so in the autumn of 1817, when the British Museum acquired numerous statues and other remains of the period of the Ramses, amongst them that impressive granite bust of Ramses II, wrongly termed "the younger Memnon", which Shelley and Smith may well have seen.[5]

A: And the Rosetta Stone.

B: Beg your pardon?

A: The Rosetta Stone was in the same consignment.

B: Ah, was it?

A: Anyway, "Ozymandias" is not about that Ramses figure exhibited in the British Museum, is it?

B: Of course not. All this is only collateral information.

A: I see. Wonderful expression. You should work for the White House. What about the "real" statue, the one that Shelley's poem is "about"?

B: The first description is by Diodorus Siculus, the Greek historian of the first century BC. It's in his universal history – *Bibliotheca Historica* is the Latin title –, and it reads: "This piece is not only commendable for its greatness, but admirable for its cut and workmanship, and the excellency of the stone. In so great a work there is not to be discerned the least flaw, or any other blemish. Upon it there is this inscription: 'I am Osymandias, king of kings; if any would know how great I am, and where I lie, let him excel me in any of my works.'"[6] And we know through Shelley's biographer N.I. White that Shelley ordered Diodorus from his London booksellers as early as 1812, that is, he read it in Booth's translation of 1700, from which I have quoted.

A: Beside the point.

B: But the ins...

A: Beside the point, I say. Because Diodorus evidently describes a *complete* statue. Where did Shelley obtain the information about the *ruined* monument?

B (*slightly uneasy*): Well, you know as well as me – since you've mentioned all these articles on Shelley's possible sources – that there is quite a list of likely candidates: D.W. Thompson suggested Claude Etienne Savary's *Lettres sur l'Egypte*, Henry Jewell Pettit Denon's *Voyage dans la Haute et la Basse Egypte*, and H.M. Richmond made a very good case for Dr. Richard Pococke's *A Description of the East, and Some Other Countries.* Even Walter Raleigh's *History of the World* and Volney's *Les Ruines* have been thrown into the debate, although the one only for the epigraph, the other for the general scene.[7]

A: The general scene, I see. And what, if I may ask, is your personal favourite?

B: Well, I suppose Johnstone Parr summed it up neatly in 1957 when he said "we are still unable to do more than speculate".[8] You see, even when Richmond, five years later, proffered Pococke, he didn't claim him as a source in the sense that Shelley sort of found a specific paragraph in Pococke and then wrote his sonnet. Pococke, says Richmond, had some "suggestive details", a series of random observations, which Shelley then worked into "a brilliantly symbolic unity, fused by his passionate hatred of tyrants and his desire to pass judgement on their aspirations."[9]

A: But the broken statue and the inscription are in Pococke?

B (*hesitatingly*): There are various broken statues that Pococke claims to have seen at Thebes, and he mentions the inscription.

A (*a bit too sharply*): He quotes the inscription mentioned by Diodorus and then continues, "This statue, without doubt, has been broken to pieces and carried away, *as there is not the least sign of it.*"[10]

B (*defensively*): He's not a source in the original sense. He has a trunk here, a foot there, a pedestal in another place. Admittedly, he's also a bit confused...

A: And confusion spreads: Parr has him give the measurements of the monument *in its broken state*, although Pococke says "there is not the least sign of it"! And then Parr even presents drawings and photographs of the "Statue of Ozymandias" at Thebes.

B: They're evidently speaking about different statues – Parr's is not that of the inscription.

A: Aha. Let's get this sorted out: Pococke and numerous other 18th-century travellers to Egypt quote, in their respective accounts, the famous epigraph "I am the king of kings..."

B: They do, indeed.

A: It's even in the Fourth Edition of the *Encyclopedia Britannica* of 1810.

B (*temporarily relieved*): It was all around, it was well known.

A: "[S]omething about the [...] Ozymandias 'epitaph' seized the imagination of these European tourists."[11]

B: Indeed, indeed.

A: The original inscription, I take it, was in hieroglyphics?

B: Of course.

A: And one knew its meaning from Diodorus' transcription?

B: One would.

A: The Rosetta Stone was deciphered in...?

B: Around 1820?

A: 1822. (*Long pause.*) If they knew the statue and the pedestal and knew the meaning of the epigraph through Diodorus, why did they have to wait for Champollion to come along? They had the perfect code-breaker at their hands all the time. (*Another pause.*)

B: From which it follows...

A: From which it follows that *they didn't know the statue.*

B: But their accounts...

A: None of them found it, *none of them saw it.* There's a field of broken and half-broken statues and other debris at the Ramesseum at Thebes, very confusing. What those travellers did was that they used Diodorus as a guide – Diodorus in hand they would try and identify what they were looking for. It wasn't that their descriptions were sparked off by their encounters with the broken statue – quite the reverse: *text in hand*, they were looking for it, didn't find it, copied Diodorus – and left it at that.[12] It's not only that Shelley assembled his impressive ensemble – trunkless legs, head, pedestal with legend – from *various* textual passages, it is also that the broken monument of Ozymandias *is nowhere to be found in physical reality.* It exists nowhere but in the Romantic imagination of the time.

B: I take your point. The critical history of "Ozymandias" is almost exclusively the history of the quest for its sources, its origin, textual or extra-textual. But the outcome of that quest is ...

A: ... that there is no "origin" outside this discourse, no *object*, but only other texts that, drawing on an earlier one, are looking for the physical representation of an imaginary construct that haunts and fascinates this very imagination. Our present-day source-hunters are only continuing, on another plane, what (with better reason) these 18th-century travellers did: to refer the text to something external. But Shelley's poem can't be anchored to something extra-textual. It does not have a referent. His statue can only be found in the poem. So much for the positivist's short-cut to reality. So much for "facts". (*Leaning forward*) Tell you a secret: even if there *was* this statue, *Shelley's* would still be only in his poem.

B: So it's back to square one? – Excuse me for a moment.

A (*relaxed*): When you come back, can we talk about *the poem*?

BREAK

B (*returning, composed*): I grant you that this kind of source-hunting is largely futile...

A: No, no, quite the contrary. I find it extremely illuminating and instructive.

B: ... but your debunking doesn't really affect the poem's message, does it?

A: Which is?

B: How the mighty have fallen. Tyrants don't last forever. Through the passage of time Ozymandias' preposterous and presumptuous claim has been converted into its exact opposite. The desert sands surrounding the broken monument pass a devastating judgment on the king's exaggerated and shortsighted boast, and the whole scene reveals a cutting irony in the word "despair": Those who would try and emulate Ozymandias will not, as Ozymandias would have it, despair of the enormity of the task, but rather despair of the completeness of his defeat – and of anyone's who would follow his footsteps. The inscription tells the truth, although it is one to which Ozymandias, *in his time*, was blind – it only came out *in the course of time*. Thus ironically Ozymandias' boast of power has been converted into an apt admonition and warning to the likes of his. At the same time the poem is kind of reassuring to radical reformers because it points out that *in the long run*, i.e. measured against the epochs of world history, but even more so measured against the epochs of natural history, despotism won't last. Neither the individual tyrant, nor despotism as a form of government. In a way, it's part of the *pre*-history of mankind.

A: The idea is ubiquitous in Shelley: you find it all the way through from *Queen Mab* to *Prometheus Unbound*, "Thou hast a voice, great Mountain, to repeal / Large codes of fraud and woe ..."

B (*puzzled*): *Mont Blanc.* Does that mean you agree with my reading?

A: Absolutely. It would be foolish not to. This general political message is also borne out by a comparison to Horace Smith's companion poem. Shelley omits all specific references to Egypt, the Nile etc.[13], and gives the statue a face that is definitely not a pharaoh's: frown, wrinkled lip, sneer, all indicative of inward passions – that's nowhere near the mild, almost Buddha-like serenity we know from statues of Egyptian pharaohs, especially of Ramses II.

B: It reminds one rather of an archetypal villainous oriental despot...

A: *Sardanapalus*, by Delacroix.

B: So you agree with my reading – but still you wouldn't teach the poem like that?

A: Let's take a look at what you presumably call the "form" of the poem and see in how far it supports its "message".[14]

B: It's a sonnet.

A: How do you know?

B: Everybody says so and it's got 14 lines.

A: Two equally weak justifications. But let's pretend. "Sonnet" connotes what?

B: Formal excellency, the transcendence of oppositions into unity, the victory of art over the disquieting hazards of life, the triumph of form.

A: Fine. Which type? Petrarchan? Ronsard? Shakespeare?

B: Well, let's see, "land/stone/sand/frown/", I guess we can let "stone/frown" pass as a half-rhyme, so we have abab; "command" – eeeh – if we let "stone/ frown" pass, then "command" would be another a – "land/sand/command" –, and "read/things/fed" would give us acdc.

A: AC/DC? Your students will like that.

B: You're out of time, my friend. "Things" stands out in this second quatrain, it's not exactly regular.

A: No, you're right: Things stand out in this poem – isolated ruins in the desert.

B: I didn't know Shelley was such a punster.

A: Most poets are, inveterately.

B: Now for the sestet. "Appear", we haven't had that, that's e then, "Kings" – wow! – , that's d again – the "King of Kings" is connected with "these lifeless things"!

A: A truism.

B: But it shouldn't be!

A: Why?

B: It ties the sestet firmly to the octet, "things" and "Kings" have no rhymes their side of the dividing line.

A: Which dividing line?

B: The one an ideal sonnet would have.

A: I like that. You say "Ozymandias" is a sonnet, then you discover it doesn't quite fit the type and therefore conclude it's an imperfect specimen.

B: You can't deny it's written against a pattern.

A: Oh yes, definitely. Written *against* a pattern, *against* a tradition. We can come back to that. But see how it ends.

B: "Appear/Kings/despair/decay", that's edf, no, ed*e* – hold on, let's work our way backwards from the end: "despair/decay/bare/away" – that's as perfect a quatrain as you could wish for.

A: So how do you fit in the "appear"?

B: Well, if we didn't accept "appear" as a slant rhyme on "despair", it would be totally isolated in the poem.

A: It appears so, indeed. But it *is* also a poem about appearances, isn't it? It *would* make sense.

B: Possibly. Arguing from the end of the poem, I would accept it as an extreme slant rhyme – you know like the ones Wilfred Owen uses systematically – and read edefef instead of edfgfg.

A: So the truth of the matter is you can only place "appear" in hindsight, in retrospect?

B: Yes, it's...

A: The truth of that rhyme is revealed in time? You couldn't tell it when it first appeared?

B: Well, it was a beginning of sorts. It would have been e in any case, wouldn't it?

A: But it didn't establish its own tradition. What came of it sounds rather different.

B: But like enough to see a similarity.

A: Despair!

B: Huuh?

A: "Despair" in the beginning, "despair" 2 000 years gone. It's even *identical*, yet opposite in meaning. The truth will out, but it's a matter of *time*, you need the long perspective. – Do you still think it's a sonnet?

B: Looks like a wilfully ruined one to me. I mean, all those slant rhymes, no complete octet, no complete sestet, at least three caesuras.

A: You can still discern the form...

B: He's even bracketed the stone blocks – "things/Kings" – as if to keep the structure from collapsing. And at the bottom, there's this beautifully preserved quatrain ...

A: The legs of stone.

B: Above, it's sort of slanted, broken, not like it should be. Looks like a pattern is imperfectly *imposed.*

A: ... that is *human.* Nature *produces* patterns: "*b*oundless and *b*are", "*l*one and *l*evel". So the poem is a monument, a fake ruin, or rather one about to crack?

B: A work of art.

A: Subject to time?

B: Don't press me. Up till now our formal analysis has only supported my reading, hasn't it?

A: Wait till it tips over.

B: Show me.

A: The poem's first word is "I", but after less than one and a half lines, the "I" hands over to the traveller. The rest of the poem is in inverted commas, direct speech as recorded by the "I".

B: Agreed, the description is the traveller's.

A: It's not only a description. In part it's also an *interpretation*, it's a *reading* of the statue and its surroundings, its context. The traveller understands the frown, the wrinkled lip, the sneer as clearly and indubitably expressive of the despot's inward passions and applauds the sculptor for his skill. But certainly those very same facial expressions cannot have displayed the same meaning at the time the statue was sculptured.

B: Otherwise Ozymandias would have had the sculptor decapitated, or whatever the capital punishment was for sculptors in ancient Egypt.

A: Exactly so. The truth of the representation is one that wasn't obvious *at the time*, it came out *in the course of time.*

B: We've had this before.

A: It's a recurrent figure in this poem: Truth isn't something that is there and given, truth is something that *reveals itself* in a *process.* It comes out and then you see it. Truth isn't something that lies *in the beginning*, truth is something that is discovered, truth evolves, truth ripens. It is realized it time. Truth lies *at the end.* It's a bit like Gadamer: The full meaning of the text lies in the future.

B: Will it ever arrive?

A: Let's talk origins first. Ozymandias decreed the statue ...

B: In ancient Thebes did ...

A: ... and ordered the sculptor to chisel his words into the pedestal. Spoken language into writing.

B: Just like the traveller's report in the poem: spoken words taken down.

A: Because only when spoken language is recorded does it have the chance to survive. Ozy's no dupe. The spoken word perishes. Writing takes the word out of time, preserves it.

B: If we pick up the monument/poem-analogy and generalize, it means that art survives power. Ozymandias' reign is long passed but the statue, albeit broken, is still there.

A: But the "albeit broken" is of supreme importance. Think of the poem's mock ruin structure. Art isn't out of time, it's subject to it, like power. It's more permanent, but not absolutely so. We're not dealing with a dyad – art vs. power – but with a triad: power – art – nature. The poem makes every effort, contentwise and formally, if you like, to make this point: the pen (or chisel) is mightier than the sword, but no match for erosion, no match for the processes of time. "Ozymandias" is about the transience of despotism, but it doesn't follow that therefore it must celebrate the permanence of art. Time defeats tyrants, yet art defeats time – that complacent message is certainly *not* the message of "Ozymandias". Its artefacts are too markedly time-worn.

B: But why then your harping on the twice-over transformation of spoken word into writing? It seems to be a conspicuous movement, Chinese-box-like, or, seen from the other end, like telescoping: Ozymandias' spoken words are chiseled into stone, then reported, in spoken language, by the traveller, before his account is likewise written down by the "I".

A: Remember that you said, or implied, the core of the poem was in the ironic reversal of the meaning of the word "despair"? How could it come about? What was the essential precondition? I'll tell thee: *that it was written down.* Only because it was written down it could be de-temporalized, taken out of its original context and – ironically, by time – be inserted into another one in which it acquired its secondary, "true", ironic meaning. It's a paradoxical double-gesture: Writing preserves, but at the same time, since through preservation it is then subjected to new contexts, it doesn't preserve at all, it changes, and it changes drastically. And don't forget: Twice it changes *for the better*, as it were, because twice the supposedly "real" meaning – of the features, of the inscription – comes out. Written words are subject to new contexts, the poem seems to say, and adds: and that is a good thing.

B: But then "Ozymandias" is deeply and irretrievably paradoxical. It says that written texts have no stable meanings and never could have, because as long as they exist they can and inevitably will be inserted into new contexts. But since "Ozymandias" is itself a written text ...

A: It even highlights its mode of being by those inverted commas: it's demonstratively spoken word *set down.*

B: ... it makes a statement about itself. It is self-referential not only in the Jakobsonian sense that it draws attention to itself and to the way it is written but also in the more rigorous *logical* sense: It is a statement about a class of statements of which it is itself a member. It's about itself. Its message is that written texts can have no stable messages. It paradoxically or ironically undercuts itself. By pointing to the fact that it is only *provisional*, it negates its own stability and definiteness. It's *a temporary gesture, deferring its ultimate meaning.*

A (*serenely*): Welcome to the club. Will you teach that?

BREAK

B: Is it "teachable"?

A: Depends on what you understand by "teaching". If you're looking for neat messages that can be extracted from the poem and held up for inspection, you'd be far better off with all those 18th-century ruin poems with their open didacticism and their explicit moralization.[15] There you can find what you first proposed to be the 'message' of "Ozymandias". Compared to them, "Ozymandias" as we have read it now, isn't teachable, because it refuses to make such an unambiguous statement. The one aspect in which it differs most from its tradition – because it's written both *in* and *against* the tradition of the ruin poem, just as it is written *in* and *against* the tradition of the sonnet – is exactly that it withholds its message.

B: It works by implication only.

A: It works by implication only and can't do otherwise, because otherwise it would fall behind its own insight into its essential temporality and provisionality.

B: Its irony is deeply Romantic then?

A: It is. Not the irony of "despair", that's simply situational. But the self-reflexive irony of the text knowing and performing its own limitations, that is, yes.

B: Again: Can it be taught?

A: I believe poetry is "essentially" non-teachable, or more precisely: to the degree that a poetic text is poetical, it cannot be "taught", if teaching means: using it in order to show something, reifying the text in order to produce "correct" readings which can then be reproduced (and marked) in examination papers.[16] It's Ozymandias' mistake: to try and stabilize texts, to erect a monument, to want to keep and hold something. Wrong from the start. It's a question of power, too, just as in the case of Ozymandias. Poetry, at its best, is the kind of writing that refuses this treatment. In a very technical, non-Romantic sense it is elusive, evasive und knowingly performs its precarious mode of being. Therefore, to use it in order to dispel notions like "poetry is fuzzy", "the message of a poem is not palpable" etc., is – to misquote Milton – "to kill poetry, as it were, in the eye". If it's poetry, you can't teach it; if you do, it's no longer poetry. You miss its defining quality. It escapes you. And, what is worse, you're systematically misleading dependents.

B: But what keeps you from teaching *that*? What keeps you from showing that poetry works like that? It would still be teaching, wouldn't it?

A: It's a question of precedence. There isn't anything that could reasonably be said about "Ozymandias" that the poem doesn't already say or display itself. It's tautological to say so.

B: Sacra scriptura sui ipsius interpres?

A: Who was it that said that "Ozymandias" speaks for itself and needs no intermediaries? It wasn't *me*, was it? – The poem is always already *there*. You cannot overtake it. You can try and trace it, but you're always following a movement that has already been performed and continues to happen. You can only point out this motion, this temporary gesture.

B: But this pointing out would still be a kind of teaching. You'd make that poem more accessible.

A: I wouldn't. I'd only teach inaccessible poems and point out in which particular way they are inaccessible. I'd trace their withdrawal, the deferral of meaning, their paradoxical status. Pursuing this end, it goes without saying that I'd only "teach" *non-teachable poems*, the only kind of poetry that is worth talking about.

B: You sound like the last high-priest of Modernism.

A: I am, dear friend, I am. But still I'll be mistaken for a deconstructionist.

B: You puzzle me endlessly. But I refuse to be appeased. *You'd still be teaching.*

A: You know, "teachable poems" suggests to me there are poems which can be made amenable to teaching – and others which are less suitable (or malleable), and you question the poems which side they're on. Now in my case, *it's the poetry that questions the teaching.* The problem is not to find a poem that fits your teaching or which can be made to fit your teaching, but how to *widen* your teaching so that it opens up a space where poetry can happen. Is your teaching up to the poetry? Is it large enough to encompass it? These are the decisive questions. Is your teaching open, open-minded, flexible, responsive enough? Or does it lag behind in any of these respects? The question is not the teaching of poetry but, quite the reverse, *how to poeticize teaching.*

B: A Romantic programme.

A: Call it what you will. The best poem is one that can't be taught – no matter whether it's fringe or mainstream (just like I've always held that it's not *what's* on the canon but rather *what's done with it once it's there* that matters). And the "teaching it" would consist in the showing that this is so – that it can't be done – *daß der Text uns über ist.* "Look on my *Works*, ye Mighty, and despair!" This showing will, of course, always be more of a dialogue – text/reader, teacher/student than the usual classroom subjection.

B (mumbling to himself): With him, it's sometimes hard to tell the difference. (*Slyly*) Much like this dialogue?

A: Pretty much so, I suppose.

B: Except that this is only between you and me.

A: It always is, my friend, it always is.

Notes

1 The text is the one given in D.H. Reiman, S.B. Powers (Eds.): *Shelley's Poetry and Prose. Authoritative Texts, Criticism.* New York, London, 1977. For an informative discussion of textual variants see K. Everest: "'Ozymandias'".
2 See also ibid., p. 25: "Its length, and the accessible directness with which its irony appears to work, make it ideal for study in schools."
3 G.C. Martin: "Look on my Words", p. 65.
4 Ibid., p. 66.
5 Cf. R. Holmes: *Shelley*, p. 410.
6 Quoted in A. Janowitz: "Shelley's Monument", p. 480.
7 There is a comprehensive bibliography of the debate in A. Janowitz: "Shelley's Monument", p. 489, fn. 3, and an excellent overview over the present state of the art in M.A. Quinn: "'Ozymandias'", p. 49, fn. 1.
8 J. Parr: "Shelley's *Ozymandias*", p. 35.
9 H.M. Richmond: "Ozymandias and the Travelers", p. 71.
10 Quoted ibid., p. 68.
11 A. Janowitz: "Shelley's Monument", p. 481.
12 Obviously, A. is here heavily indebted to Janowitz' excellent article on "Ozymandias", the best, along with William Freedman's, to have appeared in decades.
13 Compare M.K. Bequette: "Shelley and Smith".
14 The most extensive "formal" analysis so far can be found in K. Everest: "'Ozymandias'", pp. 26ff.
15 Cf. A. Janowitz: "Shelley's Monument", pp. 478, 483ff.
16 The classic essay on this aspect is, of course, H.M. Enzensberger's "Ein bescheidener Vorschlag zum Schutze der Jugend vor den Erzeugnissen der Poesie".

Bequette, M.K.: "Shelley and Smith: Two Sonnets on Ozymandias". *Keats-Shelley-Journal* 26, 1977, 29-31.
Enzensberger, H.M.: "Ein bescheidener Vorschlag zum Schutze der Jugend vor den Erzeugnissen der Poesie". *päd.extra* 18/19, 1976, 34-36.
Everest, K.: "'Ozymandias': The Text in Time". – In idem (Ed.): *Percy Bysshe Shelley. Bicentenary Essays.* Woodbridge/Suffolk, Rochester/New York, 1992, pp. 24-42.
Freedman, W.: "Postponement and Perspectives in Shelley's 'Ozymandias'". *Studies in Romanticism* 25, 1986, 63-73.
Griffiths, J.G.: "Shelley's 'Ozymandias' and Diodorus Siculus". *Modern Language Review* 43, 1948, 80-84.
Hall, J.: *The Transforming Image. A Study of Shelley's Major Poetry.* Urbana, Chicago, London, 1980.
Holmes, R.: *Shelley. The Pursuit.* London, 1976.
Janowitz, A.: "Shelley's Monument to Ozymandias". *Philological Quarterly* 63, 1984, 477-491.
Lengeler, R.: "Shelley's Sonett 'Ozymandias'". *Die Neueren Sprachen* 68, 1969, 532-539.
Martin, G.C.: "Look on my Words, ye Mighty, But Don't Despair: Teaching 'Ozymandias'". – In Hall S. (Ed.): *Approaches to Teaching Shelley's Poetry.* New York, 1990, pp. 65-66.
Notopoulos, J.A.: "Shelley's 'Ozymandias' Once Again". *Modern Language Review* 48, 1953, 440-443.
Parr, J.: "Shelley's 'Ozymandias' Again". *Modern Language Review* 46, 1951, 441-442.
–: "Shelley's *Ozymandias*". *Keats-Shelley-Journal* 6, 1957, 31-35.
Quinn, M.A.: "'Ozymandias' as Shelley's Rejoinder to Peacock's 'Palmyra'". *English Language Notes* 21, 1984, 48-56.
Richmond, H.M.: "Ozymandias and the Travelers". *Keats-Shelley-Journal* 11, 1962, 65-70.
Shelley, P.B.: *Shelley's Poetry and Prose. Authoritative Texts, Criticism.* Eds. D.H. Reiman, S.B. Powers. New York, London, 1977.
Thompson, D.W.: "Ozymandias". *Philological Quarterly* 16, 1937, 59-64.

Peter Wenzel, Bochum/Bayreuth

Be Prepared: Das Sonett

1. Gründe für die Wahl als Examensgegenstand

"I intended an Ode;/ But Rose crossed the road/ In her latest new bonnet;/ I intended an Ode;/ And it turned to a Sonnet", so heißt es scherzhaft in einem kleinen Gedicht des Spätviktorianers Austin Dobson.[1] Auch den Examenskandidaten, die infolge eines ähnlichen Schicksals bei ihrer Suche und Sichtung geeigneter Themengebiete unter Zeitdruck geraten, kann man raten, wie Dobson von einem zunächst anvisierten umfangreicheren Projekt auf das verlockend kurze Sonett umzusteigen, denn ein Korpus von 35 bis 40 Sonetten, wie es vielerorts im Examen verlangt wird, liest sich nun einmal schneller als ein umfangreiches Romangebiet von mehreren tausend Seiten, und man kann die gesparte Zeit gut in die intensivere Vorbereitung der einzelnen Texte investieren.

Der Examensgegenstand 'Sonett' bietet aber nicht nur gegenüber allzu umfangreichen Prosathemen, sondern auch gegenüber anderen Lyrikgebieten besondere Vorteile. Sonette zeichnen sich durch ihre klare Strukturierung aus. In überschaubare Sinnabschnitte gegliedert stellen sie ein System aus Gleichungen und Ungleichungen dar. Stärker als bei anderen Formen der Lyrik kann man seine Analyse beim Sonett daher an der äußeren Struktur und den hilfreichen Entsprechungen zwischen dieser Struktur und dem Gehalt orientieren.

Ein Vorzug ist schließlich, daß Sonette in fast allen Epochen der englischen Literaturgeschichte geschrieben worden sind. Die Beschäftigung mit dem so knappen Texttyp des Sonetts kann deshalb paradoxerweise ein breiteres Überblickswissen vermitteln als die Auseinandersetzung mit den meisten übrigen literaturwissenschaftlichen Spezialgebieten.

2. Die Struktur des Sonetts

2.1 Ein Beispiel

Die strukturellen und ästhetischen Attraktionen des Sonetts sollen hier an einem Text verdeutlicht werden, der als Sonett über das Sonett den Vorzug hat, diese Attraktionen selbst zu thematisieren. Obwohl der Text nicht besonders bekannt und in seiner Reimstruktur nicht besonders typisch ist – ein in seiner Form völlig typisches Sonett kann es ob der großen Wandlungsfähigkeit der Gattung ohnehin nicht geben -, ist er auch in formaler Hinsicht von besonderem Interesse, da er auf alle drei in der englischen Geschichte der Gattung wichtigen Reimschemata zurückgreift und sie zum Zweck einer geschickten Strukturierung des Gehalts miteinander verbindet.

The Sonnet

	VR	PeR		ShR	SpR
There are who say the sonnet's meted maze	a	a		a	a
Is all too fettered for the poet's powers,	b	b		b	b
Compelled to crowd his flush and airy flowers	b	b		a	a
Like pots of tall imperials, ill at ease.	c	a		b	b
Or should some tiny thought his fancy seize,	c	a		c	b
A violet on a vase's top it towers,	b	b		d	c
And mid the mass of leaves he round it showers	b	b		c	b
Its little cap and tippet scarce can raise.	a	a		d	c
Others assert the sonnet's proper praise,	a	c	c	e	c
Like petalled flowers to each its due degree;	d	d	d	f	d
The king-cup five, the pilewort eight bright rays,	a	e	c	e	c
The speedwell four, the green-tipped snowdrop three:	d	c	d	f	d
So mid the bard's all-petalled sorts is seen	e	d	c	g	e
The sonnet - simple flowret of fourteen.	e	e	d	g	e

John F.M. Dovaston (1825)[2]

V.R. = Vorliegendes Reimschema / Pe.R. = Petrarkisches (oder: italienisches) Reimschema / Sh.R. = Shakespearesches (oder: englisches) Reimschema / Sp.R. = Spensersches Reimschema

Vor allem wegen seiner zahlreichen Pflanzennamen konfrontiert das Sonett den Leser zunächst einmal mit einer Reihe von Vokabelproblemen, die nur mit Hilfe eines größeren Lexikons, wenn nicht gar nur mit Hilfe eines historischen Wörterbuchs wie des *OED*, gelöst werden können ("meted maze" = wohlabgemessener Irrgarten; "flush" = [hier:] übervoll blühend; "imperials"[3] = Kaiserkronen [eine stattliche, mit den Lilien verwandte Pflanzenart]; "ill at ease" = sich nicht wohlfühlend; "tippet" = Pelzkragen; "king-cup" = Sumpfdotterblume; "pilewort" = Scharbockskraut; "speedwell" = Ehrenpreis; "snowdrop" = Schneeglöckchen). Selbst wenn dem Leser einige dieser Vokabeln fehlen, ist der grobe Sinnzusammenhang des Gedichts wegen seines sonettypischen sehr symmetrischen Aufbaus leicht zu durchschauen: Im ersten Quartett - also in den ersten vier durch das Reimschema gebündelten Zeilen - geht es um die These, die Sonettform sei zu eng für die Einfälle des Dichters - so wie die Blumentöpfe für die stattlichen Kaiserkronen. Das zweite Quartett wiederholt den Grundgedanken von der Unangemessenheit der Sonettform, jedoch mit dem umgekehrten Argument: Für einen kurzen Gedanken, der die Vorstellungskraft ("fancy") des Dichters ergreift, ist das

Sonett möglicherweise zu lang – so wie die Vase für das Veilchen, das deshalb mit einer großen Anzahl wertloser Blätter zu einem stabilen Halt gebracht werden muß. Das dritte Quartett und das Couplet stellen schließlich die Antithese zu den vorausgehenden Behauptungen auf: Das Sonett mit seinen vierzehn Zeilen hat genau die richtige Länge – so wie auch jede der genannten Pflanzenarten eine ganz bestimmte, arteigene Anzahl von Blütenblättern hat.

Der besondere ästhetische Reiz des vorgestellten Sonetts liegt nun darin, daß es dem Dichter gelungen ist, sein in drei Schritten vorgetragenes Plädoyer für die Sonettform nicht nur mit der Blumenmetaphorik, sondern auch mit der Reimstruktur in eine geschickt konstruierte Übereinstimmung zu bringen. Das Reimschema des Textes – abbc/cbba/adad/ee – weist dabei sowohl Elemente des sogenannten petrarkischen (oder: italienischen) als auch des shakespeareschen (oder: englischen) sowie des daraus abgeleiteten spenserschen Grundtyps auf (vgl. oben). In Übereinstimmung mit dem petrarkischen Typ gliedert sich das Sonett in eine von umschließenden Reimen geprägte Oktave und einen von alternierenden Reimen geprägten Schlußteil, der hier allerdings nicht wie in den beiden möglichen Varianten des petrarkischen Sextetts über sechs, sondern nur über vier Zeilen durchgehalten wird und dann – in Übereinstimmung mit dem shakespeareschen Typ – in ein *couplet*, also einen Paarreim, übergeht. Der Gegensatz zwischen der am petrarkischen Reimschema orientierten Oktave und dem dem shakespeareschen Reimschema folgenden zweiten Teil des Sonetts spiegelt dabei formal die thematische Grundopposition zwischen der These von der Unangemessenheit und der Angemessenheit der Sonettform wider. Auch die zweite, in der Oktave vorgetragene Opposition des Gedichts – nämlich die im ersten Quartett referierte These, das Sonett sei zu kurz, und die im zweiten Quartett vertretene These, das Sonett sei zu lang für die Einfälle des Dichters – findet auf der Ebene des Reimschemas eine sinnfällige Entsprechung, stellt doch das Reimschema des zweiten Quartetts – cbba – die genaue Umkehrung des Reimschemas des ersten Quartetts – abbc – dar.

Unser Textbeispiel weist neben den genannten Mitteln zur deutlichen Untergliederung seiner Struktur aber auch Elemente auf, die seine Sinnabschnitte miteinander verknüpfen, und zwar wiederum sowohl auf der Ebene des Gehalts als auch auf der der Form. Ebenso wie auf der Ebene des Gehalts die Blumenmetaphorik das gesamte Gedicht durchzieht und ihm Kontinuität verleiht, haben auf der Ebene der Form der nach dem Vorbild Spensers konstruierte quartettübergreifende Paarreim sowie der in allen drei Quartetten wiederauftauchende Reim a (“maze”, “raise”, “praise” and “rays”) eine verbindende Funktion. Trennende und verbindende Elemente stehen somit sowohl auf der Ebene des Gehalts als auch auf der der Form in einem ausgewogenen Verhältnis zueinander. Die für das Verständnis des Sonetts so hilfreichen Entsprechungen von Gehalt und Form setzen sich schließlich auch in den letzten beiden Zeilen fort, denn wie die durch das schlußfolgernde "so" eingeleitete Zusammenfassung dient auch der abschließende Paarreim einer deutlichen Markierung des Schlusses des Gedichts.

2.2 Möglichkeiten der Füllung der Form

Die Analyse von Dovastons Blumensonett macht in exemplarischer Weise klar, worauf es bei der Beschäftigung mit Sonetten ankommt: Es gilt, die durch Analogien von Gehalt und Form gekennzeichnete Struktur des Textes, die in ihr enthaltenen Symmetrien und Asymmetrien sowie den darauf gestützten Argumentationsgang zu entschlüsseln. Dabei können die verschiedenen, oben bereits angesprochenen Reimschemata von Sonett zu Sonett ein formaler Rahmen für sehr verschiedene Argumentationsmuster sein. Der petrarkische Typ z.B. eignet sich besonders zu einer Gegenüberstellung dyadischer Einheiten wie Frage und Antwort, These und Antithese, allgemeiner Wahrheit und personenbezogener Applikation. Das shakespearesche Schema hingegen ist noch flexibler, da es einen Text außer in zwei auch in drei oder vier Sinneinheiten gliedern kann (wie z.B. These-Antithese-Synthese, Vergangenheit-Gegenwart-Zukunft, oft mit einem zugespitzten resümierenden oder antithetischen Schluß). Da die Strukturen von Gehalt und Form schließlich nicht in jedem Fall völlig deckungsgleich sein müssen, sondern – vor allem bei neueren, aus den letzten zwei Jahrhunderten stammenden Sonetten – auch in ein Spannungsverhältnis zueinander treten können, darf die jeweilige äußere Form nicht das allein maßgebliche Kriterium für die analytische Erfassung eines Sonetts sein, auch wenn sie gewiß immer von Bedeutung ist.

3. Die Geschichte des Sonetts

Da das Sonett in fast allen Epochen der englischen Literaturgeschichte anzutreffen ist, kann man sich bei der Examensvorbereitung leicht verlieren, wenn man seine Betrachtung des Gegenstands nicht auf einen bestimmten Zeitraum beschränkt. Andererseits sollte der Betrachtungszeitraum auch nicht zu eng gesteckt werden, weil sich sonst nicht genügend Möglichkeiten für Vergleiche und Kontraste finden. In der Regel empfiehlt es sich daher, die Geschichte des Sonetts entweder von den Elisabethanern bis zu den *metaphysical poets* oder von den Romantikern bis zur Gegenwart zu verfolgen. Aber natürlich sind auch andere, engere (z.B.: nur die Shakespearesonette) oder etwas weitere (z.B.: die genannten Zeiträume unter Einbezug einzelner Sonette aus dem Neoklassizismus) Abgrenzungen möglich.

3.1 Das elisabethanische Sonett

Von Dichtern am Hof Friedrichs II. auf Sizilien um 1230 eingeführt und bald in ganz Italien zu einer beliebten poetischen Form avanciert, wird das Sonett durch Francesco Petrarcas Gedichtsammlung *Canzoniere* (1327-1348), die einen modellhaften Zyklus von über 300 Liebessonetten enthält, auch in ganz Europa bekannt. Nachdem die Sonette Petrarcas in England zunächst von zwei adligen Diplomaten, Sir Thomas Wyatt (1503-1542) und Henry Howard, Earl of Surrey (1517-1547) nachgeahmt worden sind, kommt es dort in den Jahren von 1580 bis 1600 zu einer wahrhaften Flut von Sonettzyklen, unter denen die von Sir Philip Sidney, Edmund Spenser und William Shakespeare die berühmtesten sind. Die englischen Dichter (seit Surrey) modifizieren allerdings das Reimschema des Sonetts in der oben abgebildeten Weise, weil das petrarkische Schema zu viele gleichlautende Reime erfordert, die im Englischen schwer zu finden sind.

Allen elisabethanischen Sonettdichtern als Vorbild dient die von Petrarca entworfene Liebeskonzeption, die sich aus folgenden Grundmerkmalen zusammensetzt: (1) Der petrarkische Liebhaber wendet sich an eine von ihm verehrte Dame, die von (2) idealer Schönheit (mit bestimmten, in den Sonetten meist stereotyp wiederholten Merkmalen: *white skin*, *rosy cheeks and lips*, *a ruby-red mouth*, *lily-like hands and golden hair*) und (3) engelhafter Tugend und Keuschheit ist (so daß, dem bei den Elisabethanern beliebten Analogiedenken entsprechend, die äußere Schönheit der Dame letztlich nur ein Abbild der inneren Schönheit ist). Eben wegen dieser Tugendhaftigkeit kann die Dame jedoch (4) den um sie werbenden Dichter nicht erhören; sie zeigt sich vielmehr kühl und abweisend und treibt (5) den Dichter damit in eine tiefe Verzweiflung, für die es in der petrarkistischen Lyrik Bilder wie das der Gefangenschaft oder des Todes gibt.

Einen besonders engen Bezug weist die Konzeption des Petrarkismus zu dem noch aus dem Mittelalter stammenden elisabethanischen Weltbild auf, nach dem alle Bereiche der kosmischen, gesellschaftlichen und individuellen Existenz die eine, stets mit sich identische göttliche Ordnung widerspiegeln. Denn die verehrte Dame ist als schöner und tugendhafter Mensch ein idealer Seinsspiegel - nicht nur ein Abbild der himmlischen, göttlichen Schönheit, sondern auch ein wichtiges Bindeglied zwischen dieser und den materiellen Schönheiten der Welt. Das für das elisabethanische Weltbild so typische Analogiedenken äußert sich überdies in den häufigen, oft zu ganzen Bildketten ausgebauten Metaphern und Vergleichen der elisabethanischen Sonette[4], z.T. sogar in einem auch formal strikt parallelen Aufbau der Zeilen (parallele oder kontrastive Aufzählungen in jeder Zeile).

Die fünf oben genannten Merkmale der petrarkistischen Liebeskonzeption werden von den elisabethanischen Dichtern allerdings oft nur teilweise in ihr jeweiliges Sonett umgesetzt – es wird z.B. nur die Schönheit einer Geliebten oder nur deren grausame Kühle oder nur die Verzweiflung des Liebhabers beschrieben -, so daß der Leser die übrigen Elemente aus seinem Wissen um die vollständige Konzeption ergänzen muß. Überdies benutzen viele elisabethanische Dichter die petrarkistische Konvention nur noch als Aufhänger für die Behandlung eines realitätsnäheren Themas (also z.B.: Gefangenschaft in der Liebe als Abbild realer Gefangenschaft, Zwiespalt der Gefühle als Abbild von Zwiespalt in der Gesellschaft) oder beginnen sogar, die petrarkistische Konvention zu parodieren.

Eine starke Modifikation des petrarkistischen Modells ist auch für die 154 Sonette[5] Shakespeares typisch, von denen der erste, größere Teil (Nr. 1-126) an einen jungen Mann, den sogenannten 'Freund', und der zweite (Nr. 127-154) an eine weder besonders schöne noch besonders tugendhafte dunkelhaarige Frau, die sogenannte *dark lady*, gerichtet ist. Durch diese Änderung des Adressaten wird die Thematisierung zahlreicher neuer Aspekte einer Liebesbeziehung möglich, die im engen Rahmen des Petrarkismus nicht behandelt werden konnten. Solche Aspekte sind – mit Blick auf den Freund – die Gegenseitigkeit, Partnerschaftlichkeit und Treue der Liebe, aber auch ihre Gefährdung durch einen Rivalen (in den Sonetten Nr. 78-86) und durch die vergehende Zeit. Hinzu kommt die Reflexion über die verschiedenen Möglichkeiten der Bewahrung der Schönheit des Geliebten – wie das Zeugen von Nachkommenschaft (Thema der sogenannten *procreation sonnets*, Nr. 1-17) und das Verfassen von ihn preisenden Gedichten. Mit Blick auf die dunkle Dame ergeben sich als neue Themen Aspekte wie die Sexualität und Triebhaftigkeit der Liebe mit dem daraus resultierenden Konflikt zwischen Emotionalität und Vernunft. Schließlich heben sich die Sonette Shakespeares auch durch eine viel kühnere Sprache, insbesondere durch eine komplexe Metaphorik und eine oft elliptische Syntax, von den Sonetten der übrigen Elisabethaner ab.

3.2 Das Sonett in der metaphysischen Dichtung

Von den sogenannten *metaphysical poets*, also den Dichtern der ersten Hälfte des 17. Jahrhunderts, haben nur die beiden wichtigsten, John Donne (1572-1631) und George Herbert (1593-1633), einen bedeutenden Beitrag zur Weiterentwicklung des Sonetts geleistet. Dies gelang ihnen, indem sie – noch im Einklang mit dem alten Korrespondenzdenken, wonach die weltlichen Verhältnisse nur ein Spiegel der höheren, göttlichen Ordnung sind – das Modell der petrarkistischen Liebe auf die religiöse Thematik der Gottesliebe übertrugen. An die Stelle des sich in seiner Leidenschaft verzehrenden Liebhabers tritt somit der nach Gott suchende Dichter, und wie das petrarkistische Sonett eine Anrede des Liebhabers an die von ihm verehrte Dame ist, so ist das metaphysische Sonett eine Anrede des Dichters an den von ihm geliebten Gott. In beiden Fällen geht es um die vollständige Hingabe des Liebenden an das verherrlichte Objekt seiner Liebe, den Adressaten des Sonetts, gleichzeitig aber auch um die den Liebenden bedrückende Furcht, die ersehnte Verbindung nicht erreichen zu können. Der Grund für diese Furcht liegt bei den *metaphysical poets* freilich auf einer anderen Ebene als noch bei den Petrarkisten - nicht mehr in der kühlen Unzugänglichkeit des begehrten Objekts, sondern in der Schwäche und Sündhaftigkeit des Liebenden selbst.

Dabei ist John Donne der in seinen Selbstzweifeln radikalere und in seinem Glauben weniger gefestigte Dichter. In den sprachlichen Unregelmäßigkeiten seiner Sonette - ihren abrupten, einem verzweifelten Appell nahekommenden Anfängen, ihren Paradoxa, Oxymora, kühnen Analogien und *conceits* (d.h.: weithergeholten Metaphern oder Vergleichen mit einer nur minimalen Entsprechung zwischen dem Gemeinten und dem dafür gesetzten Bild[6]), ihrer von vielen Auslassungen geprägten Syntax und ihrer dem Rhythmus der Umgangssprache angenäherten, unregelmäßigen Metrik - spiegelt sich eine für das gesamte Zeitalter der ausgehenden Renaissance typische geistige Verunsicherung. Deren Ursachen sind nicht nur die in den Literaturgeschichten oft genannten neuen Entdeckungen in Geographie und Astronomie mit der daraus resultierenden Krise des Weltbilds, sondern auch die religiösen Spannungen der Zeit, die der Suche des einzelnen Menschen nach dem wahren Glauben ein viel stärkeres und problematischeres Gewicht geben mußten als in Epochen konfessioneller Einmütigkeit.

Allenfalls von ihrer Datierung, aber keineswegs von ihren charakteristischen Merkmalen her gehören die Sonette John Miltons (1608-1674) noch in diese Zeit, denn sie unterscheiden sich sowohl durch traditionellere, schon bei den italienischen Humanisten anzutreffende Themen (Politik, moralischer Appell, Lobpreis von Freunden) als auch durch eine viel ruhigere Form (Rückgriff auf das petrarkische Reimschema, viele *run-on lines*) deutlich von den Sonetten der *metaphysical poets*.

3.3 Das Sonett im Zeitalter des Neo-Klassizismus und in der Romantik

Das Zeitalter des Neo-Klassizismus, also die Periode von etwa 1660 bis 1800[7], ist die einzige Epoche der englischen Literaturgeschichte, in der das Sonett ohne besondere Bedeutung geblieben ist. Der Grund dafür ist wiederum in den Idealen des Weltbilds der Epoche zu suchen, namentlich in den Paradigmen der Vernunft und der vollständigen Symmetrie, die sich in längeren, streng nach dem Prinzip der Binarität gestalteten Gedichten (vorzugsweise einer Abfolge von *couplets* mit strikt parallelistischer Syntax) viel besser realisieren ließen als in einer Form wie dem Sonett, das ja vom Widerspiel zwischen symmetrischen und asymmetrischen Elementen lebt. Sonette aus der Epoche des Neo-Klassizismus erweisen sich daher bei genauerem Hinsehen auch meist als übertrieben symmetrische Gebilde, in denen die Zweizeiligkeit ein wichtigeres Strukturprinzip ist als die Gliederung in Quartette (eine Tendenz, die bis zu einem gewissen Grade auch in dem bereits behandelten Blumensonett von Dovaston zu erkennen ist).

Ob der Sonettfeindlichkeit des Neo-Klassizismus erscheint es nur konsequent, daß sich die Romantiker als Dichter der nächsten, gegen die Konventionen des Klassizismus gerichteten Epoche (ca. 1800-1830) erneut dem Sonett zugewandt haben, obwohl das Sonett als eine Struktur mit fester Länge und weitgehend festen Reimschemata den romantischen Idealen der Spontaneität und der Freiheit der dichterischen Form eigentlich völlig zuwiderläuft. Da es den Romantikern aber gelang, die Sonettform – in der bereits von Milton aufgezeigten Weise – durch die Einführung von *run-on-lines* und durch den verstärkten Rückgriff auf das petrarkische Reimschema flexibler als in früheren Epochen zu gestalten, konnten sowohl William Wordsworth (1770-1850) und Samuel Taylor Coleridge (1772-1834) als die wichtigsten älteren wie auch Percy Bysshe Shelley (1792-1822) und John Keats (1795-1821) als die wichtigsten jüngeren Vertreter der Romantik der Gattung zu einer neuen Blüte verhelfen.

Zu den möglichen Themen ihrer Sonette zählen alle typischen Motive der Romantik – also vor allem die Natur (die jetzt nicht mehr, wie bei den Elisabethanern und selbst noch bei den Neo-Klassizisten, als ein statischer Spiegel der kosmischen Ordnung, sondern als ein dynamischer Organismus betrachtet wird, in dessen wilde Schönheit sich der Mensch mit seiner Vorstellungskraft hineinversetzen und an der er seine Gefühle schulen kann), ferner die Fähigkeit des Menschen zur Imagination und zur Introspektion, seine Freiheit, sein Glück in der Kindheit oder in einer einsamen, gesellschaftsfernen Situation, aber auch (vor allem bei den jüngeren Romantikern) seine unerfüllten Sehnsüchte, seine Ängste und inneren Konflikte. Zwischen der Natur und den Gefühlen des Menschen wird dabei meist ein enger Bezug hergestellt, sei es dadurch, daß Elemente der Natur zum Auslöser oder gar zum Bildspender für religiöse Gefühle und menschliche Werte werden, sei es daß umgekehrt die Natur selbst in einer personifizierenden Metaphorik beschrieben wird. Eine besonders geeignete Methode zur Analyse romantischer Sonette ist daher die Suche nach sogenannten *patterns of meaning*, strukturbildenden Bedeutungsmustern, die als *pattern of nature*, *pattern of religion*, *pattern of light* oder *pattern of night and darkness* das gesamte Sonett durchziehen und in einem Verhältnis der Entsprechung oder des Gegensatzes zueinander stehen.

3.4 Das Sonett bei den Viktorianern und in der Moderne

Der häufig gegen die Dichter der viktorianischen Epoche (ca. 1830-1900) erhobene Vorwurf des Epigonentums hat ohne Frage auch im Hinblick auf die Geschichte des Sonetts seine Berechtigung, setzen doch die meisten viktorianischen Sonette die oben genannten Themen der Romantik fort. Neu ist allerdings, vor allem in den Sonetten von Elizabeth Barrett Browning (1806-1861) und Christina Rossetti (1830-1894), die Rückkehr zum Thema der Liebe, und auch wenn die viktorianischen Liebessonette – im Falle Brownings wegen struktureller Schwächen, im Falle Rossettis wegen ihrer übertriebenen Sentimentalität – gewiß nicht zu den Meisterwerken der englischen Lyrik zählen, können sie zumindest als Objekte der kritischen Auseinandersetzung für die Aufnahme in das zusammenzustellende Textkorpus geeignet sein.

Bei der Auswahl der für die Moderne typischen Sonette steht man vor der Schwierigkeit, daß es hier kaum noch gemeinsame, für alle Werke der Epoche charakteristische Themen und Strukturmerkmale, sondern nur noch den auch für andere Bereiche der modernen Literatur typischen Pluralismus gibt. Es lassen sich aber zumindest einige Autoren und Autorengruppen nennen, deren Sonette von solcher Wichtigkeit sind, daß sie sich für die Bildung eines größeren Schwerpunkts in dem zusammenzustellenden Korpus eignen, nämlich: 1. Gerard Manley Hopkins (1844-1889), seinen Lebensdaten nach ein Viktorianer und in der Thematik (Verknüpfung von Natur und Religion) noch ein Nachfahre der Romantik, ob seiner äußerst eigenwilligen, zu extremer Verknappung tendierenden Sprache – mit vielen kühnen Metaphern und Neologismen und einem besonderen Rhythmus, der nur die betonten, nicht aber die unbetonten Silben zählt (*sprung rhythm*) – jedoch ein wichtiger Erneuerer des Sonetts; 2. die stilistisch sehr konventionellen, aber wegen ihrer Thematik interessanten Kriegsdichter Rupert Brooke, Wilfred Owen, Siegfried Sassoon, Edmund Blunden und Charles Hamilton Sorley; 3. W.H. Auden (1907-1973), der sich in seinen Sonetten ebenfalls mit Krieg und Politik sowie mit universalen Themen wie der Entwicklung der Menschheit befaßt[8], aber auch in stilistischer Hinsicht ein moderner Dichter ist; 4. der Amerikaner E.E. Cummings (1894-1962), der die stilistische Kühnheit eines Gerard Manley Hopkins noch einen Schritt weiter treibt und von extremen lexikalischen und grammatischen Deviationen geprägte Sonette schreibt, deren zunächst völlig rätselhaft erscheinende Bedeutung durch eine konsequente Analyse ihrer semantischen *patterns* schließlich doch entschlüsselt werden kann.

4. Hinweise zur Literatur und zu Techniken der Vorbereitung

4.1 Zur Erschließung der Gattung und einzelner Epochen

Die Auswahl des eigenen Textkorpus erleichtern die in der Auswahlbibliographie genannten, zum Teil ausführlich kommentierten Anthologien. Über die äußere Form des Sonetts und die verschiedenen Möglichkeiten ihrer strukturellen Füllung informieren Kapitel in Crosland, Fuller, Mönch und Schlütter sowie Aufsätze von Mönch, Oliphant und Scott. Ein Problem der historisch orientierten Überblicke (vgl. Crosland, Cruttwell, Mönch 1955, Schirmer, Spiller) ist, daß sie ihren Schwerpunkt in der Mehrzahl auf die Elisabethaner, Shakespeare und Milton legen, die übrigen Phasen der Sonettgeschichte hingegen knapper und das 20. Jahrhundert meist gar nicht mehr berücksichtigen. Eine ähnliche Diskrepanz besteht zwischen der Reichhaltigkeit der epochenspezifischen Sekundärliteratur zu den elisabethanischen und Shakespearesonetten – aus der in der Auswahlbibliographie deshalb nur einzelne, besonders wichtige Titel genannt werden (vgl. Ferry, John, Jones, Lever, Marotti, Muir und Neely) – und der spärlichen Literatur zu den Sonetten späterer Epochen und Autoren. Eine unverzichtbare Hilfe bei der Suche nach Arbeiten zu allen Phasen der Gattungsgeschichte sowie nach Interpretationen zu einzelnen Sonetten leistet die Bibliographie von Donow.

Mindestens ebenso wichtig wie die Auseinandersetzung mit den strukturellen und historischen Möglichkeiten des Sonetts ist bei der Vorbereitung eines Sonettgebiets für das Examen die Beschäftigung mit den allgemeinen Merkmalen der Lyrik in den betreffenden Phasen der Literaturgeschichte. Wertvolle Hilfe leisten hier zum einen Sammelbände und Nachschlagewerke mit Überblickskapiteln zu den verschiedenen Epochen der englischen Lyrik[9] und zum anderen einführende Monographien wie die aus der *Longman Literature in English Series.*[10] Besonders groß ist die Zahl der Einführungsbücher zur *metaphysical poetry*;[11] man findet aber auch einzelne nützliche Einführungen in die übrigen Epochen.[12]

4.2 Zur Erschließung des einzelnen Sonetts

Einige Anregungen zur eigenen Textarbeit an den Sonetten kann man einem Aufsatz von Slogsnat (vgl. Auswahlbibliographie, Abs. 2) sowie einschlägigen Lehrbüchern mit Musterinterpretationen entnehmen.[13] Im wesentlichen wird man sich für das Vorgehen bei der Analyse der einzelnen Sonette jedoch ein eigenes Konzept zurechtlegen müssen. Welche Faktoren dabei berücksichtigt werden können, soll das folgende Schema zeigen, das um der besseren Merkbarkeit willen in vier Blöcken angeordnet ist: Auf der linken Seite des Schemas findet man die traditionell der Form, auf der rechten die traditionell dem Inhalt zugerechneten Faktoren. Auf der oberen Seite stehen die Faktoren, die den Gesamtaufbau des Textes prägen und daher beim Beginn der Analyse zu berücksichtigen sind, auf der unteren Seite die Faktoren, die der Verfeinerung und Vervollständigung der Analyse dienen.

1. *sequential structure of the sonnet*	2. *spatial structure of the sonnet*
1.1 the rhyme-scheme	2.1 the communicative situation
1.2 repeated words, phrases, sentences	2.2 patterns of meaning
1.3 sentence- and clause-boundaries	2.3 patterns of figurative meaning
1.4 contrastive and other sequence forms	2.4 text and title
3. *poetic devices of the sonnet*	4. *contexts of the sonnet*
3.1 figures of speech	4.1 sonnet and sonnet-cycle
3.2 tropes (metaphors, paradoxes, etc.)	4.2 intertextual relations
3.3 sound patterns	4.3 historical and ideological background
3.4 rhythm and metre	4.4 literary period

Die große Bedeutung des Reimschemas (1.1) für die formale Gliederung des Sonetts in Sequenzen wurde bereits bei der Diskussion der Textbeispiele von Dovaston deutlich. Neben dem Reim als einer Wiederholung von Endlauten tragen auch andere, breitere Wiederholungsmuster – wie z.B. die Wiederholung von Wörtern am Zeilenanfang (*anaphora*) oder die Rekurrenz ganzer Zeilen (1.2) – und die Markierung der Satzgrenzen (1.3) zur formalen Gliederung des Sonetts bei. Während diese verschiedenen Indikatoren der formalen Gliederung einander in Sonetten der älteren Epochen fast immer entsprechen, ist das bei den Sonetten seit der Romantik oft nicht mehr der Fall. Hier werden durch den Abschluß syntaktischer Einheiten innerhalb einer Zeile oder durch das Übergreifen des Satz- und Sinnzusammenhangs auf nachfolgende Zeilen (*run-on lines, enjambement*) Spannungen zwischen dem Reimschema und der Syntax aufgebaut, die auch von inhaltlicher Bedeutung sein können. Einen weiteren Ansatzpunkt für die sequentielle Analyse eines Textes bieten schließlich Funktionswörter wie *but*, *yet* oder *so*, die – von Egon Werlich in seiner Textgrammatik des Englischen[14] als *sequence forms* (1.4) bezeichnet – die wichtigsten Umschwünge, Übergänge und Zusammenfassungen im Argumentationsverlauf markieren und gerade in schwierigen, dialektisch aufgebauten Sonetten, wie man sie von Shakespeare und den *metaphysical poets* kennt, einen wichtigen Zugang zum Sinnverständnis eröffnen.

Die Struktur von Gedichten stellt sich ihren Betrachtern nicht nur als eine Kette von Sequenzen, sondern auch als eine Konstellation von gleichzeitig präsenten Elementen – Figuren, Begriffen und Werten – dar. Dieser zweite Aspekt der Strukturierung ist gerade für das Sonett von besonderer Wichtigkeit, weil man es ob seiner Kürze wie ein Bild auf einen Blick betrachten und in wiederholter Lektüre vorwärts und rückwärts lesen kann. Dabei fällt neben der im Text implizierten Kommunikationssituation (2.1) – also der Konstellation von Sprecher, Adressat(en) und möglichen weiteren in der Situation des Sonetts präsenten Figuren – vor allem die Wiederkehr sinnverwandter Wörter auf, durch die ein oder mehrere *patterns of meaning* (2.2) – sinntragende Bedeutungsmuster – gebildet werden. Es empfiehlt sich, bei der Texterschließung solche *patterns of meaning* mit verschiedenen Farben zu markieren und sie dann nach den Kriterien der Entsprechung und des Gegensatzes zu ordnen, denn auf diese Weise gelangt man zu einem System semantischer Parallelen und Kontraste, das den Kern der Bedeutung des betreffenden Sonetts ausmacht.[15] Bei manchen Sonetten – besonders der metaphernverliebten elisabethanischen Zeit – können sich die sinntragenden *patterns* auch ausschließlich aus figurativen, bildhaften Elementen konstituieren (2.3), so daß der Text in seiner Gesamtheit oder zumindest in einigen seiner Sinnabschnitte den Charakter einer ausgedehnten Metapher annimmt. Bei anderen Sonetten bietet der Wechselbezug zwischen Text und Titel (2.4) einen geeigneten Zugang zur Analyse.

Ist mit Hilfe der bisher beschriebenen Ansatzpunkte eine Strukturierung des gesamten Sonetts erfolgt, kann man sich in einem zweiten, der Vertiefung des Textverständnisses dienenden Schritt der Analyse einzelner rhetorischer Figuren (3.1), Metaphern, Vergleiche, Wortspiele und Paradoxa (also der sogenannten Tropen, 3.2) sowie der Analyse klanglicher (3.3) und rhythmischer Muster (3.4) zuwenden[16], die entweder eine bedeutungsverstärkende Funktion haben oder auch bloßes Schmuckwerk sein können.

Eine besonders wichtige Aufgabe der Sonettanalyse ist schließlich die sogenannte Kontextualisierung, d.h. die Ermittlung der Bezüge zwischen dem Einzelsonett und (soweit vorhanden) dem gesamten Zyklus (4.1), den potentiellen intertextuellen Anspielungsfolien (wie z.B. der Bibel oder der klassischen Mythologie, 4.2), dem jeweiligen historischen und ideologischen (4.3) sowie dem literaturhistorischen Hintergrund (4.4). Dabei ist zu beachten, daß diese Kontexte den konkreten Einzeltext niemals völlig determinieren, sondern lediglich Bezugsrahmen sind, in die sich der Text bis zu einem gewissen Grade einfügt, gegen die er sich aber auch durch Techniken der leichten Modifikation, der deutlichen Abweichung oder gar der offenen Parodie mehr oder minder deutlich absetzt. Die Problematisierung solcher Differenzen des Einzelsonetts gegenüber seinen typischen Kontexten wird im Examensgespräch oft von größerem Interesse sein als die bloße Kontextualisierung selbst, lassen sich doch gerade aus ihnen besonders gut die Variationsvielfalt, Entwicklungstendenzen und Umschwünge in der Geschichte des Sonetts ablesen.

Anmerkungen

1 A. Dobson: "Rose-Leaves". – In *Collected Poems.* London, ²1897, S.462.
2 Zit. nach E. Blunden, B. Mellor (Eds.): *Wayside Sonnets 1750-1850.* Hong Kong, 1971, S. 25.
3 Die Entschlüsselung dieses Pflanzennamens macht besondere Schwierigkeiten, da er von Dovaston in verkürzter Form genannt wird (eigentlich: "crown imperials").
4 Zu einer genaueren Darlegung dieser Zusammenhänge vgl. U. Suerbaum: *Das elisabethanische Zeitalter.* Stuttgart, 1989, S. 475-540, bes. S. 507 f.
5 Da die Autorschaft Shakespeares bei den letzten beiden Sonetten des Zyklus umstritten ist, wird in manchen Darstellungen die Zahl von nur 152 Shakespearesonetten genannt.
6 In einer viel zitierten Definition nennt Helen Gardner das *conceit* daher "a comparison whose ingenuity is more striking than its justness" ("Introduction". – In dies. (Ed.): *The Metaphysical Poets.* Harmondsworth, ³1972, S. 19).
7 Diese Datierung folgt M.H. Abrams: *A Glossary of Literary Terms.* New York, ³1971, S. 104.
8 Besonders zu empfehlen ist die Beschäftigung mit dem aus 27 Sonetten bestehenden Zyklus "In Time of War", der auf Audens Erfahrung des Chinesisch-Japanischen Krieges fußt, aber auch eine starke überzeitliche Komponente hat.
9 Vgl. z.B. K.H. Göller (Ed.): *Epochen der englischen Lyrik.* Düsseldorf, 1970; A. Preminger (Ed.): *Encyclopedia of Poetry and Poetics.* Princeton/N.J., ²1974; M. Coyle et al. (Eds.): *Encyclopedia of Literature and Criticism.* London, 1990.
10 Vgl. G. Waller: *English Poetry of the Sixteenth Century.* London, 1986; G. Parfitt: *English Poetry of the Seventeenth Century.* London, 1985; J.R. Watson: *English Poetry of the Romantic Period, 1789-1830.* London, 1985; B. Richards: *English Poetry of the Victorian Period, 1830-1890.* London, 1988.
11 Vgl. z.B. G. Evans: *The Age of the Metaphysicals.* Glasgow, 1978; J. Winny: *A Preface to Donne.* London, ²1981; J. van Emden: *The Metaphysical Poets.* Basingstoke, 1986; J. Trevor: *The Metaphysical Poets.* Harlow, 1988; D. Mackenzie: *The Metaphysical Poets.* Basingstoke, 1990.
12 Grundwissen über den Petrarkismus als gesamteuropäisches Phänomen vermittelt z.B. G. Hoffmeister: *Petrarkistische Lyrik.* Stuttgart, 1973; zur klassizistischen Lyrik siehe P.M Spacks: "Introduction". – In dies. (Ed.): *Eighteenth-Century Poetry.* Englewood Cliffs/N.J., 1964, S. xvii-lii; zur Romantik siehe L.R. Furst: *Romanticism.* London, ²1976, und St. Prickett (Ed.): *The Romantics.* London, 1981; zur modernen englischen Lyrik siehe J. Williams: *Twentieth-Century British Poetry. A Critical Introduction.* London, 1987.
13 Vgl. z.B. E. Werlich: *Poetry Analysis. Great English Poems Interpreted.* Dortmund, ³1972, und H. Meller: *Zum Verstehen englischer Gedichte.* München, 1985.
14 Vgl. E. Werlich: *A Text Grammar of English.* Heidelberg, 1976, S. 157-177.
15 Zu weiteren Informationen über das Verfahren der *pattern*-Analyse vgl. Vf.: "Textanalyse nach System? Kritische Bemerkungen und Vorschläge zur Praxis der Gedichtinterpretation". *anglistik & englischunterricht* 15. *Learning English Humor I.* Trier, 1981, 163-188, hier 172-178.
16 Zu einer genaueren Beschreibung dieser und weiterer *poetic devices* vgl. G.N. Leech: *A Linguistic Guide to English Poetry.* London, 1969.

Auswahlbibliographie

1. Wichtige Anthologien

Bender, R.M., Squier, Ch.L. (Eds.): *The Sonnet. A Comprehensive Anthology of British and American Sonnets from the Renaissance to the Present.* New York, 1965.

Blunden, E., Mellor, B. (Eds.): *Wayside Sonnets 1750-1850.* Hong Kong, 1971.

Booth, St. (Ed.): *Shakespeare's Sonnets.* New Haven/Conn., London, 1977.

Evans, M. (Ed.): *Elizabethan Sonnets.* London, 1977. [Enthält Sonette von 14 verschiedenen Autoren.]

Hiller, G.G. (Ed.): *Poems of the Elizabethan Age. An Anthology.* London, 1977. [Enthält einen umfangreichen Teil mit Sonetten von 11 verschiedenen Autoren.]

Honigmann, E.A.J. (Ed.): *Milton's Sonnets.* London, New York, 1966.

Ingram, W.G., Redpath, T. (Eds.): *Shakespeare's Sonnets.* London, 1964.

Kallich, M., et al. (Eds.): *A Book of the Sonnet. Poems and Criticism.* New York, 1973. [Mit Textauszügen zur Reflexion über die Gattung und einem Index zu den in den Sonetten behandelten Themen.]

Nye, R. (Ed.): *The Faber Book of Sonnets.* London, 1976. [Umfangreiche, repräsentative Sammlung zu allen Epochen der englischen Sonettgeschichte.]

Sharp, W. (Ed.): *Sonnets of this Century.* London, 1887. [Sammlung romantischer und viktorianischer Sonette.]

Smart, J.S. (Ed.): *The Sonnets of Milton.* Oxford, 1966 (Glasgow, 1921).

Waddington, S. (Ed.): *English Sonnets by Living Writers.* London, 1881. [Sammlung viktorianischer Sonette.]

2. Literatur zum Sonett allgemein

Crosland, T.H.W.: *The English Sonnet.* Norwood/Pa., 1975 (London, 1917). [Ältere, noch stark präskriptive Arbeit; zum Sonett allgemein, zu den Elisabethanern, Milton, Keats und Wordsworth.]

Crutwell, P.: *The English Sonnet.* London, 1966. [Gut zu einer ersten Einarbeitung geeigneter Abriß der Gattungsgeschichte von den Anfängen bis zu Auden.]

Donow, H.S.: *The Sonnet in England and America. A Bibliography of Criticism.* Westport/Conn., London, 1982. [Umfangreiche, auf Vollständigkeit abzielende Bibliographie der Anthologien und Sekundärliteratur zur englischsprachigen Sonettdichtung von den Anfängen bis zum Ende des 19. Jhs.]

Fuller, J.: *The Sonnet.* London, 1972. [Knappe Einführung; zu Form, Struktur und Variationsmöglichkeiten des Sonetts.]

Mönch, W.: *Das Sonett. Gestalt und Geschichte.* Heidelberg, 1955. [Standardwerk zur äußeren und inneren Form, Thematik und europäischen Geschichte der Gattung.]

Mönch, W.: "Das Sonett. Seine sprachlichen Aufbauformen und stilistischen Eigentümlichkeiten". – In Reichenkron, G. (Ed.): *Syntactica und Stilistica. Festschrift für Ernst Gamillscheg.* Tübingen, 1957, S. 387-409.

Oliphant, E.H.C.: "Sonnet Structure: An Analysis". *Philological Quarterly* 11, 1932, 135-148.

Schirmer, W.F.: "Das Sonett in der englischen Literatur". *Anglia* 49, 1925, 1-31. [Noch immer lohnender Gang durch die Gattungsgeschichte mit Schwerpunkt auf der Entwicklung der Form.]

Schlütter, H.-J.: *Sonett.* Stuttgart, 1979. [Behandelt Herkunft, äußere und innere Form, Wertung des Sonetts, seine Geschichte in der Romania und in Deutschland sowie – in einem Beitrag von R. Borgmeier – das Shakespearesonett.]

Scott. C.: "The Limits of the Sonnet: Towards a Proper Contemporary Approach". *Revue de la littérature comparée* 50, 1976, 237-250. [Zum Verhältnis von Konstanz und Wandlungsfähigkeit der Form.]

Slogsnat, H.: "Eine Sonettfolge als Index epochaler Prozesse". *anglistik & englischunterricht* 11. *Unterrichtsreihen Englisch I.* Trier, 1980, 115-164. [Unterrichtsreihe, illustriert u.a. Möglichkeiten der konkreten Textarbeit am Sonett.]

Spiller, M.R.G.: *The Development of the Sonnet. An Introduction.* London, New York, 1992. [Gründliche Untersuchung der italienischen Ursprünge und der englischen Entwicklungsgeschichte des Sonetts bis zu Herbert und Milton.]

3. Zu einzelnen Epochen und Autoren

Bhattacharyya, A.: *The Sonnet and the Major English Romantic Poets.* Calcutta, 1976.

Ferry, A.: *The 'Inward' Language. Sonnets of Wyatt, Sidney, Shakespeare, Donne.* Chicago, 1983.

Göller, K.H. (Ed.): *Die englische Lyrik. Von der Renaissance bis zur Gegenwart.* 2 Bde. Düsseldorf, 1968. [Sammlung exemplarischer Gedichtinterpretationen, mit Beiträgen zu Sonetten von Wyatt, Surrey, Sidney, Shakespeare und Drayton in Bd. 1; E.B. Browning, D.G. Rossetti und Hopkins in Bd. 2.]

John, L.C.: *The Elizabethan Sonnet Sequences. Studies in Conventional Conceits.* New York, 1964 (11938).

Jones, P. (Ed.): *Shakespeare, The Sonnets. A Casebook.* London, 1977.

Kaiser, R.: "Das naturbeschreibende Sonett bei Wordsworth". *Die Neueren Sprachen* N.S. 11, 1962, 11-23.

Kaiser, R.: "Vier Sonette: Eine vergleichende Interpretation". *Die Neueren Sprachen* N.S. 12, 1963, 252-263. [Zur Sonettdichtung der Romantik.]

Lever, J.W.: *The Elizabethan Love Sonnet.* London, 1956.

Marotti, A.F.: "'Love is not love': Elizabethan Sonnet Sequences and the Social Order". *ELH* 49, 1982, 396-428.

Milward, P. (S.J.): *A Commentary on the Sonnets of G.M. Hopkins.* London, 1970.

Muir, K.: *Shakespeare's Sonnets.* London, 1979.

Nardo, A.K.: *Milton's Sonnets and the Ideal Community*, Lincoln/Neb., London, 1979.

Neely, C.T.: "The Structure of English Renaissance Sonnet Sequences". *ELH* 45, 1978, 359-389.

Stull, H.L.: "Sacred Sonnets in Three Styles". *Studies in Philology* 79, 1982, 78-99. [Über religiöse Sonette der Elisabethaner, *metaphysical poets* und Miltons.]

Zillmann, L.J.: *John Keats and the Sonnet Tradition. A Critical and Comparative Study.* New York, 1966 (Los Angeles/Cal., 1939).

Acknowledgements

For permission to reprint poems in copyright, thanks are due to the following: For STING's "Sister Moon" to Magnetic Publishing Ltd; for U.A. FANTHORPE's "Not My Best Side", from *Side Effects* (1978), to Peterloo Poets; for Michèle ROBERTS' "rite de passage" to R.I.B. Library Reed Book Services; for Derek WALCOTT's "The Sea is History" to Random House UK Ltd.; for SISTA ROOTZ' "Dictionary Black (Trap)" to the author; for Grace NICHOLS' "Sugar Cane", from *i is a long memoried woman*, to Karnak House; for PHILIP LARKIN's "The Building" to Faber & Faber; for ADRIAN MITCHELL's "Autobahnmotorwayautoroute" to Peters Fraser & Dunlop Ltd; for IRENA KLEPFISZ's "Fradel Schtok" to Eighth Mountain Press.

Anschriften der Autoren

Dr. Elfi Bettinger. Ludwig-Maximilians-Universität München. Graduiertenkolleg "Geschlechterdifferenz und Literatur". Schellingstr. 3, 80799 München.

Prof. Dr. Christoph Bode. Otto-Friedrich-Universität Bamberg. Englische und Amerikanische Literaturwissenschaften. Weide 18, 96047 Bamberg.

Prof. Dr. Gisela Ecker. Universität/Gesamthochschule Paderborn. Fachbereich Anglistik/Amerikanistik. Warburger Str. 100, 33098 Paderborn.

Dr. Klaus Ensslen. Ludwig-Maximilians-Universität München. Amerika-Institut. Schellingstr. 3, 80799 München.

Dr. Karl. J. Häußler. Auweg 7, 83334 Inzell.

Prof. Dr. Günter Jarfe. Universität Passau. Anglistik und Amerikanistik. Innstr. 25, 94030 Passau.

Prof. Dr. Evelyne Keitel. Technische Universität Chemnitz-Zwickau. Fachgruppe Anglistik/Amerikanistik. Postfach 964, 09009 Chemnitz.

Prof. Dr. Barbara Korte. Technische Universität Chemnitz-Zwickau. Fachgruppe Anglistik/Amerikanistik. Postfach 964, 09009 Chemnitz.

Dr. Andreas Mahler. Ludwig-Maximilians-Universität München. Institut für Englische Philologie. Schellingstr. 3, 80799 München.

Prof. Dr. Manfred Pfister. Freie Universität Berlin. Institut für Englische Philologie. Gosslerstr. 2-4, 14195 Berlin.

Dr. Ingrid von Rosenberg. Universität-Gesamthochschule Duisburg. Studienfach Anglistik/Amerikanistik. Lotharstr. 65, 47048 Duisburg.

Prof. Dr. Hans Ulrich Seeber. Universität Stuttgart. Institut für Literaturwissenschaft. Neuere Englische Literatur. Keplerstr. 17, 70174 Stuttgart.

Dr. Anna Maria Stuby. Universität Hannover. Englisches Seminar. Welfengarten 1, 30167 Hannover.

Dr. Peter O. Stummer. Ludwig-Maximilians-Universität München. Institut für Englische Philologie. Schellingstr. 3, 80799 München.

Prof. Dr. Peter Wenzel. Ruhr-Universität Bochum. Englisches Seminar. Universitätsstr. 150, 44801 Bochum.

RECLAMATIONS OF SHAKESPEARE

Ed. by A.J. Hoenselaars

Amsterdam/Atlanta, GA 1994. 317 pp.
(DQR Studies in Literature 15)

ISBN: 90-5183-606-6 Bound Hfl. 160,-/US-$ 94.-
ISBN: 90-5183-639-2 Paper Hfl. 50,-/US-$ 29.-

CONTENTS: Introduction. *Andrew Gurr*: Shakespeare and the Visual Signifier. MIEKE BAL: *The Rape of Lucrece* and the Story of W. ROBERTA E. PEARSON and WILLIAM URICCHIO: "Shrieking from below the Gratings": Sir Herbert Beerbohm-Tree's *Macbeth* and His Critics. HELEN WILCOX: Gender and Genre in Shakespeare's Tragicomedies. WILLEM SCHRICKX: Elizabethan Drama and Anglo-Dutch Relations. ANTHONY PAUL: The Poet Laureate's National Poet. PAUL J.C.M. FRANSSEN: Portraits of Mr. W. S.: The Myth of Sweet Master. Shakespeare in Asimov, Wilde, and Burgess. AART BALK: Revolting against the Legend: Anti-Shakespearean Elements in Jules Laforgue's *Hamlet*. M. T. JONES-DAVIES: Shakespeare and the Myth of Hercules. C. C. BARFOOT: News from the Roman Empire: Hearsay, Soothsay, Myth and History in *Antony and Cleopatra*. MARK BERGE: "My Poor Fool Is Hanged": Cordelia, the Fool, Silence and Irresolution in *King Lear*. HENK GRAS: Enchanting Metadrama: Shakespeare and the Use of the Boy Actor in *As You Like It*. PIERRE ISELIN: Myth, Memory and Music in *Richard II*, *Hamlet* and *Othello*. JULIA MULLER: Music as Meaning in *The Tempest*. P. J. GABRINER: Hierarchy, Harmony and Happiness: Another look at the Hunting Dogs in the "Induction" to *The Taming of the Shrew*. J. J. PEEREBOOM: Every Word in Shakespeare. MICHAEL GREEN: Sixth Form and Pressure: Why Teach Shakespeare at 'A' Level? Notes on Contributors. Index.

USA/Canada: Editions Rodopi, 233 Peachtree Street, N.E., Suite 404, Atlanta, GA 30303-1504, Telephone (404) 523-1964, Call toll-free 1-800-225-3998 (U.S. only), Fax (404) 522-7116

And Others: Editions Rodopi B.V., Keizersgracht 302-304, 1016 EX Amsterdam, The Netherlands. Telephone ++ (0) 20 622 75 07, Fax ++ (0) 20 638 09 48